Compound D

The Struggle to Build a Home
in the Heart of
America's Most Dangerous City

DAVID SUTTNER

PAGE PUBLISHING, INC.
Conneaut Lake, PA

First originally published by Page Publishing 2020

ISBN 978-1-64628-616-4 (pbk)
ISBN 978-1-64628-617-1 (digital)

Printed in the United States of America

Purpose

This book has two purposes. First is to encourage adventurous and clever young men and women to take advantage of the tremendous opportunities in land, business, and housing that are available from time to time, usually after a recession in the inner cities and urban areas. We are talking about those risk-takers willing to work hard and face the dangers of life. You see, our slums—created by years of neglect, liberal governmental programs, blight, violent crime, and poverty—are, at times, for sale, often at bargain-basement prices. True, you're competing with the greed of speculators who bank land and pay the minimal taxes to keep the property out of foreclosure and wait for the big developer; but if you look around, a property can be acquired.

A neighbor, a few years ago, bought a foreclosed home two doors down from his house for about $25,000. The house had sold five years earlier to a young computer programmer from New York for $125,000, but he had lost his job in the last economic downturn and then lost his house during the economic "bust" of '09. My neighbor was in a position to do most of the work himself and, more importantly, protect his investment by living nearby. He's now renting it out to students and living the good life.

Society gave up on Detroit's neighborhoods after the Riot of 1967. For decades, much of Detroit looked like third-world dead zones that are reminiscent of bombed-out Berlin circa 1945. A block or two over, you might find a little jewel of an old neighborhood that had avoided the direct hit.

It's like that big gothic cathedral in Cologne, Germany. At the end of World War II, the neighborhood around it was bombed to rubble; but somehow, by the grace of God, the bombs missed it. Keep an eye on those neighborhoods that were missed by the economic bombs. They have a special place in our cities. For one thing, they are loved. We live in one such neighborhood (it's called Woodbridge), but it's life is on a razor's edge.

Let me use an analogy. If you walk into a darkened room, your eyes don't see very well; you must take time to adjust. You can't clearly see the objects around you. If someone turns on a bright light, you have to wait awhile—both in the dark and in the bright light—to get a good look at your environment.

The darkness of depression, poverty, and violence keeps you from seeing the opportunities that exist around you. The bright lights of a supercharged economy also blind you to the dangers of overinvesting and risks of the community and the neighbors around you. Detroit, as well as many other cities, is exiting from a full-blown depression. There are opportunities if you are able to see them.

My wife, Erma, and I have lived all our adult lives in Downtown Detroit. We were kids in our early twenties when we moved in to do graduate work at Wayne State University in the late sixties. We liked it, even during the rough years, and stayed on. We raised our son, and after fifty years of work and careers, we are now enjoying retirement. I know this city as only a white man living in a black city can know it. I know its dangers, its excitement, and its opportunities. Much of what I have to say will resonate with interested readers, and heads will nod in agreement that I speak the truth.

During good times, the money flowed in from Lansing and Washington, DC, making the inner city livable for the middle class but just barely. By inner city for Detroit, I mean the areas encompassed by the horseshoe-shaped East and West Grand Boulevards that surround the central core of this city.

Unfortunately, the rising tide of economic prosperity never really seems to lift all boats, as the old saying goes. Detroit has a permanent underclass of discontented folks who continue to have babies out of wedlock, commit crimes, and generally muck up things. It's not that they are evil or inherently criminal, but society has relegated them to the lowest position on the economic totem pole and they are not happy about it.

The second purpose is more personal. It is to justify, at least to myself and my family, why we chose to live our lives in this situation. To help me understand how I fell in love with this beaten-up, old battered city that is on its comeback.

We may have different goals in life, but all hope our lives have value and our work is meaningful. When we look back, can we say it has had meaning to us, our family, and community? Before my dad died, I had the opportunity to ask him what he was most proud of. After thinking about it for a while, he said that he had lived a hard life, followed construction projects during the depression. He was most proud of the fact that he had never killed anyone, but (with a twinkle in his eyes) he said, "But more important, I was never killed by anybody." I hope when it's my time, I can say the same thing.

Prologue

Woodbridge community, Detroit, Michigan
April 2019

Retirement is great; don't let anyone tell you otherwise. I got my first social security card and a real part-time job, working for my dad's construction company as a grease monkey in 1957. Retirement, some sixty plus years later, is like a winning endgame of chess against a conniving and treacherous opponent. It's what we all work and strive for.

Mornings, I'm not so far from my work world that I can't still enjoy listening to the weather and traffic reports. You can find me smiling the whole time. I enjoy sitting on the back porch, looking at nothing in particular, and sipping from a mug of steaming hobo coffee (a drink made simply by pouring boiling water over coffee grounds, allowing it to sit until the desired strength is obtained, then straining the black liquid into a coffee mug.) In life, I've learned to go for simplicity and quality.

My mornings are spent in exercise and hours reading piles of books that I've accumulated through a lifetime but have not had yet the time, energy, or inclination to read. At other times, I work on the yard and watch the garden grow. There is a pleasure in listening to the early morning exciting and confusing chorus of the birds tuning up, not quite ready to meld into a harmony of a song, and then I take our dogs for a walk.

On nice days, I watch our dogs playing tug-of-war in our fenced-in backyard (the neighboring house is rented out as a town house without a "backyard" and has been incorporated into our fenced-in compound.). The birds in the huge blue spruce my son and I planted when he was just a little tyke, now sing and chirp a beautiful medley.

I have a wonderful loving wife who dotes and spoils me and a beautiful granddaughter who moved in to go to college. I read much and have my family, friends, church, workshop, garden, and travel plans, plus I discovered Google and YouTube.

We love black culture, music, food, and have been made to feel welcome by the overwhelming majority of black residents. I can probably count the number of racial incidents directed at me on one hand. In this narrative, it may seem as if black thugs and punks play a major role. Well, Detroit is 80 percent black; of course, the majority of crimes are going to be committed by blacks, but it's usually on other blacks.

Though I'm enjoying my retirement and my life, something was missing. I needed to complete one last life's goal, or maybe two. So I decided to set aside time and work this year on my remaining goals. I always wanted to write and have published a Western fiction. Yes, a short cowboy story and a book entailing some of life's little lessons.

I'll try for truth and honesty in this telling. What I have to say may just be of interest to today's young risk-takers, those who were not born with silver spoons in their mouths or with trust funds set up by wealthy grandparents. My target audience is those young, predominately white kids who want to build a better life and are not afraid of hard work and a little danger, excitement, and loads of adventure.

Why white kids? Because I'm white and I was young once, many decades ago, well into the prior century, when we first moved into Detroit.

This is not a manual of "do's and don't" of urban survival, though it may have some of that; nor is it a simple recounting of old war stories of foiled robberies and prevented assaults, though I'm sure it will have some of that. But it's about understanding and acquiring the skills necessary not only to survive but to also thrive as a member of a small white minority in a once-great American city that is now fighting its way back from a third-world status. Over the years I've picked up some street smarts, and I'm willing to share them if you'll listen.

Life is about attitude and risk-taking, about setting goals and living up to them. It's about when to stand tall and when to duck low. This is written for the young men and women who are willing to take chances and work hard to build a secure future in the changing and dangerous inner cities of America, for there are great opportunities in the cities.

Our little family of three plus pets not only survived against the odds but also thrived in the inner city of America's most dangerous city, Detroit. Some of the events happened years ago, and my memory may be vague on some or a few details. I have also changed a few names to avoid embarrassing some good folks, but the facts are real and the lessons learned are true, as they say, to the best of my knowledge and belief.

As a kid, my father often told me that I was not very smart but I was very lucky. He was correct on both points, and I believe, after a lifetime of hard living, that we generally make our own luck by hard work, by tenacity, and by making good choices and avoiding bad ones. For example, it took me a lot of years to appreciate the fact that nothing good happens after midnight while drinking with friends.

I was at the right place at the right time and lived through one of the most turbulent periods of unrest in our modern history. I witnessed firsthand the decline and fall, and now the rebirth, of a great American city, Detroit.

If you are thinking about moving into a city to take advantage of a downturn in the economy that happens with regularity in our economy or to jump onboard the current economic train that's leaving the station or if it's just for the culture and entertainment or even if you just dream of living in a handsome old Victorian house or a spacious loft apartment downtown, I think you'll find this an interesting read.

CHAPTER 1

Life's First Lesson

Fisk, Southeast Missouri
Winter 1949

As a child, I grew up in the backwaters of southeast Missouri, near the Arkansas line. After years of following my father, a heavy equipment operator on major projects, our mother finally put her foot down and told my dad that we needed to settle down. The first five years of our family life had been spent in trailer courts and small apartments. Finally, with a new child on the way, we settled down in the small city of Poplar Bluff, Missouri, near my mother's family. Women have always played a central role in our family life.

I was very imaginative and impressionable as a child, and frankly, often my own shadow scared me out of my wits. I was often my own worst enemy. After a Saturday filled with work, chores, and play at the farm, we, the grandchildren and extended family on my mother's side, would gather at night, in front of a crackling fire, to listen to my maternal grandmother's ghost stories and sing old-time religious hymns reflecting her Pentecostal persuasion of hellfire and damnation in true Scotch-Irish tradition.

As the last embers died, we were off to the large bedroom in the attic where all the children slept together in real feather beds. The brick chimney that came up through the floor and went out the raftered ceiling was warm to the touch. I loved to squeeze next to it on a winter's night and feel the warmth and security radiate from its bricks, surrounded by my family.

One of Grandmother Myrtle's ghost stories dealt with the creatures that came up in the middle of the night from an old cistern in the cellar. They would grab a child stupid enough to allow an arm to dangle off the bed. With a swift jerk, the creature would pull the child off the bed and drag the child down those cold stone stairs to the cellar.

We sat openmouthed in wide-eyed terror as she told us, with increased inflection in her voice, how we would hear a loud *thump* as the body hit the floor to be followed by muffled screams and cries for help. After the echoes of the screams died away, we were told that the child was never heard from again. None of us children had ever heard the cries personally and no one could recall ever missing a cousin, but we never doubted the stories. I wondered if my grandparents would come out and try to save me if I were the victim. I decided early on that you had to depend on yourself if you wanted to survive in this world. We kids often discussed whether or not, upon hearing cries in the night, we would come to the aid of the unfortunate victim or hide under the covers. It was decided that you could avoid this fate if you hid very still under the covers.

The stories worked if a grandchild rolled over and an arm slid out from under the covers or the hand fell to the floor. The survival instincts kicked in, and the little hand was snatched up back to safety under the covers. During my entire childhood, we never lost a child to the night creature.

The children learned "to hold it" for fear of getting up in the middle of the night to use the chamber pot under our bed. This was before my grandparents had indoor plumbing. In those days, everyone had an outdoor outhouse (with a *Sears* catalog for paper) known as a privy.

The little children would only venture out there after dark with an escort of older cousins and a lantern. I once heard my father say that the difference between a rich man and a poor one was that a rich man had a canopy above his bed. The poor man had one under his.

I heard years later from an uncle that the old farmhouse had a problem with rats and mice moving in out of the cold each winter and that the stories were told to keep the children's hands and feet off the floor where they might suffer a bite. Let me tell you, the story worked.

My grandmother's stories were so vivid and real that even today, I can get goose bumps thinking about them. They dealt with basic fears and superstitions and the dangers of panic. Some nights I went to bed so frightened that I magnified every sound of the old farmhouse settling in for the night into monsters and demons. One story that particularly affected me was called "The Grave." It's a simple little tale, and I remember it word for word, even after all these years.

Once, when I was a little fellow of about five years of age, I had only been home for several days after a long weekend visit to my grandparents' farm and the ghost stories kept playing in my head. I would get scared and cry out for my mother and sob and cry in her warm, loving arms. I would beg to be allowed to sleep with my parents.

My dad worked construction around the country and returned every few months for a home visit. On that occasion, I was warned by my father that if I continued with the "nonsense and childish behavior" of being afraid at night, I would not be allowed to spend the night at my grandparents ever again. I loved my grandparents, and heck, I was just a kid at the time. I couldn't help it. I got scared at night. Both my older sisters got to sleep together (this was before my little brother came along). I didn't understand why I couldn't sleep with my mother at night. When Dad was away working construction, Mom would often let me sleep with her, especially if I was afraid of something.

My dad had put me to bed that night and told me to sleep tight and not to let the bedbugs bite, one of his favorite sayings. Heck, we didn't even have bedbugs that I knew of. On that particular night, on his way out of the room, my dad turned off the light and closed the bedroom door, causing an old raincoat to sway and move. I could clearly see, with the aid of the moonlight streaming in through the open bedroom window, its movement back and forth between light and dark shadows.

I knew that it was just an old raincoat hanging on the door. Why, heck, I had stood on a chair to hang it up there myself. It was just an old raincoat, that's all. But the more I looked at it, the more it came alive—a man but not just any man. It was the man in one my grandmother's story, the one entitled, "The Man with the Golden Arm." He stood there swaying back and forth, just standing there watching me. First I tried pulling the blanket up over my head, but I had trouble breathing. My heart thumped so loudly in my chest I thought it would burst. If I couldn't see it, maybe it couldn't see me; but I knew in my heart that wasn't true.

Slowly, I peeked out from under the blanket, and sure enough, it really was a man or creature standing there. And it was watching me watch it. Goose bumps crept up my arms and shoulders, and my hair at the back of my neck stood on end. Waves of cold chills and shivers came over me. I felt sick to my stomach.

I could clearly see its red eyes watching me, and it held something long and sharp in its hands. It was just waiting for me to go to sleep and then…then it would attack me.

I started to cry out, to scream for my mother, but I knew that if I did, my father would come in and the thing would turn back into a raincoat. I would never be allowed to visit the farm again. I had overheard my father telling my mother that he didn't like all those ghost stories that Grandmother told the children. "It scares them needlessly and fills their heads with nonsense," he had said.

My mother answered, "Perhaps you're right. He wet his bed again last week after his visit. He said he was afraid to get up and go to the privy. Maybe he shouldn't sleep over until he's older." Didn't they know that I didn't have any older brother to take me out at night and watch over me?

Slowly, taking a deep breath, I braced myself. With prayers to the Blessed Virgin and all the saints for help (we were a hard-core Catholic family), I pulled the blanket aside and ever so slowly crept out of bed, and grabbing hold of a baseball bat, I moved toward the door and the thing watching me.

Reaching out with the end of the bat, I hesitated, dreading to touch, dreading to disturb, and fearful as to what would happen if I did or didn't act. Suddenly, I used the bat to strike the raincoat. I tore it from the hook and flung it to the floor, and then I kicked it into the corner and began to breathe again. To this day, I hate to sleep with a bedroom door closed, and I never hang up a garment on the back of a door. It was a hard lesson, but I learned to get over the fear and not to hide under the covers.

There are a lot of things that go bump in the night; and some of them are mean, dangerous, and real. But fear, though it alerts us to danger, is often exaggerated and can lead to panic. We should listen to that inner voice that alerts us to the dangers of life and not just dismiss it and hide under the covers. You cannot allow fear to control you. Excessive fear often leads to indecision and panic. And panic kills.

I learned early on that you must deal with life's problems yourself. You can't always depend on your parents, the police, or a governmental agency to solve your problems.

CHAPTER 2

Getting the Job Done

Mingo Swamp, Southeast Missouri
August of 1959

As a kid, I thought of the possibility of becoming a Catholic priest along with that of a mercenary for hire (of course, always fighting for the good guys), a teacher of the poor loved and respected by his students, or a cop taking on the worst of the worst, all in no particular order. But I knew deep down that I didn't have the temperament or the academic ability for most of these avocations. I could barely read, write, or spell and was an absolute failure in math. By age fourteen, I had flunked the third grade once, been passed "on condition" twice, and was in danger of failing the eighth grade. I had not gotten off to a good start.

It's funny how life turns out. Sixty-plus years ago, I didn't know I'd wind up as a high school teacher, a principal of a grade school and a high school, a college professor, and an attorney with five degrees under my belt.

As a kid, I had gotten into too many scraps and fights and had a tendency to goof off any chance I got. I was seriously considering the occupation of the class clown, a position for which I was well suited. I was locked in battle with the nuns, and only as an adult did I begin to feel sorry for them and for my parents, who put up with me. I was once called a holy terror and wore that badge with honor for the remainder of the school year.

It wasn't that I was necessarily a bad kid or went out of my way to aggravate my teachers; I just didn't fit nicely into a small world with few options. True, I wasn't the most cooperative kid and got spankings so often that I would slip extra papers in my back pockets as padding before heading for school with my two older sisters and little brother, just in case.

On holidays, Saturdays, and vacations I loved going out with my dad on construction jobs and hanging out with the men in the brush crews. They were tough, raw men without families like ours. Many had been jailed and had served time on chain gangs for petty offenses or had served in the military. None had an education beyond grade school and didn't seem to need it.

They lived a hard life by a stern code of loyalty to your friend, hard work, and hard play. They acted and reacted with violence. There was not much thinking or pondering the results of one's actions for these men. Someone hit you, then you hit him back—harder. We seldom had a thief in the crew—they were roughly dealt with and discharged—but we did have our share of outright liars and tellers of tall tales. I fit right in.

Once I saw a knife fight between two of the men. A few minutes before, they had been sitting beneath a tree in the shade during the lunch break. The brush crew that day was small, only four men in number (all hard cases), plus Cecil, my dad's assistant, and me. It was hot, dirty work and hard to get good men, men willing to work in ninety-five-plus temperature with high humidity.

Cecil and I were sent over to work with the brush crew and keep them moving, cutting, chopping, and burning the path the dragline and equipment would follow down a ditch bank. We were clearing the way for the heavy equipment that would dig the canals and drain the swamps in southeast Missouri and create farmland. Cecil, a Korean War vet, was the straw boss, and I was his newly minted assistant, all of fourteen years of age.

All morning we had chopped, dug, cursed (yes, I learned a few choice words to call a stubborn tree root or a swarm of wasps.), and cut through the tangle of bramble, vines, thorns, and saplings so we could bring in the fuel, stored in fifty-five gallon drums, up to the dragline where it was hand-pumped into the machines. It was hot, dirty, gut-busting work with bonfires blazing, burning off the excess tinder that had piled high in clearing the path. The big trees we couldn't go around were cut with chain saws and double-bit axes and brought down to either be dragged off or piled for burning.

Suddenly, one of the men jumped up and tossed his water cup aside, saying, "You take that back, you..."

Threats and oaths erupted from his companion, and in a hot minute, both had squared off, suddenly appearing with sharp knives. The other men moved out of the way to watch and to give them some room. I looked around, but Cecil had left to scout out the route and plant flags to mark our path. The two men no longer spoke, they just hunched forward with feet moving, arms extended with knives, balanced and tense, ready to lunge and cut.

I called for them to stop, to no effect. I yelled for Cecil.

A few grunts and slices resulted in a scream and a curse as one man slashed the other's arm. They grappled, and the man with the bleeding arm fell to the ground, cursing in pain. It was over. Cecil trotted back and went over to assess the damage. He ordered them to put their knives away and ordered me to get the first aid kit from the truck.

The uninjured man who had done the cutting helped the other to his feet and watched as his friend's wound was washed and antiseptic applied. It was then bandaged expertly by Cecil. I thought Cecil was going to fire them both, but instead, he called them over behind the truck and talked quietly for a while. They nodded and came back after the break to resume their work. Cecil had ordered them to work together, and the uninjured man was responsible for helping his mate with his rough work.

Later I asked Cecil what he would tell Dad. "Oh, I'll tell Mr. Joe all right. It just that I ain't quite figured out how and when I'll do the telling. In the meantime, don't say anything, okay?"

"Okay," I promised. I didn't feel right in keeping a secret from my dad, but it wasn't long before Cecil went up to the dragline and hopped up on the cab as Dad brought the machine to rest and idled back on the diesel engine. I could see them talking. Dad glanced toward me and the brush crew and nodded his approval. Cecil hopped off the dragline, and we resumed our work of widening the clearing along the canal.

In talking it over later, Cecil said, "A lot of the time, it's how you tell the story." He smiled his crooked smile. "Always tell the truth, but put it in a good way to help folks. I told Mr. Joe what happened and what I did about it. The job is to get the brush cleared, so I put them back to work. No serious damage was done, just a minor cut. I will follow up with them…give 'em a good warning. If it happens again, they'll be fired and charges brought. Your dad agreed that the job was the main thing." I learned a lot about leadership from Cecil. It's about getting the job done.

CHAPTER 3

Initiation

Jefferson City, Missouri
September 1959

At that time of my life, I wanted to get out of Poplar Bluff, Missouri, in a bad way. The opportunity came during eighth grade to enroll at La Salette School, a boy's college prep school in Jefferson City, Missouri. The French Catholic order was accepting in-state students on much-reduced tuition for their high school seminary in hopes that some would become Catholic priests or brothers. My father thought it a waste of time; but Mother, who believed in education, talked to him, and finally, they agreed that I could try.

My dad told me that I didn't have to go unless I wanted to and that he'd have a job open for me at the construction site when I returned. The only problem was I had no interest in becoming a heavy equipment operator.

All went well for the first two weeks of school, even though I was completely lost in French, Latin, algebra, ancient history, religion, and English. I was taller and stronger than any of the other freshmen and most of the upperclassmen. Besides, I fancied myself a bit of a tough guy. No surprise that I was left alone by the bullies.

One kid in particular caught my attention—a little guy named Hank, who hailed from New York. I never knew if it was the city or the state. Back then I really didn't know the difference.

I had never met anyone like him before. He couldn't fight worth a darn and had no ability in sports. He was weak and tired easily and wasn't good at physical work. We were each assigned tasks around the facility, and I found myself being paired with him in raking leaves, washing the school's vehicles, or anything that involved physical labor. I didn't mind doing his work plus mine because he was funny and very smart. He had a cutting wit and could come up with gags and jokes on the spur of a minute. He was great at imitating the voices and manners of our teachers. He had them down to a T, and we roared with laughter at his antics.

The only problem was that Little Hank didn't know when to keep his big mouth shut. He would smart off to anyone and, likely as not, get punched in the gut and often get knocked down for his trouble. Upperclassmen would take no crap from a freshman, especially if no one in authority was watching.

Even after being hit and still be lying on the ground twisted in pain, he would call the aggressor a biting name, based on the person's appearance, hair, odor of breath, or shape of his nose, ears, etc. This would get him a kick in the rear end. He would fight his way through the pain and just laugh at them. At that time, I didn't have a dog in the fight, so I stood off to the side and watched. Besides, Little Hank got exactly what he deserved.

On one particular occasion, Little Hank smarted off to a junior and got the punch hard on the shoulder. The blow—which, in truth, might have been pulled a bit—sent him sprawling head over heels down a slope into high grass. No problem, he deserved it; and I just stood there leaning against a rake and watched. But then the upperclassman decided to teach him a lesson and went down and began delivering some sharp kicks to Little Hank's rear end.

That's when I stepped in and told the upperclassman that he should pick on someone his own size. After some words, the upperclassman backed off with a statement I didn't quite understand at the time. "We'll deal with you later," he called back over his shoulder as he walked away. I helped Little Hank to his feet and helped him hobble back up the hill. By the time we reached the crest, we had formed a friendship.

That Monday in English literature, the professor lectured about Charles Dodgson. Never heard of him? Don't feel bad, neither had I. In fact, I had never heard of his pen name, Lewis Carroll of *Alice in Wonderland* fame, either. The professor talked about how some boy not particularly good in sports would be called a muff. I think he said it came from an old sports term meaning to "drop the ball."

It seemed as if young Dodgson had a gift for math and literature, but when it came to sports, he much preferred croquet to the physical games played in England at that time. With croquet, he would use geometry and physics to plot angles and vectors and thus demonstrate keen shots to his fellows. The professor talked about how, often, a young muff would be protected by a guardian angel, usually, an upperclassman of strong moral fiber, a young modern knight who righted wrongs and protected the weak. In other words, one who was a true hero.

I liked the idea of being a protector of the weak. I would save my friend from a pack of bullies. I don't know if young Dodgson was a friend with his protector or not, but it looked as if I had become Little Hank's friend and protector. After all, Little Hank was great in math and English and was beginning to help me in my classwork.

That evening, after dinner and before study hall, I asked Little Hank if he liked croquet. He told me he had never played, and I suggested that we go to the prefect and see if we could get up a team and play on the lawn. We did just that, and to my amazement, I found that I liked the game and wasn't too bad at it. I had to ponder on that for a while.

Sometimes it seemed as if Little Hank would start the fights just to watch me finish them. We had a rule in the school against spontaneous fights. Anyone caught fighting would soon have a visit with the prefect and face the board of education, have extra duties, and worst of all, have his privileges curtailed. For example, not being allowed on Sunday afternoon to walk with your mates into town and go to a bookstore, see a movie, or go to an ice-cream shop.

But anyone could call out another student and challenge him to a boxing match in the gym, which was located in the basement of the church. The students would gather around the ring as a brother or monk would referee rounds that were of no set length. The cheering and calls would go on until the referee saw blood (and often lots of it) and called the fight and declared the winner. There were no draws. That usually ended the problem and allowed for a pecking order.

I loved to fight and had no problem being Little Hank's champion. In turn, he tutored me in my lessons, and I'm sorry to say that I wasn't much of a student. Even with his help, I was barely passing most of the subjects, just by the skin of my teeth. But somehow I learned to read and began to remember facts and formulas for the next day's classes.

Three weeks into the school year, things were settling down nicely. I was getting a feel for the routine and division of the day between schoolwork, sports, hobbies, work, and study.

One thing did worry me though. Each student, beginning with the seniors, had to read aloud during the evening meal from a book approved by the prefect, who was the boss of the place. I was scared to death because each day my turn to read drew closer. I was terrified at the prospect of standing up in front of a crowd of people and trying to read. I knew I'd be laughed off the podium.

I began to practice reading aloud and, with Hank's help, began to plod and stumble through the readings. My mouth got dry and my hands shook as I stammered out the words. Hank very patiently corrected my pronunciation and gave me encouragement. Up until that time, I thought that the past participle of a word ended in *et* (e.g., I *learnet* the lesson, not *learned* the lesson or I *burnet* the book, not I *burned* the book).

Hank always treated me with respect, and I was the only one he didn't jab and cut with his sarcasm and biting humor. At that time, my ego was so fragile that it would have cracked under the sarcasm, and I probably would have beaten someone half to death.

At the end of the third week of school, during the dead of night, I was sleeping soundly when I was suddenly pulled from my bed and rolled up in my blanket and pulled to the floor by three figures clad entirely in black. Each was shouting at me and hitting me with gloved open palms.

I was pulled to my feet, blindfolded, prodded and shoved, stumbling down the hall, to line up with other freshmen and then marched (arms to the shoulder, hands holding to shoulders of the one in front) down the hall and around the building. We were told to shut up. Anyone caught talking was beaten. The night was broken with smacks from the paddles and cries and screams of pain. It was like a scene from Dante's *Inferno* that the professor had gone on about. I shut up and silently placed my arms as directed on the shoulders of the student in front and walked as directed.

Suddenly, we jerked to a halt, and I was pulled out of line, dragged by two guards, and slammed into a chair. I knew where I was (the barber shop) even before my mask was removed. I could hear the buzz of the electric clippers and smell the machine oil and Old Spice that lingered in the air. I had long dark-brown hair with, believe it or not, a touch of gray at my temples when I was shoved into the barber chair. At first glance, I appeared to be older and more mature than I really was.

The electric clippers began to do their job, and my hair fell to the floor. I had received my first buzz cut. I was truly a skinhead. Everything was cut off the top, low and tight. I glanced in the mirror and saw a scarred, bald-headed kid sitting in the chair. I looked years younger, and I didn't recognize my image.

Then I was placed back into the marching line, reblindfolded, and moved around the building until exterior doors were opened, and then I was pushed into the cool night air. Next, we were forced to stumble down a long flight of stairs; it had to be into the basement gym because the screams and cries echoed just like at a basketball game. To this day I hate basketball and gyms. I won't join one or watch games there.

My mind wasn't working right. I was blindfolded and stupid with fear. I was in a fog as to what was going on. Rough hands shoved me against a wall and we were told to reach for the sky and climb the wall. Every few minutes someone would come up from behind and smack our rear ends with a paddle and tell us to "climb the wall higher." *Smack* went the paddle. "Higher, you fish, higher." This was followed by another smack from the paddle.

I did what I was told. I tried to really climb that wall until I was pulled off the wall with the statement "This one for special treatment." I recognized the voice. It was the same upperclassman who had bullied Hank. *Oh my god,* I thought, *how is Hank taking this?* But I was too busy worrying about myself to spend much time thinking about anyone else.

By this time, I was shaking, and for the first time since being a little kid, I was really scared. Suddenly, my hands were tied behind my back and my blindfold removed. The bright lights of the gym stung my eyes, and for a moment, I was dizzy. I was swung around (first one way, then another) and, finally, abruptly stopped.

Now I was really living a scene from Dante's *Inferno*. All the freshmen were lined against the walls, screaming and whimpering and trying to climb the wall. A handful of black-clad upperclassmen wearing ski masks wielded paddles and roamed up and down the walls, whacking rear ends and laughing and screaming like demons. The freshmen, though outnumbering their tormentors ten to one, begged and pleaded between screams as they made ridiculous efforts to climb a wall. With that glance, I learned how the few could control the many with intimidation and violence.

On the stage at one end of the gym, a student was screaming and begging for his life. Everywhere students were crying out in terror or calling for their mothers. The black-clad figures were joyous with whoops of delight. I was shoved toward a ladder leaning against the basketball hoop. On its rim, with his back against the backboard, his legs in black pants, black shoes and socks straddling the rim and dangling down, sat the executioner. He was the only devil not entirely in black for his chest was bare and he wore black gloves and a black hood that came down to his shoulders. He looked like a medieval torturer I had once seen pictured in a book. The eyes and mouth had been cut out from the black hood, and he yelled, "Welcome to hell, freshman. You'd better say your final prayers because you are going to die." He then laughed a deep evil laugh. He lifted up a hangman's noose and slapped it against a gloved hand.

"Bring up the next victim," he demanded. I was again blindfolded and pushed, prodded, and forced up the ladder.

I heard a maniacal laugh as a noose was placed around my neck. I tried to turn my head one way then another in order not to accept the noose, but it was firmly placed around my neck. A moment later I was pushed back off the ladder into space. I had no way to regain my balance and fell backward straight down.

Suddenly, I hit the floor hard. I later learned that a mat had been placed beneath me. I lay there dazed, winded, scared, and mad as hell. I was sucking in air in great gulps when, suddenly, I was pulled up and shoved back to a place on the wall as other students were pulled off for "special treatment."

The screaming and smacking went on and on and on. Then it was my turn again to be in the barrow, so to speak, to receive a little special treatment. As before, my hands were quickly tied behind my back and the blindfolded tightened. I was pushed toward the stage.

On the stage, I was forced to kneel and my pajama top was unbuttoned and pulled down over my arms, further restricting movement. My blindfold was removed to reveal two devils dressed entirely in black standing before me. One was holding a branding iron, now white-hot, into the flame of a torch while the other laughed and hooted in joy.

"Is it ready to apply, brother?" said the one. The one holding the white-hot branding iron moved it close to my face. I felt the wave of heat dry my skin and the moisture from my eyes, which were dilated wide open in fear.

"Yes, my brother, it's ready," he answered.

"Good," the first one continued. "We can now proceed with the branding by which this poor soul will always be ours. Blindfold him and let's do this…NOW."

They both laughed as the blindfold was again slipped over my head and tightened. Instantly, a flaming pain stabbed my chest, and I screamed out in agony. "Please, no! No!" I howled above the chaotic noise of the gym.

The reaction was hoots of laughter from the black devils, and I was kicked, stumbling, back to a place on the wall. I don't know how long I remained on the wall. By this time, I was numb and shaking with cold and terror. All the other emotions had been drained out of me. Eventually, we were pulled off the wall and marched back to our dorms. We were finally shoved back into our beds, and the black-clad figures disappeared. I slid under the covers and fell fast asleep, hearing the sobbing and moaning from my fellow freshmen.

The morning bell sounded at the normal time, 6:00 a.m. For a moment, I thought I had had the worst nightmare ever. I rubbed my eyes and ran my hands over my face. I was so tired. Then, I rubbed my head and discovered that I had no hair but I did have a bright red spot on my chest. I later learned it was caused, not by a branding iron, but rather by a cube of ice.

CHAPTER 4

Failure

Jefferson City, Missouri
1959/1960

I had just been initiated into the French religious order of La Salette with the hell night's ordeal. Then began a school-sanctioned week of organized humiliation and hazing by upperclassmen. We were slaves assigned to upperclassmen as their personal servants. We carried their books to and from class, shined their shoes, cleaned their rooms, and in general, put up with their crap. Whenever we met an upperclassman, we had to kneel before him and repeat, word for word, a little prayer of subjugation we were told to memorize. Some were even forced to wear dog collars. I can still repeat it after all these years:

> O majestic upperclassman, I kneel before your august presence and worship at your feet. I am not worthy to be in your presence and am but like whale shit on the bottom of the sea. I have no other purpose in life but to serve you. Your slightest wish is my greatest command. I live to serve you now and forever. What would you bid me do?

We would then be commanded to do something silly. I was once ordered to climb a tree and eat an unripe persimmon—without making a face. I failed that test. Have you ever eaten an unripe persimmon? I had to eat another one and wound up with the runs.

Thank God the hazing only lasted one week and ended with the school resuming its normal routine. I had spotted several upperclassmen for some special treatment of my own in the ring. Over the next few months, I had my share of fights. I won some, lost a few, and had a couple of bloody draws; but it felt darn good, and I had made my point. I always hated punks who hid under hoods and masks, but sooner or later, the truth would out! Revenge is sweet, but I was getting a reputation for being a big dumb country kid who could take and give a whooping. In football, I was on the line, guard or tackle, and used as cannon fodder. "Kill the bastards. Hit 'em harder" was our chant.

As for Little Hank, they really gave him the full treatment during the initiation. The rest of the term, he kept his mouth shut around upperclassmen.

With Little Hank's tutoring, I somehow passed into the tenth grade on condition and went back home to Poplar Bluff for the summer vacation. I worked for my dad again that summer on the dragline, pumping fuel and cutting brush. It was one of the best summers of my life. I hated to see it come to an end.

Unfortunately, Little Hank did not come back in the fall of the new school year. I was told that he had suffered a serious illness during the summer and had had to drop out. It wasn't long before my grades were also in the failure range. I really missed Little Hank, and I wonder if he knows how much he influenced my life. I learned from him the dangers of putting your mouth in action before your mind is in gear.

During my tenth grade, the initiation for the freshmen was planned in meticulous detail in secret meetings during the first three weeks, and I'm sorry to say that I participated with gusto and assumed the role of the hangman sitting atop the hoop.

We followed the same script as in the prior year. The staff absented themselves during hell's night. We loved the theater of acting our parts as fiends and devils. We tried to live up to the script or even to exceed it. We took delight in scaring the hell out of a bunch of incoming freshmen, and I wonder how many we left with lifelong emotional scars. For this I am sorry and openly apologize for my actions.

My grades continued to fall during the year; and fortunately for me and the rest of the world, after midterms, I was demoted back to the ninth grade. I began to fail at the same material I had passed, just barely, the year before.

Then that winter, I suffered a compound fracture while skiing. It was a bad break and had to be rebroken and set a second time. Wow, I was thinking things couldn't get any worse when I was caught with half a bottle of vodka in my locker. I had appropriated it from the faculty dining room one evening, thinking that they would never miss it.

Unfortunately for me, the good priests and brother keep track of such things, and the administration had a "pop" locker inspection. I was expelled from the school prior to the finals. Here I was, sixteen years of age, and I should have been going into the eleventh grade of high school the next year. But I would be going back to start ninth grade over for the third time. Wow, could it get any worse?

On my train trip home, I reflected on my failures and actions at the school. I was returning in disgrace, a sixteen-year-old failure, and would probably leave school. Sixteen was the legal age in Missouri to drop out and go to work for my dad, if he would have me.

I also began to understand how a few Nazis could control the many with fear, intimidation, and violence, but it had to have the cooperation of the authority. During that initiation night, all the staff were absent from the facility. During the initiation week to follow, the staff turned a blind eye to the insults and humiliating treatment of their freshmen students.

Organized violence and intimidation have to have at least the tacit approval of those in charge. By doing nothing, the staff gave approval to the system. I remember reading in college about the Milgram study of 1963 in which students were requested to give electric shocks to subjects who got wrong answers on a test. Though many expressed great anxiety at doing so, they followed orders and continued to increase the dial into the danger zone. The study was rigged only to look and sound like the test student was being shocked.

The study has recently been challenged as flawed, but I know from personal experience that people, good people, will follow orders and do some very bad things. Somehow we must each develop our own internal compass and find direction not just in following orders of authority but by following the small internal voice we call our conscience.

I've often thought about the initiation and come to the conclusion that they really didn't hurt me that much. I came out a bit bruised and hurt but stronger for the experience. I learned many valuable life lessons that I was able to put to good use in future years.

CHAPTER 5

Life's Lessons

Summer of 1960

I worked vacations and Saturdays with my dad as an oiler (nick-named grease monkey) for his construction company. I had driven a tractor at age eleven and our pickup truck at age four-teen. Early one morning, we were in the '49 GMC pickup driving to a work site deep in the country. On such trips, my dad would give me bits of wisdom that have served me my entire life.

One recurring theme was as follows: "Son, 90 percent of virtue is lack of opportunity." He often talked about the virtue of honesty. He had these little aphorisms that he lived by and explained that it was the duty of those in positions of authority and stewards of other's property not to tempt weaker men who had little or nothing to lose.

"You must always lock doors and chain down equipment to keep folks from stealing from you. Anyone, if placed in the right situation, will steal, lie, cheat, or even do worse," he warned. "When you make it too easy and they steal from you, they also become vic-tims of sorts because it steals their dignity and willingness to work. We have a duty to make it as difficult as possible for weaker folks to steal from those of us who do the real work of society. Otherwise, you have anarchy." Yes, he really did talk like that.

I once asked Dad what he thought of Marxism. "Hmm." He thought for a moment. "Let me put it this way. Once I was working on a big dam project, this was during the Depression. This one evening, a real communist came into the camp, climbed up on a table, and talked to the men about organizing a union and calling a strike. He told us about the evils of capitalism, the oppressors of the working man, and the coming industrial revolution, which would lead to class warfare."

"The agitator said that under communism, all men would be able to share equally according to their needs, not their abilities. So after the speech, I asked him, 'You mean to say if you had a million dollars, you would share it equally with us?' He answered, 'Yes, I'd share it equally.'" Then Dad continued, "So next I asked him, 'You mean that if you had $20, would you share that equally with us too?' 'Heck no,' he answered. 'I've got $20.'" Dad roared with laughter, and I was left to work out my own interpretation of Marxism.

One evening, I noticed that a fifty-five-gallon drum of diesel fuel was a little light and told Dad about the suspicious disappearance. We had a supply dump of oil drums that we kept on a county road close to the dragline, tractor, and equipment. My job was to man-handle the fuel drums on the hydraulic lift on the rear of the tractor and haul it through a path I had cleared to the machine. Finally, I would hand-pump the fuel and grease all the fittings. I would climb up the boom, rising one hundred or so feet above the water surface of the ditch (hence the name grease monkey), and grease the fittings at the tip of the boom.

Several gallons of ten-weight motor oil had also disappeared. Dad had studied the tire prints and the boot marks in the thin layer of powder-dry dust at the site. It would be another scorcher, and we hadn't had rain in almost a week. He told me to keep my eyes open for an old pickup truck with a bald left front tire that would be badly burning oil. He said that they were probably mixing some diesel with their gasoline and we should see a blue plume of exhaust smoke following the vehicle.

"How do you know that?" I puzzled.

"The tire tracks." He patiently pointed them out to me. "Son, they show no respect for me. They probably live right around here, and they'll be back right after we leave for home. But I'll have a little surprise waiting for them. We have a duty not only to keep ourselves out of the occasion of sin but also to do our best to keep our fellow man on the straight and narrow."

Dad was a big believer in self-help. I never knew of him reporting a theft to the sheriff or ever filing an insurance claim. He dealt with things himself and in his own way.

"Dad, I can hang out near the fuel dump and see if anyone comes along and tries to take anything." I nodded toward a small brush pile under a shade tree that would offer seclusion and shade.

"No, but they'll be back. You wait and see."

The next morning, after parking the pickup at the dump site, Dad removed a mason jar of dark heavy liquid from under the seat and poured its content into a two-gallon oil can then topped it off with fresh oil from another can.

"Molasses," he said. "Leave this oil can next to the fuel oil drum."

Sure enough, the next morning, we found the can of oil had disappeared, along with several more gallons of diesel oil.

A few days later, we heard from a landowner, who had come out to discuss putting in a stock pond with Dad, that one of his share-croppers had the engine of his pickup seize up on him and left him and his family stranded along the side of the road. It's funny, but we never had any more problems at that site.

That philosophy of self-help expounded by my father served me well. For decades, during the worst period of violence and chaos in Detroit, I dealt with problems in my own way and never did call the police unless it was to get my side of the story on paper first.

CHAPTER 6

Love of My Life

Poplar Bluff, Missouri
Fall of 1961

I landed on my feet, and again luck was with me. When I went to register at the Poplar Bluff High School, the secretary asked for my age and grade. I told her that I was transferring from Jeff City and that I was entering the eleventh grade. They gave me the normal classes with one exception. My dad wanted me to take the machine shop. Dad had a high opinion of machinists and blacksmiths.

He thought I could help make some of the parts for the machines and that it was a good skill to fall back on. My dad didn't think much of formal education. Often, I heard him say, "He's so educated he thinks he's too good to work," and "Education makes a man so he doesn't think he needs to work." Dad thought all a man needed was to have enough education to read the Bible and the newspaper and do his ledger books. The eighth grade was enough for him.

It's strange, but I was the dumbest kid in the entire school in Jeff City. I had been kicked out in disgrace. I was supposed to be re-entering the ninth grade again! Suddenly, in Poplar Bluff, I was treated as if I was the smartest kid in school. I had plenty of good clothes from Jefferson City, so I dressed in black slacks, black shoes shined to a high gloss, and socks. I wore a dress shirt, either blue or white, and had two sports jackets that I wore to school on Fridays and special occasions. Teachers began calling on me and smiling and asking my opinion.

I had a few little spats with some of the locals, but after standing up to them, they backed down and life was good until, one day, I was called into the office. The secretary had a transcript from my school in Jefferson City. It documented my educational failure. "What do you say about this?" she demanded.

"Hmm." I pursued the document. "There must be some mistake. That's obviously not me. Ask any teacher. Look"—I pulled out an assignment with a B on it and pointed out that this was an inferior example of my current work—"they must have made a mistake." This was a time before computers when people wrote letters to gain information. No one called. That was long-distance and costly. The US Mail Service took its time to deliver.

I left the office in the status quo, but I knew it was only a matter of time before the hammer fell. What to do? I'd have to give that some thought.

One Saturday evening—September 29, 1961—my buddies and I were in the balcony at the Rodgers Theater watching a silly film starring Fred MacMurray called *Flubber* or something. I was bored and a little put out. My girlfriend, Dottie, had bailed on me to attend her girlfriend's fifteenth birthday party; so I sat with a bunch of loudmouth, wisecracking teens busy throwing popcorn down on the patrons below and making catcalls. We sat in the balcony, which had previously been reserved for "coloreds." But now the entire theater, like our high school, was open to both races.

Suddenly, Dottie appeared behind me and, leaning over the seat, gave me a little kiss and hug. "What are you doing here?" I asked. "I thought you had a birthday party to attend."

"Yes, that's why I'm here. Round up your buddies. We're headed back to the party. Only the girls showed up. We need some guys for a real party. Come on."

We loaded up into Dottie's parents' station wagon and headed to the junction of 67 South and Highway 53. "Say, Dot, what gives? There aren't any houses around here, only junkyards and car lots." I scanned the area. As far as the eye could see were wrecked cars and trucks by the thousands, many piled up waiting for scrap.

"Don't worry," she said as she pulled into a dirt drive, going around several wrecked cars. "My friend Erma lives upstairs. Her dad owns all of this."

"Wow, look at all the car parts." I looked around in amazement, a high school boy's dream come true. It was like entering an enchanted palace.

That evening I met Erma, a cute skinny little girl with dazzling brown eyes. On my turn at Spin the Bottle, it landed on her. I always said I was lucky, and I gave her a real kiss square on the lips. She, in turn, slapped my face so hard I heard bells ringing in my ears. The crowd hooted with laughter, all except Erma and Dottie.

"Wow," I said to my buddy next to me, "that's the girl I'm going to marry."

Surprise, surprise, on Monday I learned that we were both in Mr. Miller's geography class. I immediately moved from the rear of the class with the goof-offs to the front row to sit next to Erma, and at the end of the first class, I asked her out on a date.

"I thought you and Dottie are a couple," she replied.

"No, we're just friends, that all. We're not going steady or anything." I was already thinking of ways to break off the budding relationship with Dottie.

"Are you on the honor roll?" she asked. "I can't go out on a date unless he's on the honor roll. That's my folks' rule."

"Honor roll?" Was she serious? I had never been on the honor roll in my life. But I answered, "I'm new here, but I will be at the end of this term."

"How do you get on the honor roll?" I asked around and learned that the student had to have a B or better average. How do I get a B-plus average? Simple, cheat! I began a methodical plan to bring all my grades up. I began using crib sheets for exams. Simple enough! I just tucked them into a sleeve and removed them as needed. I started doing homework and turning it in on time. Then I began to study the assignments and read the texts. Finally, I began to study after school with smart kids and copied a lot of answers from them.

Suddenly, I found myself getting first Bs and then an A- and, finally, a majority of As; and to my amazement, I found that I didn't need to pull the crib sheets out during the test. It was just enough to know that I had them in reserve, if necessary. The act of creating a crib sheet fixed the items in my memory. I discovered that I had excellent short-term memory.

The grades came out at the end of the first term, and lo and behold, there was my name actually on the honor roll printed in black and white in the *Daily American Republic* for the world to see. My folks had trouble believing it.

"Well," I asked Erma on Monday morning, "did you see my name on the honor roll?"

"Well," she replied, "that's an awfully deep subject for such a shallow mind." That's been one of her favorite phrases throughout her life.

"Did you see it or not?" I insisted. She nodded in the affirmative. "Then are we going out this Saturday? You said you'd go on a date with me if I made the honor roll. Let's go to a movie. I'll take off early Saturday afternoon. My dad will let me off for the afternoon if I ask him, maybe." I knew that Mom would see to that in light of my recent academic achievement.

"Can I pick you up?" I inquired. Mom let me use her '58 Buick if I did something good. Things had improved at our household, and Dad now had the county drain commission's contract to clean out all the irrigation canals in Butler County. Mom had her own car and, on special occasions, would lend it to me.

After some conversation, Erma said, "No, I'll meet you at one o'clock this Saturday at the Rodgers Theater."

That Saturday I had lunch at the grill at the Rogers Drugstore and sat at the counter with a good view of the box office and the street. I had bacon, lettuce, and tomato sandwich; even today it's my favorite. I was nursing the last of my phosphate cherry soda when I saw Erma come around the corner and head to the ticket office. I took a final sip and almost gagged in surprise, for right behind her was a girl a few years younger than Erma followed by three boys progressively younger.

I jogged out to the ticket booth. "I've got our tickets, but I see you've brought guests."

"Yes, this is my sister, Marie, and brothers, Chris, Greg, and Leonard. They'll also need tickets."

I paid for their tickets and gave each a quarter, and once inside, they went to straight to the candy counter and then disappeared into the darkened theater. Greg, about ten years of age at the time, had pocketed his coin and, finding us in the balcony, sat behind us and spent his time leaning over the chairback, whispering in his older sister's ear. Soon, the whole gang was behind us.

"Look, can't you kids find another place to sit?" I inquired. Greg sat back in his chair, and then Leonard commenced kicking the back of my seat. After a few moments, I gave in.

"Okay, I gave each of you a quarter. What do you say?"

He kept kicking the back of my seat. "Another quarter" was his answer.

I complied, and we didn't see any of the siblings until we gathered in the lobby after the features. There Erma took a head count, lined up her little brood, thanked me, and exited. Wow, what a first date. My dad always told me that when you marry, you marry the spouse's family as well, so make sure you like them. Not only did I like them but I also fell in love with them, so much so that I always joked that if we ever got divorced, I would get Erma's family in the settlement and she would get mine. My family was great, but hers was a ball of action and excitement. And as a plus, her father owned and operated the biggest junkyard in southeast Missouri!

That Monday I was called into the principal's office once again. The new transcript, just like the older one, had arrived, and I was called to answer. But now, because I was already well into the semester and on the honor roll, it was decided that I could remain in the eleventh-grade classes, but I would have to take extra makeup classes to graduate on time. No problem. I had to give up the machine shop class the next semester so I could take three academic classes during the afternoon.

On my last day in the machine shop, a fellow student had brought in his dad's 1911 Colt .45 semi-automatic from the Korean

War. Mr. Gorman, our shop instructor, had promised to show us how to take it apart to clean it and then reassemble it. After the reassembly, he took us out back, the shop was in a separate building behind the high school and set up some old paint cans and let us fire off a box of rounds. A phone call from the main office told us to cut out the shooting or the fireworks. It was bothering the music class.

CHAPTER 7

A Call to the Front Office

January 1962

Another uncle had passed with a heart attack. This one had only been in his fifties. The men in our family don't make it to old age, most dying by their midsixties, but that was a long way off and not something for a teenager to worry about.

With Dad and Mom both working, I was selected to represent the family at the funeral in Saint Louis. I took the note with Mother's genuine signature asking that I be excused from school because of a death in the family. I took the early Friday morning train to Saint Louis where an older female cousin picked me up at the train station.

On our way to the funeral home, we talked about our respective lives, and I told her about Erma. I explained to my cousin how I needed help to bring Erma around to see my good points. Erma had already criticized me and my pals about our reckless driving and bad attitudes toward authority. I needed help. My cousin took me to a large department store where she helped me purchase a green cutstone bracelet. This was my first gift to Erma.

I thought about other ways to impress her, and then the idea came to me. I would call her long-distance (a big deal) at the high school. It was now Friday afternoon, and the lunch period would soon be over.

I found a public phone and asked the operator to look up the number and called the high school office. The operator told the school secretary that there was a long-distance call for Ms. Erma Mae Browning. She was wanted on the telephone; after all, it was long-distance.

I hung on while Erma was summoned from the classroom and brought into the office where the entire staff stopped to listen in to her end of this rare conversation.

Finally, she came on and said, "Yes, who is speaking?"

"Hi, Erma, it's me, Dave. How are you doing?" I inquired.

"All right," she hesitatingly responded. "What do you want?"

"I just called to see how you are doing. You know, just to say hello and that I'm looking forward to seeing you when I get back this Sunday."

"Oh my," she stammered, "all right. Thank you for calling. I have to go now."

"Hold on for a minute, please. I just wanted to tell you that I'm thinking good thoughts about you and miss you. Do you have anything to say to me?"

"Yes, goodbye." She hung up. I always wondered what the office staff made of that emergency long-distance call, but Erma didn't say she wouldn't see me on Sunday. Things were looking up.

A *Language Lesson*

Butler County, Missouri
Summer of 1963

The summer of 1963, I worked for my dad on a construction job putting in a drainage canal out in the rural county. I was going to college in the fall and trying to save up some money. It was a hot afternoon, in the high nineties, and forecast to break one hundred degrees with high humidity. I was sitting in the cab of our pickup truck while Dad and the county surveyor met with some townsfolk in the small Negro farming community of Morocco. This area had been farmed since after the Civil War by freed slaves and their descendants.

The surveyor and Dad were trying to explain to the town fathers why the irrigation canal had to go one way through a field and spill into the main drainage ditch No. 1 so the water could be carried down to the Mississippi all the way to New Orleans.

The discussion was getting a little long-winded and a little heated, with voices raised, and we were wasting time and time was money. Seeing that my dad and the surveyor were the only whites surrounded by a group of Negro men, I got out of the truck cab and wandered over to the group, just to listen in on the conversation. I was hot and bored.

One Negro boy, about my own age, was the center of attention. I found this strange until he said that he was a college student at a place called Howard University in our nation's capital. My dad said he didn't care what college the boy went to, this was a discussion for the men of the town council. He said, pointing also to me, "You boys go over there and wait."

"You can't call me boy," said the young Negro in a bit of a huff.

"Well, you sure aren't a man," said my dad. "What should I call you?"

"You, honky, you shouldn't call me nothing" was the reply. The town fathers all took a step back and stood in silence, not believing their ears that someone had just called my dad, who everyone referred to as Mr. Joe, a "honky." My dad hired lots of colored folks from this area for work on the brush crews. There would be consequences.

"Honky," my dad barked back, "you call me a honky?" His face turned bright red as the rage built in him. I had never seen him this angry before, and frankly, I was afraid that he was going to blow a gasket. I saw my father's fingers clench into fists, and he stepped forward toward the kid. Was he going to punch out this impertinent kid?

"Dad." I stepped into the circle between my father and the kid. "It's no big deal, it's just a term colored folks use for white people. It doesn't mean anything. That's all it is. It's no big deal."

"No big deal?" he scoffed. "It doesn't mean anything to you, maybe." My father turned to the kid and looked level into his eyes. "I'm no bohunk," he said. (What the heck did that mean?) "I'm sure not a damned honky, a peasant just off the boat." I'd never heard my dad swear before, so I knew, along with everyone else, that this was very serious business. "I'm German. Why would you call me a honky?"

The group was suddenly silent, each of us trying to process this new information. A German! What the heck was going on?

The young Negro kid looked just as confused as I felt. "What did you say?" he stammered. "Look, I'm sorry Mr., ah, Mr. Joe." His demeanor entirely changed. "I didn't know exactly what it meant, ah, you know, that word I used. I thought it was a just a white man, you know, like he said"—he nodded in my direction—"only…well, mister, I just didn't know what it meant."

"Very well," my dad went on, "but you shouldn't use terms like that about people you don't even know. It can cause problems."

"Sorry, Mr. Joe," he repeated.

The tension was now diffused, and the men drew away, leaving the two of us standing there looking at each other, both of us feeling a little ill at ease. The black kid (I now knew not to call him a boy.) walked over to a fence post and leaned against it in deep thought.

My father, the white county surveyor, and the townsfolk closed in among themselves, forming a sort of a circle, the men squatting down on their heels or kneeling and following the surveyor as he drew lines in the dust with a stick, indicating structures, fields, irrigation ditches, and the lay of the land.

Soon they were talking, and you knew they would resolve the thorny questions as to the flow of water without the interference of some half-grown kids. I knew enough to leave the men alone, and so I walked over to the Negro kid who stood idly leaning against a fence post. He looked a bit shaken. I introduced myself and pointed out that the man he had just had words with was my father.

"Man, your old man is intense," he said.

"You don't know the half of it. You ought to try living with him."

"No, thank you. I got enough problems of my own."

We talked for a while about his college classes and social life, girls mainly, and I learned something about Howard University. It turned out that we both were the first boys in our respective families to attend college. He was a year ahead, but I had failed the third grade outright. So we were both the same age. I told him that I was going to Southeast Missouri State College in the fall. In those days, it had an open admission policy with very low tuition for anyone who had a high school diploma. True, most flunked out their first year, but at least everyone had a chance.

We got to talking about insults and fighting words and name-calling and how a person can get into a whole heap of trouble without really thinking. I told him that we didn't use insulting terms like *honky* around our house and that we didn't use the N word either. Dad didn't permit any insults.

He said at Howard, they used the terms *whitey* or *honky* for whites in general and *cracker* or *rednecks* for Southerners in particular. He talked of the black man not getting a fair shake and that it was about to stop. I told him I thought that everyone got a fair deal in this county if he worked hard and followed the rules and that I'd never heard colored folks referred to as blacks before.

He told me, in a confidential tone, that blacks or Afro-Americans didn't like being called Negro and especially didn't like the term *colored* and never-ever-ever to use the N word.

"Afro-American," I repeated.

"No, that's wrong," he corrected himself. "That's the hairstyle. But you can say African-American."

I assured him I had been raised in a Christian home and would never use the N word, and then I asked what I should call his people. He said that black was fine for the time being, but it would probably change.

He said, "Haven't you heard that 'black is beautiful' before?"

Then, suddenly, the men's conversation ended. They all got up, some of the older Negro men being helped up by younger ones, and nodded to one another. One by one, they shook hands with my dad, and then we finally got back to work.

Near their little settlement, on the ditch bank, was a gigantic refuse pile. For generations, the families had dumped and burned their trash on the slope of the main ditch. Mounds of rusting cans, bottles, old bits of machinery and appliances were piled up to the top of the berm. Upon investigation, I was met with swarms of wasps, by the thousands. I told Dad that the next day he'd be at that spot and it could be a problem.

Dad told me to get a fifty-five-gallon drum of No. 2 diesel and soak the trash piles good and then set it afire. What fun I had. I man-handled a barrel of diesel onto the power lift at the end of the tractor and raised it up and drove to the ditch berm and then backed up to a spot where I dumped the drum over and opened the bung and let it spill its contents down into the dump.

By this time, the word was out that there was going to be a burning of the dump to get rid of the wasps, and a small crowd gathered to watch me set up. I noticed the black kid and waved. He waved back, and I motioned for him to come over. We found some rags and, with old wine bottles, made and tossed flaming Molotov cocktails into the piles of rubbish. There was no big explosion, like in the war films, but the fire grew and burned and drove the wasps crazy.

We burned out thousands of nests, and for the next day, I had to ride in the cab of the dragline with an oil can in each hand and squirt out a stream of diesel at the flying wasps who came too close to the machine. I got to where I could hit them on the fly. What fun, and I only got stung a few times.

The Talk

Cape Girardeau, Missouri
Summer of 1966

I was twenty-one years of age and a graduating senior in college with a good job at F. W. Woolworth Co. I was earning $1.25 per hour. I told my parents that Erma and I were planning on getting married. We had dated for five years and now maintained two apartments at college. It made no sense. I knew she was the one for me.

Dad had always liked Erma and thought it was all right for me to date Catholic girls, but he often said that I should find a good Protestant girl to marry—after she converted to Catholicism, of course. Dad had met and married Mom, who was from a Southern family of Protestant persuasion, and I was expected to do the same. Of course, my sisters were expected to marry either Catholic boys or, convert them prior to the marriage.

Mom, on the other hand, wanted me to marry up the social ladder. She already had a girl picked out; but when I told her that I was only interested in Erma, she relented a bit.

Dad's only talk with me that resembled the "birds and bees" talk was the night before my wedding when he reminded me that, as Catholics, we only get married once. He wanted to know if I was going into this with my eyes open. I wasn't even allowed to go out drinking with my buddies that night. I had to enter this thing called marriage stone-cold sober. Funny, I wonder if a twenty-one-year-old man today would obey his father when told to stay home the night before his wedding. It was a different world then, and I had a different old man for a father.

Dad explained that Suttner men took their family responsibilities seriously. He had delayed marriage until he was in his midthirties when he could support a wife and family. Mother was just eighteen when she married. He said he never wanted to hear about any problems we were having between ourselves and said that he would not take sides.

Dad had lots of funny rules. Children were not allowed to ride bicycles but could drive cars and pickup trucks when their feet reached the pedals and they could see over the dash. We could own shotguns and rifles, but no one living under his roof could have a pistol, at least until age twenty-one. The strangest rule was no rolling pins in the house. All pies, dumplings, and loaves of bread had to be rolled out with a bottle or a wooden dowel. I suspected that Dad must have witnessed some act of violence done with a rolling pin and had banished it. To the day he died, we were never able to learn the particulars of the story. Mom would never tell us anything except that it was one of Joe's rules. I asked my sister Barbara if she knew the reason for the "no rolling pin" rule. It was a mystery to her also.

He explained to me that there was no excuse for fighting or fussing in front of any third party. A wife in an abusive situation has the duty to move out if no one can be found to counsel or "adjust" her husband's attitude.

Usually, this job, "being a Dutch uncle", fell to the father-in-law, an uncle, or a brother. A woman couldn't stay in a bad situation and be a punching bag. Every time the husband hit her, he committed a mortal sin; and as long as she remained, she was committing a sin also by putting them both in the occasion of sin. If the situation couldn't be resolved, the wife and children, if any, had to move back to her parents' home, to the disgrace of her husband. Hard as it might sound, even though the wife was the victim, in our family, she was also wrong if she allowed herself to be a doormat.

The wife was also not allowed to be abusive toward the husband. She needed to treat him with love and respect, especially in front of others.

"Son, a woman needs to feel loved, but a man needs to feel respect." My dad continued. "There are two kinds of men in this world. Those who believe that you should never marry a woman that you can't knock out with one punch, and then there are those of us who believe that you should always take care of the cook."

"Dad, I know that we are not in the first category because we believe that a man never hits a woman." In my whole life, up to that point, I had never witnessed any man abusing a woman. This only happened in movies and books, not in our world. In our world, wives respected and loved their husbands, at least in public.

"Just think about it." Dad smiled. "If you don't take care of the cook, she'll take care of you, and it could be permanent." Dad told me of cases where the wife had resorted to poison to end an abusive relationship. The husband had been verbally abusive and then had begun to slap her around when he had too much to drink. He liked to consume a glass of buttermilk with corn bread before going out drinking with his friends. His last night on earth, he quaffed down a large glass of the stuff and got ready to go out when stomach cramps hit him. He died later that night. Somehow, he had consumed a quantity of ground glass. It seems that he was unable to detect it in the buttermilk with the corn bread. No charges were ever filed.

These lessons served me well in life. No matter how down or disappointed we felt, we never took out our anger and frustration on each other. Sure, once in a great while, Erma and I would have a disagreement and raise our voices a little to each other for emphasis, and then we'd both feel bad and go off by ourselves and sulk until one or the other or both came together to apologize.

We never blamed each other for life's problems, figuring that it was just our turn to be in the barrow, so to speak. And we found out that often, when bad news came calling, it brought company. We firmly believed that bad news came in threes. We would brace ourselves for the worse and felt elated when we dodged a bullet. We would keep track of misfortunes, accidents, and equipment failure and found that old saying to be true.

In our lives together, now moving well into its sixth decade, we have never hit or abused each other, nor has Erma ever used a rolling pin to bake a pie. But I do hope this is the last generation to ban rolling pins.

Why do I spend time talking about our relationship? Because when you take on the challenges of inner-city living, with your nearest relative or support system seven hundred miles away, you must depend on your partner completely.

You won't have time to be distracted by petty arguments and spats. Life can be hard; but if you have a mate you trust, someone who has your back and is unafraid to stand next to you during the battles of life, you'll make it. Sure, we've had our share of failures and missed opportunities, but we've had our share of successes and triumphs.

We were married over the Fourth of July holiday of 1966 and began our real life together.

CHAPTER 10

Welcome to Detroit

*Michigan
1967–68*

I n June of 1968, after resigning from F. W. Woolworth Co. as assistant manager and a year teaching in Charleston, Missouri, Erma and I put everything we owned into a small U-Haul trailer pulled by our 1966 Pontiac Tempest and, along with the baby, moved up north. We landed first in the small community of Milford, Michigan, but we soon discovered that we were attracted to the university cities. But which one, Ann Arbor or Detroit? I must admit that as an antiwar student, it was nice to be near enough to Canada to make a run for the border if my number came up.

Both were close and both had good universities. We visited each city and looked at the universities and the cost of living. Ann Arbor was upscale and expensive, even back then. I thought we could afford to live in Detroit, and so in the summer of 1969, we again loaded up our car and a small U-Haul trailer and moved into Downtown Detroit on a hope and a prayer. We knew no one and had no relatives in the state.

We bought a *Free Press*, noting that nothing was free in Michigan, and began our search for an apartment near the campus. On Trumbull Avenue, we spotted a sign stating "Apartment for Rent." But upon inquiry, we were told by an older black lady that she didn't rent to white folks but we might want to try across the street. She had heard the old white woman there had an empty apartment and was looking to rent to white folks.

We hurried over and found an old frame house at Calumet and Trumbull and found a young white man mowing the yard. We explained that we were students looking for an apartment near campus. We couldn't afford much but were good people and willing to work in lieu of part of the rent.

We chatted for a while and finally got him to show us the unit. It was on the first floor with two bedrooms, a living room, a kitchen, and a bath. The rent was $45 a month and included water and heat, but there were conditions: we would have to pay our own electricity and shovel the sidewalks in the winter. No problem. We had paid $100 a month for a smaller apartment in Milford. What was the deal here?

He explained that the little old lady living upstairs was his mother. Since the '67 Riots, the young man had moved out to the suburbs, but his mother refused to leave the family home. He wanted someone to look after her and do some maintenance around the house. We paid a security deposit and the first month's rent in advance, with the security deposit refunded to us from Milford.

Each morning the old lady was out sweeping the sidewalks and picking up the trash blown in or dropped by pedestrians from the night before. We soon discovered that she spoke only a little broken English and, like so many Detroiters, had moved to the city as a child from somewhere in Eastern Europe.

By September, our apartment had been robbed twice, in spite of the iron bars I installed on all first-floor windows. During the last robbery, they had broken a plate glass window facing the alley a good eight feet above ground level. We were sleeping when a rock smashed the window. I ran out of the bedroom, careful not to cut my feet on the broken glass, with my little .22 revolver aimed at a figure reaching through the window and grabbing the little television that we had just purchased. I yelled, "Drop it," which he did. The TV toppled out the window and fell crashing to the alley below. I had the thief in my sight but had been warned not to shoot an intruder still outside the house (and warned that if I did, I should pull him back in before the police arrived). I didn't shoot, and the shadow disappeared down the alley and escaped.

While cleaning up the shattered glass, I found a perfect palm print where the thief had touched the glass. We carefully wrapped it in a newspaper and put it aside, thinking that the police would want it as evidence. We then waited several hours for the scout car to arrive.

Finally, two police officers, both white, arrived to take our statement; but they refused to take the glass containing the fingerprints. "There won't be any proof that it is connected to the B&E," they insisted. I told them it was a ten-foot drop to the alley and no one else could have left the print. "That may or may not be true," I was told, but it didn't matter anyway because I had broken the chain of custody. They both kind of smiled.

In my statement, I told an officer that the intruder was a middle-aged colored male and was about to give a description when he pulled me aside and warned me not to use the word *colored* to refer to blacks.

"They don't like it. It sounds like you are a racist."

I assured him that I was not a racist and would never use that word again to refer to black folks.

He then asked where I was from. I told him that we were from Poplar Bluff near the Bootheel in southeast Missouri, near Arkansas, I added by way of explanation.

The officer just smiled and repeated the town's name incorrectly. "Popular Bluff?"

"No, Poplar Bluff, you know, like the trees—Lombardy poplar trees that grew on a bluff above the river," I explained. He just smiled. I didn't get the joke.

He informed us that his report was for insurance purposes and that we could pick it up at the precinct in three days. When we told him we didn't have renters' insurance, he just smiled to himself and shook his head and suggested that we move out to the suburbs. We were really babes in the woods.

Wow, did we have a lot to learn about Detroit police practices. Today, when we watch those *CSI* crime shows on television, we chuckle with the knowledge that Detroit's crime lab was so inefficient and corrupt that the state had to close it down years ago. They had no laboratory to match fingerprints, even if they had taken them.

The next day I installed a heavy four-foot-by-eight-foot plywood over the opening. I then tightly screwed it in place with one-way lag bolts (you can screw them in but can't screw them out). That should slow them down. It seemed as if the bad guys knew when we came and went. I would have to do something about that, but I needed a job first.

CHAPTER 11

Employment

Detroit, Michigan
Summer 1969

By the summer of 1969, we were settled in our new apartment. We painted the rooms, bought used carpet from the auto show, and carpeted the rooms in commercial gray. We had no furniture to speak of, so I sanded and stained a sheet of plywood and put it on some cinder blocks. That was our dining room table. We had a couple of beanbags for chairs. A two-burner hot plate, a tiny refrigerator, kitchen utensils, and a little black-and-white television completed the inventory of our worldly possessions, except books. We had transported my collection of books and shelves (Dad had given us the bookshelves he received when he purchased a set of *World Book Encyclopedia* years before). Life was simple.

True, we had moved to Detroit to pursue educations, but another powerful reason was to be near enough to Canada to make a run for the border in the event my draft number was called.

Detroit was a hop, skip, and jump away from Canada. By then I was totally committed against the war in Vietnam. I argued from a historical point of view that we had turned our backs on our earlier allies, the Vietminh, in our battle against the Japanese in the Pacific. I reminded people that we had been allied with the Communist Soviet Union against a greater evil, Nazi Germany.

To add insult to injury, we had supported French efforts to regain mastery and control of their former colonies in French Indochina, and this was when they had done nothing to help us in the fight against the Japanese. Thinking about it, they had done nothing but surrender to the Germans in Europe.

The old joke seemed true, "Do you want to buy a slightly used MAS rifle (the French infantry weapon of World War II)? Never fired and only dropped once." Then the teller of the joke would raise his arms in surrender. This always got a good laugh.

During this period, there was some bureaucratic holdup on my references and transcripts from my college in Missouri, preventing me from getting a job with the Detroit Public Schools. So I worked day labor and any odd job I could find.

I would get up early and walk, or take the bus, to the hiring hall on Henry Street in the downtown area and wait, along with a mixed group of men of nationalities and races that I never knew even existed before, for the minimum-wage assignments that were doled out. My first few trips, the jobs ran out before my name was called.

Sometimes I would find a group outside, and we'd stand around smoking and, at times, passing a bottle around on cool mornings, waiting for our names to be called. One such morning, I stepped into a group of black men engaged in an ongoing conversation about local history. I nodded a greeting and stood silently, listening.

"Oh man," a large black man with a watch cap pulled down low on his forehead continued, "that ain't nothin', you don't know no fear until you run up again' the Big Four." His comment was followed with a chorus of affirmative "Um hmms" and "That's right."

He continued, "One Saturday night, I was with some of my n—s, and we was walking over to the Fox Theater (he pronounced it like "tree-a-ter"). We was staying down in the Black Bottom when the Big Four pulls up next to the curb and a big cop gets out all by himself and asks us n—s where we are a going."

"Who was it?" someone asked.

"It was Nat Turpin himself, don't you know, and he was looking for some young brothers who had pulled a heist earlier. But we wasn't them. I was young, but I wasn't stupid." He continued, "I didn't give him no sass. I just answered his questions real polite like. He was carrying a blackjack and slapping it in the palm of his other hand—*smack, smack, smack* it went. I tell you, I was scared to death. Everyone knew that he would crack a brother's skull for sassing him."

"She-it," said another black man who had been listening in silence, "I wouldn't put up with that crap. I'd a take that blackjack of his and shoved it up his black ass." The group hooted and laughed with derision.

The man telling the story said, "You didn't grow up around here, you don't know shit from Shinola. Everyone called him Mr. Ben, even the whites. He carried two big pearl-handled .45 revolvers. This was during the time when most cops carried little .32 revolvers or those little.38, not the big .38 Specials we have today." The group nodded in agreement. "Besides that," he continued, "he wore some kind of bulletproof armor under his shirt."

"He killed more men than Billy the Kid," one man stated, "even killed a white man once. Turned out to be a member of the Purple Gang, and he got a medal for it. Yes, sir, he knew how to keep these young n—s in their place and to show a little respect for their elders. You know, of all the killing he did, he never killed a kid."

"Come back tomorrow at 7:00 a.m." was shouted out of the window separating the clerk from us, and then the window was slammed closed.

As time went on, I learned how the system worked. Everything has a system, and I began to get some assignments. I began to be one of the first in line, and once I bought doughnuts and coffee for the clerks with my last change. Each morning I shaved and combed my hair and was ready to work. I stayed away from the drunks and addicts who were just looking for a quick score. Once, we spent the day moving file cabinets, fully loaded, and office furniture from one floor of a high-rise office building to another. *Boy, it would be cool to work in an office like that someday,* I thought. It was hard work, but I was used to it and didn't mind.

At the end of each day, we'd get our pay envelope, taxes withheld, and I would be sure to give a tip of a quarter to the hiring agent. Unlike the lord in the Bible parable about hiring workers for his vineyard even late in the day, our employer never gave a full day's pay for working for the last few hours. It was only later that I learned that that parable had nothing to do with fairness but was rather about the concept of God's grace and design. Later, I took a job as a bill collector, one of the worse jobs I've ever had, and prayed for my teaching credentials to come through.

I was the possessor of a Missouri life teaching certificate, something unheard of today. When I finally did get a letter from the Detroit Public Schools allowing me to be an unlimited substitute (that is, one who will go anywhere in the city and teach any subject at any middle, junior high, or high school grade), I was finally able to register at WSU in a master's program in general secondary education. Life was improving.

As the years passed, the war in Vietnam wound down and my number had not been called. We stayed on, whether out of guilt for not serving or, as I like to think, because of a commitment to help our neighbors and the city of Detroit. The neighborhood was getting worse. But the rent was cheap, and it was near to the university where both Erma and I had decided to get advanced degrees.

CHAPTER 12

The Welfare State

Detroit, Michigan
November 1969

Our first Thanksgiving in our little apartment was cheerful. We hadn't been broken into for the past few months. For several days, I would make a big show of going to work and driving away, then I would circle back and park on a side street and enter through the rear of the house and lie in wait. On the third morning, I heard a sound like someone was trying to tear the house apart. Running outside like a madman with my little .22 pistol in hand, I caught two black men with a crowbar trying to pry out the lag bolts I had installed into the window frames to hold the iron bars in place. The iron bars bent but held.

I screamed and charged them. They broke and ran in different directions, one of them dropping the crowbar (which I still have). After placing the crowbar inside the house (spoils of war), I locked the door and thought about calling the police. But I thought better of it and went to work. Life was getting better.

Erma had a job as a secretary at R. L. Polk & Co., and I was bringing in a few dollars each week. Our wants were modest; and we hired a local lady to watch our son, Bobby.

The Wednesday before Thanksgiving was the last of a three-day assignment with the day-labor people. That evening, I got my pay envelope from the hiring agent but was told that there was no work on Thanksgiving Day.

We bundled up our baby and off we went to the Farmer Jack's grocery store on Grand River Avenue to buy some milk and food for our first Thanksgiving meal in Detroit. I remember studying the prices of the produce and carefully keeping track of our purchases. We had to save at least $5 for gas. Instead of a ham or a turkey for our main course, we could only afford to buy a package of thin-cut pressed ham. But that was fine with us. We were going to have our Thanksgiving dinner together. We were young, in love, and very happy about our prospects.

In the checkout line we saw shopping carts piled high with the bounty of American goodness and the lively predominantly black crowd of shoppers paying with food stamps. Beer, wine, and cigarettes were segregated and paid with cash out of pocketbooks and coin purses, often on chains, hidden in the blouses of the female customers. It seemed as if the women in the black community controlled the money. I looked around and didn't see many black men shopping with their mates. The women seemed to come with a number of little children holding hands and pointing at objects of desire. Hands were often slapped and one could hear the sharp rebukes of mothers telling children to "Leave that alone" or "Don't touch if you know what's good for you."

As I looked down at our few items in our cart, I noticed that not only were we the only white folks in the line but we also had the smallest number of items for checkout. And we were also the only ones paying the entire bill in cash. The cashier, a well-endowed Middle Eastern lady in a low-cut blouse and large gold hooped earrings, smiled and played peekaboo with Bobby for a few seconds before ringing up our purchases.

"Don't you have any food stamps?" she asked.

"No," I answered, "we are paying with cash." She thought that was strange and just smiled and shook her head as if to say "Why not?"

At home, as we were putting away the groceries, we talked about the clerk, the customers we saw, and the use of food stamps and welfare. We could qualify, but we never really considered that as an option. We discussed the fact that in a year or two (or maybe three at the most), we would be in a nicer apartment or maybe even a house and how those folks, both blacks and poor whites, would still be on welfare.

In those days, there were hundreds of poor whites living in apartments and houses along Trumbull Avenue. It was called Little Appalachia. Most of the families had moved up from the South for the factory jobs during the war years when Detroit was truly the Arsenal of Democracy or later as sharecroppers were displaced by huge agrofarms in the 1950s.

The factories in Detroit, for the most part, were being closed; and the white folks no longer had the farms to go back to. They had adapted to the city and its streets. The young white men were as tough and mean as any other city thug, and often, their families were criminal enterprises. Many of the young white girls were busy selling themselves on the streets, having babies, and collecting welfare. These criminal families had one or more members in prison, and between legitimate jobs, they set up B&E's, armed robberies, and theft from those few who still worked. In our neighborhood, you had to look out for three types of dangers: the roving gangs of black thugs from the Jeffries project; the lone punk, usually black but often white, who roamed the streets seeking crimes of opportunity; and the white trash families waiting for the chance to rip you off.

We decided that getting on assistance wasn't worth giving up our dignity. I was proud of the fact that even during the Great Depression, my folks had never gone on relief. My father told me that it got so bad during the winter of 1931–32 that he moved back to the farm and lived off the land. He told me that they were trying to sell some cattle that winter but the cost of shipping them to the Kansas City market was more than they brought on the exchange. They couldn't afford the grain, so they slaughtered the herd and neighbors from all around came and hauled away free sides of beef. My grandparents were almost self-sufficient on their farms, but those days were long gone. We had to make it. We had no farm to go back to.

As you can see, we were raised to work hard, take our turn, treat people fairly, and stand up for our rights and what we believed in. We would not go on welfare, not then, not ever. We cooked our simple meals on a simple two-burner electric hot plate that we had received as a wedding gift and were darned happy to have it. I put the milk away in the small mini-refrigerator that my brother sold me for fifty dollars when he left for the military. Sure, life was tough, but we were in love, had a great little kid, and life would get better. And it did, but it took a while.

CHAPTER 13

Daily Life in the City

Detroit
1969–70

We secured our little apartment as best we could and made as good a life for us as possible. We joined Saint Dominic's Catholic Church and learned that its older parishioners were a source for answers to life's pressing questions. Where is the best place to have your car repaired or the best place for auto insurance? Where can we get someone good to take care of Bobby?

We had hired an older white lady on Trumbull Avenue, but luckily, I got out of work early one day and decided to pick up Bobby. After repeatedly knocking with no response, I looked through a window and saw Bobby standing in a crib, whimpering. His cries and screams had no effect on our babysitter, who was sitting in an armchair next to an empty bottle of gin, sound asleep.

With my trusty pocketknife, I was able to move the bolt of the lock over to allow me to enter and collect our son and the diaper bag. I left a note and a little money to cover what we might possibly owe and told her we no longer required her services.

Through the church, we were lucky to find an old Irish family that had been in the neighborhood for generations; and they lived just a few blocks away. Ella, the matriarch of the family, met us, fell in love with Bobby, and said one more child more or less wouldn't matter. Bobby wound up being an only child with seven brothers and sisters.

Later, on a Sunday morning, I told him that after church, we would walk to the corner market on Trumbull to buy Popsicles. On the way home, a huge Lincoln town car jerked to a stop at the curb in front of us. The driver, a large black man dressed in a flamboyant suit wearing a wide brim hat of matching color, jumped out and slammed the car door. He bounded up the steps of an old apartment building and commenced pounding on the doors and shouting. We stood on the sidewalk licking our Popsicles and watched.

Screaming insults at someone inside, the man finally kicked open the doors and went in. There was a loud explosion, and he was thrown back out the door as if snatched by an invisible hand. His body, or what was left of it, hit the lower steps and flopped on the sidewalk a few yards away. A pool of dark blood formed around his remains.

A white lady in a bathrobe came out on the stoop to look at her handiwork. A 12-gauge pump shotgun, with smoke still curling from its muzzle, was cradled in her arms. She seemed satisfied with her work and, shifting the weapon in her arms like an infant, returned back into the apartment. We finished our treats before the police arrived. A crowd of onlookers had gathered to share information on the shooter, a known whore, and the victim, her pimp. Everyone agreed that it was rough justice of sorts. He was known to beat his women.

She was cuffed and taken away, and a meat wagon arrived to cart off the body. The landlord was called to repair the door, and an old lady with a broom turned on the water and hosed the area and swept away the bloody stain.

Detroiters love a free show. After each event, the neighbors and street people collect to look at the carnage. They seem to be especially attracted to fires and police cars, not so much with ambulances. We watched for a while and then walked home.

One bad event was quickly being followed by another. We had another B&E at the apartment. Someone kicked in the rear door and, after searching all the drawers and cupboards, found and stole my little Rohm .22 revolver.

I was made to feel like a criminal when I reported it at the local police station. "Now another weapon on the streets," I was told, "a real Saturday night special, a cop killer." I felt bad, and determined to get a real gun and do everything I could to obtain a carry permit so as to keep the weapon secure on my person at all times.

Trouble always comes in three, or so it seemed. Soon thereafter, Erma was accosted by two young black punks who tried to take her bicycle as she rode home from work. We only had one vehicle, and I needed the car in my position as a bill collector. Erma fought them off, and by the grace of God, she kept both her life and her new black three-speed ladies' bike.

Erma was really ticked off, and that evening we drove the alleys and streets near where it had happened slowly, street by street, looking for the punks. I had recently bought a used .38 Charter Arms pistol on a trip to Missouri and had slid it under my seat.

We were both upset, and I wasn't sure what we would do if and when we caught them. I was planning on making a citizen's arrest. My weapon was licensed but only for home or business, not to carry. This would be tricky.

Lucky for everyone concerned, Erma never spotted them. Was it worth it? I wondered why I felt the need to stay in Detroit. Erma and Bob stayed because I stayed, but why did I stay? If I wasn't going to serve in Vietnam, then I would stay in Detroit, at least through the end of the war.

I began to view street crime as a force of nature, like a tornado or blizzard, something beyond our control. We hunkered down and did our best to prepare for it, and then we dealt with it and cleaned up the resulting mess. I came to the realization that I knew why I remained in Detroit. I could not bear to think of myself as a coward.

I had declined to volunteer to fight in Vietnam, my generation's war. Deep down, I felt shame and guilt. So many of my generation, especially the working and lower classes, went to Southeast Asia to fight and many to die while I remained stateside.

True, I had moved to Detroit, just across the river from Canada; but I didn't consider myself a draft dodger or coward. After all, my number had not yet been called. I decided that as long as there was a war in Vietnam, I would remain in Detroit, doing my best to help the folks and be a good neighbor. I would use self-help and a little street justice as needed to survive. Welcome to our world.

CHAPTER 14

Unlimited Substitute

Detroit
1970–71

Our first year in Detroit, just after the 1967 Riots, went from bad to worse. Jobs were hard to obtain, and I took any work I could find. But I hated my job as a bill collector. It was the worse job I've ever had in my life. But finally, my credentials were approved by the Detroit Public Schools, and I could apply for a teaching position.

For the first time in months, we had a modest income, and I enrolled in the master of education program at Wayne State University. The campus was only a twenty-minute walk or a ten-minute bike ride. We had previously scraped up the money to buy a pair of beautiful his-and-her British black three-speed bicycles. At about this time, Erma found work as a secretary at a publishing firm in Detroit. Things were looking up.

I accepted substitute teaching positions in the Detroit Public Schools as an unlimited sub. The pay was good, thirty-five dollars a day.

Once I was called to substitute for a teacher who had gone out on disability at a west side junior high. I had received the call late and arrived just as the class bell was ringing. I parked in the fenced-in lot marked for staff and visitors and jogged, briefcase in hand, around the building to the main entrance.

Hearing a second-floor window open above me and the sudden chaotic banging and screams of unsupervised children, I looked up just in time to see the first book, followed by several other textbooks, come flying down at me. I jumped to the building and pressed against the bricks as several heavy books hit the pavement where I had stood a second before. Running like a football player, I luckily avoided several more books, hearing them smack the sidewalk behind me.

I jogged up the steps to the first-floor office and walked in and introduced myself as the substitute teacher for the day. I saw the principal, a little white woman hiding in her office, wave me away without a word and close her office door. The black secretary exhaled in sympathy and tried on a smile. The noise of desks hitting the floor startled us both and caused us to look up the stairs.

"You have world history, Ms. Anderson's class. It's room 204." She scrutinized me closely as I signed the forms. "You have substituted before, haven't you?"

I assured her that I was a professional unlimited substitute and there was nothing for her to worry about.

She said, "I truly hope so." She came to the top of the steps with me and pointed at a room from which banging, shouts, screams, and peals of laughter were emanating. It sounded like the students were trying to tear the place apart. It was the same room the books had been thrown down at me.

Upon entering the room, I saw the majority of the students cowering in a corner as a busy group of boys and girls pushed the desks toward the huge double-hung windows. Two boys were up on the windowsill, trying to open them. They had the desks lined up ready to toss out the window.

"Good morning, students," I commanded in my best teacher voice, ignoring the chaos. "Please arrange your desks in order and take your seats. We don't have much time. You'll find this the most interesting and, I dare say, the most important class you've ever had in school. Quickly! Quickly! We don't have all day."

I erased the gang signs, four-letter words, and graffiti from the chalkboard and, careful not to turn my back to the class (an unlimited sub learns to write on the blackboard while facing the class), I wrote my name on the board while looking at the class. I pronounced it for the class and said, "Quickly, quickly. I'm your teacher for today. You are lucky to have me, so let's get started."

The students looked at one another in stunned silence as I opened my attaché case and removed some papers.

"First, we must take attendance. It's the rule," I explained. "Quickly, or you are going to miss out on a fascinating experience that you can tell your mothers about this evening."

The majority of the students approached their desks and began righting them and moving them in rows. I started picking up papers, binders, and books off the floor and returned them to students as I patrolled up and down the aisles, straightening a desk here and there.

In a few minutes, the room was somewhat orderly and a little neater, so I began by telling the students that I was not only a master teacher but also a student at Wayne State University and that I was studying American folk literature. I would jot a few terms on the board to make it look good for the administrators and staff who would always peek in and then give them an example of a folktale.

It just so happened that my grandmother, Myrtle McKuin (my mother's mom), often told us kids ghost stories; and I remembered the scary ones. As children, we would sit on the floor at her feet, hugging our knees and scooting closer to one another during the scary parts. It was better than going to a drive-in movie, and I still remember the chills of fear running up and down my spine. I actually had enough stories, games, and activities to keep the rowdiest group of kids attentive and quiet for three days, then I'd have to move on to another assignment. I always began with the best of my grandmother's stories, "the Grave." It held the students' attention for a full period. By the way, Rod Sterling did an updated version of the story in the *Twilight Zone* series. I believe he still called it the Grave, but it was set in the Old West and starred Lee Marvin.

This was followed on the second day with "Rasputin, the Mad Monk of Russia." I had done extensive research for a paper on this topic in college in Missouri. The third day, I let the students tell their own stories and family folklore and we would begin to work on writing. This was the most fun. In addition, I carried a set of word games and age-appropriate puzzles that the students enjoyed.

Normally, on the first day substituting, the secretary would find some excuse to come to the room to check on things. Looking through the window in the door, she would find the students eagerly leaning forward in their seats, deeply engrossed in the tale. I would be at the front of the room, jotting something on the blackboard, or moving up and down the aisles. From the outside, it looked like I was really teaching. I always had a list of words on the board, as if somehow we were discussing these topics. Soon the principal and other teachers would find an excuse to peer in and watch.

I always got invited back and was often offered permanent jobs on numerous occasions, but I turned them down after the third day. I was a storyteller and a babysitter, not a teacher. Also, I was enrolled at WSU in a masters of education program and had no time to prepare lesson plans and grade papers. I knew that the administration wanted a quiet, well-managed room more than anything else. Normally, when a teacher was out, the substitute was fair game for any abuse the students could come up with. It was matters of classroom pride to have a substitute teacher fleeing from the building before the end of the school day. This was especially true if the teacher was white and the students black.

Once, while subbing at Central High School on Woodward Avenue, I was asked, along with an older white male teacher, to stand on each side of the double doors and watch the students exit from an afternoon event in the auditorium on Malcolm X Day. He was older, so I let him choose the side he wanted to monitor. We stood in the back during the presentation and listened to terms of "black pride" and "black is beautiful" and the evils of white America. When it ended, we stepped back out to our respective posts.

The doors flew open with a bang, and the students literally ran from the building, screaming with laughter and completely ignoring our pleas to slow down and walk. "Don't run," I repeated. In a few minutes, hundreds of students had departed, leaving a trail of crumpled papers, candy and potato chip wrappers, books, binders, caps, scarves, and other debris on the steps and out of the building.

I bent down to start picking up the papers when I glanced over at the other side of the door. The older white teacher was on the floor, not moving as blood pooled from a wound in his neck. He had been stabbed by one of the students as they left.

By luck, I had a clean white handkerchief in the breast pocket of my suit jacket and used it to stem the flow of blood. From that day on, I always carried a clean white handkerchief in my breast pocket and a colored bandanna in my hip pocket for daily use.

A janitor called for an ambulance, and after what seemed like an eternity, the teacher was loaded on a gurney and taken to emergency. I heard that he lived but left on complete disability and never taught again. I was told that he had been stabbed with an ice pick.

Most of the teachers during that period were white and scared to death of the students. They couldn't wait to get out of the building at the end of the day. Many would almost run over students to get away from the school. You would see a stream of cars pulling out from the teachers' parking lot, racing their motors to get away. As time moved on, my portfolio of materials expanded to where I could remain up to two weeks in one classroom before I had to move on.

It was easy to see why the students hated most of their white teachers. They did not relate to the students and had moved to the suburbs. I always carried some cheap plastic chess sets in my briefcase and often taught and played chess with students during lunch and before and after school.

Once, while subbing at Murray-Wright High School, which was within walking distance of our apartment, I was warned by one of my chess students to make sure I was out of the building by the sixth hour.

"Just be gone out'a here," I was warned without explanation.

I went to the office and tried to see the principal but was informed that she was unavailable. I explained to an assistant principal (AP) what I had been told and was given a slip allowing me to take the class to the library that period. The AP thought that, somehow, I was the target of the threat.

At the beginning of the sixth hour, I took my class to the library for research, a real treat. While there, we heard the fire alarm going off and had to evacuate the building. I learned later that the classroom next to mine had been firebombed and a teacher assaulted. Well, anyway, it was time to move on.

What did I learn from these experiences? Stay alert and move toward the problem, not away from it. Be commanding and have a real presence. I think Aristotle said it best. If you want to be brave, then act as if you are brave. Practice bravery until it becomes part of you. Control the situation with your words and appearance. Don't antagonize or inflame and never, ever lose your temper. Yes, there are times when you increase the volume of your voice and speak in short declarative sentences. Be polite and give respect, and then you can demand it. Remember, I used the same basic materials no matter the grade or the subject. Only a few times in my experience did a teacher leave valid lesson plans or exams to be given. I began to rely on my own wit and materials.

I can't count the number of fights I broke up with a commanding word and a movement toward the action. I was also slugged once in the jaw while attempting to break up a fight in a high school. Luckily for me, I turned my head in time to only have the blow glance off my jaw. The surrounding students all exclaimed with an "Uhooo" sound together and froze, waiting for the next act.

Realizing that all eyes were on me, I shook off the blow and smiled. Then I puffed out my chest and bellowed, "Enough, before someone gets hurt." I then commanded the two students engaged in the fight to follow me to my room; and surprise, surprise, they did.

We spent a half hour talking about the origins of their fight, and I asked them if they were up to a game of thumb wrestling to settle the disagreement. I showed them the basics of the game, and after three games, I declared a winner and everyone shook hands. The student who threw the punch that landed on me apologized. I told him it was nothing and thus gained school "creds" as a white teacher who could take a punch to the jaw. I also gained the respect of the principal for dealing with a problem without involving administration.

By the next day, the story had grown to my taking a massive blow from a Joe Lewis-like student and just shaking it off and smiling. I was offered a permanent position, but I left when my materials were exhausted.

You may be wondering what is meant by "thumb wrestling." It's a game of strength and skill that, I discovered, can be used as a substitute to a challenge for fists, knives, or guns. The two opponents rest elbows on a table and face off. Each grasps the hand of the other with thumbs-up. The object is to hold the other's thumb down with one's own for the count of three. I explained the rules: best two out of three wins and the loser must shake hands and congratulate the winner.

"One, two, three, begin." The thumbs dance back and forth. Each combatant is trying to gain the advantage and, with the use of leverage, feints, and rapid movement, forces one opponent into submission. Even if both are evenly matched, one will eventually allow his thumb to slide below the others and, as the opponent comes down to lock on, will make a quick movement and be on top. It's an exciting game and good fun to referee. We always allow for a rematch. This game allowed boys and girls to test their strength and agility against each other in a nonviolent game.

By the way, after years spent on brush crews, I was agile with strong hands and never lost a game to a student. The next year I accepted a regular teaching position at a regional middle school and discovered that I loved teaching and enjoyed the parents and students.

CHAPTER 15

Our First and Only Home

Detroit, Michigan
Winter of 1971–72

I heard from fellow parishioners at Saint Dominic's about a house opening up for sale a few blocks away on Avery and Alexandrine. I was told it was an opportunity too good to pass up. I felt it would be good to get our own place still within easy biking or walking distance of the campus. I was beginning to think of advanced degrees. Erma was also thinking about going back to finish her bachelor's degree.

I was told that the new owners had the title to the place but had only recently acquired it. They needed to do a quick sale and were moving out of state. I finally had a real teaching job for the Detroit Public Schools with a regular paycheck. Life was looking up.

That afternoon, after school, I met with the owners on Avery. It was a beautiful, if run-down, brick-and-stucco Victorian two floor with four bedrooms, one bathroom, a basement, an attic, and with a detached garage.

The owners had a U-Haul parked in front and were busy hauling items of furniture, boxes, lamps, and the like out to the trailer. I introduced myself and told them that my wife and I might be interested in the place. Even with the place in disarray and the trash and debris scattered over the floors, I instantly fell in love and was trying not to show it. Inside, it had high plastered ceilings with grape leaf and vine molding running around the front living room and dining room. A huge mirror rested atop a beautiful oak mantle above a brick fireplace with lots of beautiful dark oak woodwork and doors. The first-floor woodwork had never been painted (a very popular thing to do in the 1940s), as had so many of the neighbors' houses that we had visited. *Yes,* I thought, *we could be happy here.*

"Do the chandeliers come with it?" I inquired.

"Well, we had planned on taking the light fixtures," he said, "but of course, everything is negotiable. You see, we, ah, inherited the place and want to sell and, you know, move on with our lives. Are you interested?" I got the feeling he was hiding something. I thought it best to have a real estate person look over the documents.

"I might be, not sure. It's in pretty rough shape, but first I want to look around from the basement to the attic. If I like it, I'll get my wife to take a look. But the chandeliers and those carpets"—I pointed to a half-dozen old carpets rolled up, ready for removal—"they will also have to stay or it's a deal breaker."

They huddled together in a conversation for a few minutes before nodding assent.

The basement was dominated by a huge old gravity air furnace, probably installed when the house was built in 1905. It had been a coal-fired conversion to natural gas and would probably need to be replaced. The wiring wasn't just old, it was obsolete. The plumbing was shot, and the kitchen needed a new floor, all new appliances, cabinets, and windows. Other than the fact that the front porch was falling down and it had a postage stamp-sized backyard, it did have a lot of character.

An hour later, I met with the couple on the porch. "How much do you want for it, as it stands, defects and all?"

"You mean as is?"

"Yes," I replied, "as she stands, mess and all."

"We were thinking around $20,000. But for cash, we could go as low as $15,000."

I started to name all the problems and defects, including the roof, which wouldn't make it through another winter. The small pantry add-on in the rear leaked and needed major repairs or would have to be torn down. It didn't take long to agree on an even number: $10,000. That was if my wife approved and we could get a reasonable interest rate on a home loan.

Erma and Bobby came over to look at it, and after a brief inspection, she asked, "Do you really want it? It needs so much work."

I said that I did. We walked around dreaming about how we'd like to fix it up.

We went to a real estate agent to have the deeds reviewed and to a bank for our first mortgage. It stretched fifteen years into the future. Would we even live that long?

We moved in and spent the first few days hauling ladies' garments to Goodwill. The closets were crammed with clothing and personal effects. We couldn't understand why so many personal effects had been left behind.

A few days later, we picked up a certified check and gave it to the owners. They shook our hands, wished us luck, and left town. We never heard from them again.

Later we learned from the next-door neighbor that the old lady who lived here before us had also been a member of Saint Dominic Parish. She had outlived her family and was fearful of being unable to take care of herself and winding up in a nursing home. She cut a deal with a couple from the church that they would come and live with her and do the cooking and housekeeping. In turn, she signed a deed granting the property to them when she passed. We were told that she feared a nursing home more than anything else.

The couple moved in, and within a few weeks, the old lady fell down the flight of stairs, breaking her hip. After the hospital stay, she was sent to a nursing home where she promptly expired.

Erma has always believed that our house has a special visitor. Is it the spirit of the old lady? Erma can tell you a multitude of sightings and stories of strange happenings at the house. As for me, if there is a spirit, it's friendly.

Several years ago, my sister Barbara came for a visit while her husband was on his second tour of duty in Vietnam, (he volunteered both times). She reported that while occupied in the second-floor bathroom one morning, she felt a cold chill that was nothing unusual in itself for Michigan. But when she tried to exit, someone or something on the other side of the door prevented her from opening it. She said that she tried to turn the doorknob but felt a counter pressure.

Barb said that she went back and sat on the commode and had a cigarette to calm her nerves. She knew that we were both at work and had taken Bobby to the sitter.

She told me that she had called out, "Anyone there?" She said that, hearing no response, she next said, "All right now, George, stop playing games. I need to get dressed now, so stop holding the door and let me out."

Barb said that she flushed her cigarette and went to the door. The knob turned easily and the door swung open. She looked carefully around to make sure no one was lurking around a corner. The house was completely empty.

George was the name I had given to the spirit after Erma, early one morning, woke me in a fright saying that someone wearing a dark cape was standing in the corner watching. I came awake; grabbed my glasses and my .38 pistol, which was kept on the bed table; and jumped up. I turned on a light, but there was nothing to see. Erma was absolutely convinced that she had seen him, not dreamed it, so I had to conduct a search with pistol and flashlight while Erma went in to keep Bobby company. I searched the house from basement to attic, each closet, nook, and cranny; but George had vacated the premises.

CHAPTER 16

The Devil You Say

Detroit, Michigan
October 1972

When Bobby was about five years of age, less expensive smoke detectors began to appear on the market. I purchased one and put it in the hallway outside our bedrooms. I tested it with cigarette smoke and the alarm blared and it blinked. We three talked about our escape route and the dangers of fire and smoke.

One night, after coming in from an evening at the Dakota Inn (my favorite Bavarian-style drinking establishment, then as now), we picked up Bobby at the babysitter and put him to bed. Erma and I sat around for a while talking about Devil's Night coming up in a few days. It had become the custom in Detroit to burn down any and all abandoned and unprotected structures on the night before Halloween. There were so many abandoned structures to choose from. Last year, someone burned neighborhood dumpsters and an unused garage, even with our citizens on patrol.

I had again volunteered to be on the citizens' patrol, walking the neighborhood's streets and alleys and trying to prevent arson on Devil's Night. We now had the new smoke detector, a fire extinguisher in the kitchen, and a smaller one in the vehicle; but were we really ready? I decided that it would be good to test it out and see how Bobby would react under actual conditions.

Erma was reluctant at first, but I explained to her how this was actually good for the boy and that it would help him to survive. During those days, arsonists were busy burning Detroit to the ground and not just on Devil's Night. Many fires were for insurance money under the guise of general arson for fun. Often, city properties couldn't be sold for what the owners had invested in them. It was just easier to burn them and collect the cash and move out to the suburbs. Folks from the suburbs were bringing their cars into Detroit, torching them for the insurance, and leaving the burned-out hulks under overpasses and littering side streets. It was a crazy time. The sirens of fire, police, and emergency vehicles were heard 24-7.

Erma finally agreed, and with Bobby fast asleep, she hid behind a closed bedroom door opened just enough to watch his bedroom across the hall. I lit up a cigarette and blew smoke up at the new device. Suddenly, it was activated with an ear-piercing screeching sound and a flashing light. I slipped into another room with the door slightly ajar. I watched Bobby sit up and struggle with his covers. He came awake and looked around, dazed and confused, and then he stumbled out of his bed and yelled for help. Then he began running around his darkened room, bumping into things; finally, he opened his closet door and went in to hide. Had it been a real fire, his body might have been found in the closet the next morning, after having died from smoke inhalation.

Erma turned on the lights as I waved the smoke away from the alarm. We had an unnerving quiet broken only by Bobby's sobs and whimpering from the closet. Erma's comforting words brought him out of the closet and calmed him down. Between sniffles, he listened as we explained that this had been a test. We talked about the dangers of fire and about our escape plan.

Were we being cruel? Yes, you bet we were; but life in Detroit was hard then, and a little kid had to learn early the real facts of life. Panic kills!

Over the next few months, we pulled a smoke-alarm test several more times, and Bobby quickly got the hang of it. He didn't panic, just reacted. He seemed a bit put out at times but accepted the interruption of his sleep for the greater good.

I remember the night of our final test. We picked Bobby up from his second family and tucked him into his bed. He was soon sound asleep. After watching some television and having another beer, we decided to have another test, but this one with a twist. I carried some chairs and a rolled-up carpet and piled them up on the stairs at the landing. I had blocked off Bobby's primary escape route. It would be interesting to see what he would do under these circumstances.

Again, we turned the lights off, and I activated the device. It again went off with an earsplitting screech. We watched from our hiding places as Bobby jumped up from his bed, yelling, "Mom, Dad, fire!" Hearing no response, per the plan, he ran to the stairs; but he found them blocked. He paused for a second; looked around, then he suddenly jumped, and caught hold of the banister, swung himself up over the obstacles and quickly slid down. He then opened the door and exited according to the plan.

Needless to say, he had passed the test with flying colors.

His training paid off years later when he was fourteen. I had had a run-in with a gang of thugs in the area, and one afternoon, Bobby had come home from school and was eating a bowl of cereal in the kitchen when he heard a shattering crash against the steel-reinforced back door. He told me later that it sounded like a bottle crashing and then a *whoosh* sound.

He ran to the side door and looked around the corner to find the rear of the house engulfed in flames and belching a cloud of acrid black smoke. Someone had thrown a Molotov cocktail over the fence onto the back porch under which we kept the straw-filled doghouses. Bobby first ran for the garden hose and began to spray down the area. By the time the fire department arrived, he had put out the fire and had raked the smoldering debris from the doghouse under the porch into the yard. He was giving everything a good soaking. He gave the report to the arson investigator, obtained his business card, and told him I would call when I came home from work.

Erma came in shortly thereafter and found Bobby calmly sitting at the kitchen table finishing his cereal and doing homework.

Erma told me later that she had parked on the street and come in via the front door, so she was unaware of the mess in the backyard and the scorched aluminum siding on the rear of the house. "How was your day, son?" she asked.

"Oh, nothing unusual. But they tried to burn down the house, that's all."

After that incident, he was no longer called Bobby (a name he hated). We called him Bob.

CHAPTER 17

Dangers of Street Parking

Detroit, Michigan
Winter of 1979

The years quickly passed. Both Erma and I received advanced degrees and better positions (mine in education and administration and Erma's in teaching and secretarial). Each year, major improvements were made on our home and our next-door rental. The two rear yards were developed into a fenced-in compound.

On a particularly bad winter evening (with an accumulated snowfall of over twelve inches of heavy wet stuff), I had to park my car on the street. Our garage was full of building materials for another future renovation project. I, along with my other neighbors, had spent hours shoveling sidewalks and the parking spaces in front of our houses. Then we set out old kitchen chairs or milk crates etc. in the cleared spaces immediately in front of our house. Its meaning was understood by all Detroiters as "private—keep out".

I went back into the house to warm up with a cup of hobo coffee when I heard a vehicle spinning its wheels in the snow. Putting my coat, hat, and gloves back on, I picked up my shovel and went out to help. A pickup with rear wheel drive has no traction whatsoever in the snow. You have to load up the bed above the rear wheels with snow for traction and just dig yourself out of the drifts. To my surprise, the pickup was spinning back along the street into the space

I had just cleared. Its rear bumper had pushed the chair aside as its front wheels spun up against the curb and stopped.

"Hey," I called, "didn't you see that chair in my parking space?"

The young rough-looking white guy got out of his truck and started to walk away.

"Hey, you, I'm talking to you, mister," I bellowed.

He glanced back and shrugged his shoulders and said, "Not my problem, man. These are public streets. I can park wherever the f—I want."

"Whooo, hold on," I replied, "don't get all tough on me. I asked you a simple question. I would appreciate it if you would find another parking place. My wife is coming home soon, and I shoveled that space for her," I added, hoping that he might do the right thing if he knew it was for a woman. No such luck.

He replied simply, "F—you," and then turned to walk away, leaving his truck awkwardly parked in my space with its bumper sticking out in the line of traffic, blocking movement along the two deep ruts in the snow.

I called after him again. "You're not from this neighborhood? Here we work together and have rules. You don't take another man's space. I'll help you find a spot for your pickup."

"I got a spot, and I ain't telling you s—," he screamed.

"Sorry to tell you this, but move your pickup now or face serious problems. It's up to you."

"Are you threatening me?" Turning around, he approached in a boxer's stance, gloved fists clenched. He held his chest high, puffed out, and came on fast. As he approached, he slipped, almost falling backward. With arms flailing, he steadied himself on the icy sidewalk. I was wearing heavy winter outdoor work boots with thick waffled soles. He appeared to be in some kind of leather shoes, probably with slick bottom soles with no traction or stability.

Picking up my shovel—it was a steel coal shovel my father had given me when we moved north. It was great for digging out packed snow and ice and beating off punks. I rested it lightly on my right shoulder, testing its weight and getting a good grip on its handle.

"Come on," I said. Neighbors were coming out to see what the commotion was all about.

Swearing a blue streak, the young man got back into his pickup and gunned the engine, spinning snow and ice as he exited into the two traffic ruts in the snow. I replaced the chair in the middle of the space and went back inside to await Erma's return after work.

Looking out the front window, I saw the young man's pickup come sliding around the corner and parking on the opposite side of the street; and there he promptly got his truck hung up in a snowdrift up to its axle.

Enjoying my coffee from the warmth of my home, I watched him spin and accelerate his engine back and forth, spinning deeper in the snow. Jamming his transmission back and forth wouldn't do it any good. Finally, he got out and looked at the two smooth patches of ice his wheels had made. He seemed not to come equipped with a shovel or bags of salt or kitty litter to sprinkle on the slick spots. By this time, several young black men with shovels came by and offered to dig him out for a fee.

Pissed off and highly agitated, he paid them some money and finally got out. I never saw him in the neighborhood again.

I found out later that he was dating one of my tenants at the house next door. She told me, from his point of view, how a crazy man had threatened him with a shovel for parking on a public street and that he refused to ever come down to Downtown Detroit again.

"How do you feel about that?" I asked.

"Oh, I suppose not too bad. He really is a jerk, and I'm better off without him."

"Then I guess it's okay that I tell you I was the crazy man he was talking about."

"Oh," she replied, "I knew that. I heard him outside and watched the two of you from the house. He really is a jerk."

"You can really do much better than him," I commented, and she nodded in agreement and smiled.

"You know," she said, "you remind me of my father. I really feel safe living here." I thanked her.

She and her friend, two single students at WSU, stayed as our tenants for eight more years.

Now for the moral of the story, I would have been much better off if I had not needed a parking space on the street. To put your life in harm's way or, in this case, to put another's life in jeopardy over a parking space is not very smart. This was not my finest hour.

But once you say it, you have to do it. All I can say is I was younger and in much better shape, but I hadn't yet learned how to use tact and diplomacy in a high-risk situation. I would handle it differently today, but the results would be the same: he would have to move his pickup truck.

Thinking about it, if I had to do it over again, I wonder if I should have gone out and helped him dig his truck out. No, not really. It was too much fun watching him try to get out on his own and then having to pay some neighborhood kids for help. His lesson was not to drive a pickup truck in the city during a blizzard without salt and a shovel and not to park in a space someone else had spent time digging out.

CHAPTER 18

Home Sweet Home

Detroit, Michigan
Winter 1984

For several years, our luck improved. I moved from being a teacher to a department head then principal of a Catholic grade school. I was good at managing funds and writing proposals and accepted a position at the Archdiocese of Detroit in their grants and programs department. While there I met Mrs. Marilyn Lundy, a marvelous lady with a heart of gold and a will of iron. She ran a series of high-risk social service programs (pre-release programs for women offenders, community centers, a home for wards of the court, etc.) under the umbrella of the League of Catholic Women. Unfortunately, her headquarters, an eight-story brick building on Parsons Street just off Woodward Avenue, was undergoing a slow death. The elevators often broke down, the windows leaked, the electrical and heating systems often malfunctioned. The building needed a major gut rehab.

Mrs. Lundy first brought me on as a consultant to write proposals (and I included myself in each budget as a part-time manager) and soon was negotiating a deal to convert the faded old Casgrain Hall into a brand-new senior citizen apartment building. Not only did I secure a good position with Mrs. Lundy but she also encouraged and helped me to go to law school. It's good that my professional life was secure because several disturbing events fell on our little family during the winter of 1984 and spring of 1985.

The new tenants of our next-door rental property were late on their rent again, and the whole neighborhood could hear them fighting with loud voices, cursing and arguing late into the night. The family consisted of a black man, Josh, his white wife, and their little girl. He had lost his job and had asked for a delay in the rent until he could find work. He claimed to be looking for work, but I didn't see much evidence of an organized job search.

His scruffy-looking friends showed up at all hours of the day and night and played their music loud, I guess for the benefit of those living on the Far East side. I've always believed in "live and let live," but things had gotten out of hand. Erma and I talked it over and decided that I would speak with them the next day and perhaps give them a legal notice to quit the premises, a long and arduous process involving multiple hearings at the landlord-tenant court at the Thirty-Sixth District Court. And even if you were successful, it involved the hiring of the sheriff's bailiffs to evict the tenants, but it was the law. At that time, I was thinking about going to the Detroit College of Law, so I thought it might be an interesting experience.

There was no yelling that night, no noise whatsoever from the house. But I went over anyway the next day to talk to them about civility and peace in the neighborhood. I had my speech all prepared in my head. Strange, but when I pounded on the front door, it opened inward. Why would someone not lock their front door?

I entered and saw that the place was a wreck. Pizza boxes and fast-food wrappers were strewn about the hall and kitchen. I could see that the sink was heaped full of dirty dishes. A pot was on the stove, the food burnt into a black blob. At least someone had turned off the stove.

"Josh," I yelled, "Dave here. We've got to talk, man." I came into the living room and saw him standing at the television, turning knobs and hitting buttons. The unit refused to come to life. You could easily see that the cord was pulled out from the wall. Josh seemed out of it.

"Josh, what the hell is going on here, man?" I raised my voice to get his attention. He turned toward me, noticing that I was standing there. Without answering me, he began mumbling something to himself and continued twisting the knobs. Finally, he punched the television set, causing it to rock back and forth and finally crash to the floor. He just looked at the set, sort of dazed and confused.

Now I yelled at him, "You're out of here. Pack your stuff. You're evicted. Pack up your shit and get out."

"You can't evict me. I know my rights," he slurred. The sad part was that he was correct. I couldn't legally evict him, but my blood was up. We had put a lot of time and money into this rental property to make it a comfortable and inexpensive rental unit. We called it a town house. There was no yard work and no shoveling of snow. We deducted $50 a month from the rent because we had taken their backyard for our dogs. This brought the rent down to a modest price and provided protection to the rear of the property and the alley.

"I'll give you an hour to get out. If you're not out of here by then, I'll throw you out." Josh was a big man, but he seemed out of it and slow-witted. *Drugs,* I thought. I left, slamming the door behind me.

Exactly one hour later, to the second, I was back on his porch and pounding on the door. The door was still unlocked, so I walked in and yelled, "Josh, have you gone?" I knew he hadn't left for I had sat at my front window and watched the porch. No one else had left. I wondered where his wife and child were, and I hoped I wouldn't find their bodies in one of the bedrooms.

He was where I had left him in the living room, the same spot. "Josh," I asked in a loud voice, "where are your wife and your little girl?"

That's when I heard a child crying from the upstairs. I ran up the stairs and found her in a bed under a pile of rumpled blankets, peeking out and crying.

"It's all right, honey," I told her. "You know me from next door. I'm Mr. Suttner. Where is your mommy?" I asked in as gentle a voice as possible.

She stopped crying enough to tell me that her mommy and daddy had a fight last night and her mommy had left.

"He wouldn't let me go with Mommy," she sobbed.

"It'll be all right, sweetie. Do you know where your mommy is now?" She shook her head in the negative and buried her little body under the blankets.

Now I was really ticked. My heart was breaking for the little girl as I stomped down the stairs with righteous indignation in my heart.

"Where is your wife?" I demanded. "Where did she go? Tell me now, or I call the police and the Department of Social Services. If I have to call, you'll go to jail." Josh was nonresponsive, so I grabbed him by his shirt and shook him hard. It didn't take long for him to produce a telephone number. Their phone was dead. I guess the service had been cut off. I returned next door and called the number.

I got the little girl's grandmother who immediately inquired about the well-being of the child. Both grandmother and mother got on the phone, and I briefly told them what I had found and asked if they would come over and take the child. There was much crying and carrying on in the background with the lady's mother telling her, "I told you so. He's no good. You never listen to me until it's too late."

I asked the child's mother if she had called the police. She said that she was thinking about it and that Josh had slapped her around pretty good and she had the bruises to prove it. I encouraged her to make the call.

As I hung up, I recognized that my heart rate was high and I was breathing hard. My blood was up; and before I confronted this punk, I had to calm down. As I always do during times of trouble, I prayed for strength, courage, and wisdom. I asked for divine help and guidance to get me through this ordeal. I opened my desk drawer and slid a snub-nosed .38 Charter Arms pistol into my pocket. I had some second thoughts about it and returned the pistol to its resting place. With the mood I was in, it wouldn't have taken much for me to shoot Josh.

Upon my return, the front door was still unlocked. Josh had picked up some fast-food wrappers and dropped them into a trash can. He looked at me and said, "Get out of my fucking house."

"First, this ain't your fucking house. It's my fucking house." I never curse or swear, but I was ticked. I was already beginning to wish that I had brought my pistol. What had gotten into me? "Besides," I added, "you ain't paid this month's rent or last either. Your wife is on the way to pick up your little girl, so get moving. I don't want you here when she arrives. You are going out one way or another."

At first, I thought he was going to charge me or at least take a swing. I braced myself for the confrontation, but instead, Josh darted toward the couch that was behind me. Startled, I also dove for it, and we both came up with our hands on a sawed-off shotgun that was hidden under a cushion.

It was an evil-looking weapon with the stock sawed off at the pistol grip and covered in black electrical tape. After a brief struggle, I pulled the weapon toward me, careful to keep the barrel pointed at the floor, when Josh resisted by pulling back. I reversed my grip and let the weapon fly back and smack him in the face. Then I grabbed it again and pushed and twisted the weapon's muzzle out of the way and freed it from his hand. I heard a snap as his hand came off the trigger guard, and he screamed in pain. He held his trigger finger, which was bent at an awkward angle.

Pushing him out of the way, I pointed the weapon at him and motioned him toward the door. His eyes were filled with hate and rage as he nursed his injured hand, but he backed up and excited to the porch.

As cold as ice, I said, "Now get and don't come back. If you do, I'll bust you open and dump your remains in an alley for the rats." In those days, the neighborhood was plagued with hordes of great gray Norwegian sewer rats. The last I saw of Josh, he was walking north on Avery, cursing and swearing at the top of his voice. Several neighbors opened curtains and doors to peer out. These were troubled times, and most felt it best not to get involved.

After emptying the shotgun and putting it and the twelve-gauge shells in a paper grocery bag, I was concerned that Josh might return with some friends, so I retreated for my .38 and waited for the ladies to arrive. As I sat on the front porch and waited for the mom, I thought about the trash we had to deal with in the city. No wonder those who could move out fled as fast as their cars would carry them.

About thirty minutes later, a car pulled up with the wife's mother driving. She came in and apologized and offered to clean the place up and pay the back rent if she could stay. I've always had a soft spot for little puppies, children, and women in distress. The bruises and cuts about her face were raw and obvious. She had really been worked over. She said she was going to the police to file a report.

"Sure," I said, "you can stay." It seemed like it would kill two birds with one stone: she would clean up the mess; pay the back rent; and because her name was on the lease and not Josh's, I had technically not used "self-help" to evict anyone.

CHAPTER 19

Doing the Right Thing

Winter 1984

The next day, after work, I examined the sawed-off shotgun. It had been a nice single-shot Savage twelve-gauge. As a kid, I had hunted rabbits with a sixteen-gauge single shot of the same make. I still have my weapon in a closet. It was a shame what they had done to this fine old gun. Not only was it now illegal as all get out but it was also an ugly, evil-looking thing. The barrel had been roughly cut down with what looked like a hacksaw. You could see the scratch marks where it had been clamped in a vice. It had been an unprofessional cut and was very rough. My dad would have kicked my behind if I had made a cut like that. It had several slips and starts where the blade had scratched the surface.

I shook my head in disgust and thought briefly about grinding and sanding down the rough cut, but only briefly. It might be fun, but it was still illegal. It was a felony to possess one. Who knows? It may have been involved in killings.

The shoulder stock had also been roughly cut down to make a pistol grip. It looked like they had used a jigsaw, and it was poorly done. A lot of black electrical tape had been wrapped around its handle. Was it for a better grip or maybe so as not to leave fingerprints? It was hard to tell.

I had placed the weapon back in the brown paper bag and driven over to the Vernor Police Station where, years earlier, I had been a police reservist. I ran a few names by the desk sergeant, but all the officers I knew back then had either retired, been suspended, transferred, or died. I had thought about being a cop back then and really enjoyed the time spent with the officers after their shifts at the Irish bar next door.

Erma, in a matter-of-fact manner, told me that she had enrolled Bob in the Holy Redeemer Cub Scout Program, which met on Tuesdays evenings, the same night as my Detroit police reserve meetings, gun-range sessions, and time-at-the-bar sessions.

No problem, she could take the little guy to his meetings. After all, the Cub Scouts was really women's work. Fathers don't take over until their son is ready for the Boy Scouts, or so I thought. For a few months, I had a ball hanging out with cops, shooting .38 pistol service revolvers on the range, drinking at the Irish bar, and drilling and practicing riot control. What's not to like? Then Erma told me that she signed up to finish her degree at WSU, and lo and behold, her first lecture class was also on Tuesday evenings. So I would have to take Bob to Cub Scouts, and thus ended my career in law enforcement. I had been bamboozled!

I remember something about the use of cattle prods on prisoners at the Vernor Precinct, which had resulted in the termination of several officers I had known. I vaguely remembered the story. It happened after I had left the precinct. The cops found it easier to enforce crowd control and get drunks and dopers to move along with electric cattle prods. The press found out, and there was an investigation. It turned out to be a PR nightmare for the police department. The bottom line was that it was blamed on white racist cops, some of whom had been instructors for the reserves.

I told the desk sergeant that I had found a sawed-off shotgun and wanted to turn it in. His eyes got big, and he called for the supervising detective. I laid the bag containing the weapon on his desk. Both he and the detective looked like it might contain a snake and refused to touch it, so I opened it and showed them the weapon. I had it broken down and showed them that it was empty.

The detective asked where I had gotten it. I briefly told him the story.

"Look, mister," he said, "that thing violates federal law. It's a crime for you to even have it, and the paperwork!" The desk sergeant grimaced. "My advice," continued the detective, "is that you drive over to Belle Isle and toss it off the bridge. The sooner the better! Now take it with you."

So that's exactly what I did. I drove over to the east side on Jefferson Avenue and turned south onto the MacArthur Bridge to Belle Isle, an island park in the middle of the Detroit River. I stopped halfway across the bridge, looked both ways, and seeing no one around, got out and tossed the bag as far as I could into the Detroit River and heard it splash. I've always wondered how many guns have been tossed over that bridge. It might be fun for the Detroit Police Dive Team to check it out.

CHAPTER 20

Daily Perils

Detroit, Michigan

The late eighties and early nineties were busy with professional activities. I was elected chancellor of the Sigma Nu Phi legal fraternity, acquired another degree, passed the bar on the first try, and founded the German-American Lawyers Association. I was legal counsel for many of Mrs. Lundy's social service corporations. Family life was a bit stressful. Bob joined the Army during high school and began a twenty-five-year career that would eventually lead him into multiple war zones.

We hardened the defenses at home with double-planked eight-foot stockade fence around the rear parameter, dogs, weapons with permits to carry and upgraded the electronic security system. These, along with iron bars in windows and steel doors and frames, held the bad guys at bay.

While I was in law school, Bob and Erma policed the yards, shoveled sidewalks during winter, raked leaves during fall, and in general, maintained the facility. My job was to work about fifty hours a week as an administrator for Mrs. Lundy, take classes in the evenings, and study the rest of the time.

Erma would often pick me up in front of the law library at 7:00 p.m. and drive up to the Dakota Inn for dinner, where I was allowed two glasses of beer with dinner. Then at precisely 8:00 p.m., she drove us home where I would study or work on assignments until bedtime. We knew it was temporary and that everyone had to pitch in so we could all have a better life in the future.

I remember one Saturday afternoon when Bob came running into the house to tell me that there was a man beating up a lady across the street. I grabbed my .38 and ran outside. Glancing back, I noticed that Bob had taken a rifle from near the front door and stood in the open doorway as my backup, giving the scene his complete attention.

Standing at the driver's side was a black man dressed in what today is called a "wife beater shirt" and jeans. I saw him slap a black woman's face. She was holding a screaming infant, and she instinctively lowered her head to protect and cover the child. The man started to cock his arm, ready to deliver a blow, when I arrived in time to shove him against the car and scream in his face with as much spittle as possible that I would "blow his ass away" if he hit her again.

The man's eyes got big as he looked down the barrel of my .38. Turning him around, I leaned him against the car to make a citizen's arrest, a technique I had learned at police reserves. Then I saw another man, also black, rise up from behind the back seat. It looked like he was going for a shoulder holster.

"Don't do it, f—!" I screamed and cocked the weapon as I stuck it through the open window at his head.

"No, man," he cried out as he raised his hands, "I got no gun. Just getting a handkerchief from my shoulder purse, that's all." Sure enough, he wore a male version of a purse strapped under his left arm. It looked just like a shoulder holster. I slowly blew the air out of my lungs and carefully lowered the hammer. *Holy cow,* I thought, *I almost shot a guy for getting a handkerchief. How would that play on the five-o'clock news?*

I had also violated several of my rules. I shouldn't have a cocked pistol with my finger on the trigger. It was just by the grace of God that the gun hadn't gone off. I also had not properly checked out the situation and failed to notice the man in the back seat, and finally, I had almost shot a man for wanting to wipe his face.

At about that time, I heard a siren come blaring up Grand River Avenue. Backing away, I slipped the weapon in my pocket and returned to the house as the police car pulled up. The woman and the child were crying, but the two men remained stationary and silent.

Bob put the rifle back inside and came down to stand in the yard to watch the proceedings. The woman with the baby was unsure what had happened, but she didn't want to press charges. Both men made some statement and showed IDs to the officers, but not finding their names on the current list of outstanding warrants, they were warned to "take it home."

The woman with the baby got back in the car with the two men, and they drove off. The police officers remained parked for a few minutes talking and filling out some forms. Bob continued to rake leaves, and I went back to my studies. It was just another day in the neighborhood.

I knew it was stupid intervening on behalf of someone who wasn't even willing to press charges against the man. But what else could I do? I couldn't just stand by and not help. I would have to come up with a better method, and I did.

From then on, when I was driving and saw a person being assaulted or someone being chased by a gang, I would scream at the top of my voice, "Stop. Halt. Cops have been called," and then I would lay on the horn. They often ceased the assault and scattered, often with one remaining for a few seconds to deliver a farewell kick. I would stop to ask if the victim needed medical attention. The answer was always no. I used this technique several times, and after cell phones became popular, it seemed to have more of an effect.

I developed another technique while moving around Detroit. I would yell to the miscreants that the cops were coming and that they had better get the hell away. I would then back off and observe.

Later, when I got my concealed-carry permit, I didn't mind rushing a gang like a screaming banshee; but I wouldn't pull the weapon or run carrying it. There are too many chances of a slip and fall or an accidental discharge. After the event was over, I would quietly fade away. I wanted no publicity or involvement with the police.

It is a major responsibility to carry a loaded weapon in a populated area. Modern ammo can penetrate an object and still go through a hollow core door or window and kill some old lady watching television. I couldn't live with myself if this happened. I had to be extra careful. I made a commitment to go the range at a monthly minimum, often with Erma. We also formed a shooters club for monthly practice. At the range, I practice right-hand and left-hand shooting with revolvers and semiautomatics, wearing regular glasses first and then dark sunglasses (in case I might have to engage in low-light situations).

I'm always trying to find the easiest weapon to carry that I shoot the best with. On a visit home after one of his missions to Iraq, Bob and I went shooting together, and he showed me the technique of "point and shoot." You don't aim, just fire by instinct. It's interesting and good for clearing a room if you suspect an intruder in your house.

Also, he started the practice with the target only a yard away (most shooters would be embarrassed to shoot so close, but it was part of his drill). After firing all the rounds dead center, he would back the next target another yard and fire again and so on, yard after yard, until the rounds began to separate and some would go outside of the black. That's the distance he concentrates on. It's a great technique. It's great fun shooting with family and friends, and you get the bonus of cleaning the weapons and discussing grips, stances, ammo, weapons, and shooting techniques. You're never too old to learn.

CHAPTER 21

Man's Best Friend

Detroit, Michigan

Bob fell in love with the Rottweiler breed while serving in Germany in the 1990s. Upon his return stateside, he purchased Molly. We also got to know her during visits. We spent time with her and enjoyed taking her on walks. She was no-nonsense and all business. When Bob received orders to go to England, he learned that the quarantine for dogs would be six months. He asked us to take care of his dog while he was on assignment. How could we refuse?

We fell in love with Molly and the breed. They are loyal, obedient, and love walks. They are a nearly perfect urban dog. Sure, you must walk them every day, but it's great because we humans need the exercise and they protect the neighborhood while on patrol. They are low-maintenance and get along well with family members.

Also, they will take a bullet for you—I've seen them in action. I tell people that in Detroit if I had a choice between a .45, and my Rottie, I'd choose the dog. Granted, if I had my druthers, I'd have both. There is nothing that feels as good as a warm 1911 .45 tucked up under your belt on a cold morning. And since I'm an American, I can have both and I do, plus a third little friend (my .380 Kel-Tec as an "O Jesus" backup) for good measure.

I remember once when Gunner, our fourth Rottweiler, and I were on dawn patrol early one morning. We first walked north on Avery Street up to the freeway, which marked our northern boundary. All was quiet, so we turned west, for no particular reason, and walked by a fenced-in lot topped with strands of barbed wire leaning inward. This is a sign that there is something the owner wants to keep in the lot more than he wants to keep someone out.

Gunner was walking a few paces in front and to my right when two junkyard dogs, both big German shepherds, threw themselves, snarling and barking, against the fence on our left. As we walked down the sidewalk, Gunner occasionally glanced at them but did not show any signs of agitation or concern. As we walked, the dogs moved along with us on their side of the fence, creating an awful racket of yelps, snarls, and barks. Normally, they were kept in the brick building, but they had been let out early today and were in a surly mood.

I made a mental note that in the future, we would walk on the other side of the street. Suddenly, Gunner stopped, lowered his head, backed out of his collar (I always keep the collar loose so the dog can get out when necessary), and moved to my left, separating me from the fence and the junkyard dogs.

Both dogs were now filled with rage and snarling and snapping at each other as well as the fence in their attempt to get at us.

"What are you doing?" I asked Gunner as I picked up his collar and leash and continued walking. I suddenly realized that a few yards ahead, unbeknownst to the two German shepherds, the gate on rollers had been left open.

Oh boy, I thought. *This is going to be very, very bad.* I continued walking at the same pace and started to pull my pistol out of my coat pocket, first round loaded with bird shot. I hoped I wasn't too close. Gunner, a few paces in front, reached the opening in the gate first. He wheeled to face the German shepherds at the opening.

Gunner turned on them and, holding his own on the sidewalk between me and a violent confrontation, he let out a vicious series of earsplitting barks with teeth and fangs bared, snapping and growling with saliva flying in their direction. Both dogs froze on their side of the fence, not daring to take another step. They turned and tucked tails and ran back to their building. I stood there in the middle of the sidewalk holding a leash with an empty collar. I motioned for Gunner to slip it back on. I breathed a sigh of relief as I holstered my pistol and closed the gate shut and continued our walk.

I've been thinking a lot about dogs and how their domestication has brought blessings to mankind. I want to tell you a little myth that I've been playing around with to explain the unique and special arrangement man has with his canine friends. Here goes (just bear with me).

Picture a cave entrance in a valley, say twenty or so thousand years ago. It's very cold and miserable out. You see these two fierce-looking canines (probable gray wolves of some sort) lying atop a ridge looking down on the camp of early humans sitting around a smoky, sputtering fire. The early humans are on the verge of extinction. They are starving, exhausted, and scared, preparing to face the terrors of another cold night.

"What a pathetic-looking bunch of creatures," one canine says to the other. (Just work with me here. There are plenty of books where dogs can talk.)

"What are they called?" asked the companion.

"No idea, but I agree that they are really a sad-looking sight. They have no fur to keep them warm and protect them, they have no fangs or claws to fight or defend themselves with, and they can't run very fast."

The other nodded in agreement.

"Do you want to eat one of them tonight?" Both sat watching the night darken the valley.

"No," the other replied. "I don't really care much for their taste, but they may have one or two values."

"Really? What?"

"Once when I was a pup, I was scavenging around one of their camps, and some of the creature's pups gave me bits of food cooked over their fire. It was very good and warmed me. They played with me, petted me, and rubbed my belly. Wow, it was sure nice."

"Interesting. I say we go down there and talk to them."

So they went down. (Now remember, in my myth, those days man and animals spoke a common language.)

On approaching the humans, the canines asked for a parley. The humans, scared and too timid to leave the protection of their fire, asked the canines what they wanted.

"Look at yourselves," the canine with the prior experience began, "you are losing the battle of the survival of the fittest. I doubt if you'll be around a season from now. While, on the other hand, look at us. We are sleek, dangerous beasts. We run in packs and fear nothing. We'll make a deal with you. You let us live in your cave, warmed by your magic heat maker, and provide us with food. And we'll teach you how to hunt." The humans considered this offer.

The other canine continued, "To sweeten the pot, so to speak, we'll also protect your lands, patrol, and keep the dangers of the night at bay. We'll give you warnings before an attack and will defend you. In turn, you must treat us with respect, kindness, affection, and rub our bellies. We will become your faithful companions."

The humans again gathered in a discussion. "We will agree with you, but you must obey us and follow our commands."

The canines, after some thought, nodded in agreement but added, "Only if you promise to feed us twice a day and play games with us." Finally, all the details were worked out, and a solemn contract was formed between the two species.

It wasn't long before the humans began to cultivate the wild grains knowing that their fields would be protected. With the grains, they not only created bread but also learned to brew beer, the staff of life (the brewing process also killed the bacteria that had been making humans sick and killing so many, thus saving the early human race).

Soon the canines taught the humans to hunt, and meat became a regular part of their diet. Life improved for both species, and they multiplied. The cave was abandoned for skin-covered huts, and small houses were built. Soon a village grew up with buildings to store grain for the future and meeting halls to develop governance. Families developed along with classes, skills, art, music, religion, and law. Life was looking up for humans. Civilization was dawning on mankind when tragedy struck.

An invasion of small rodent-like animals burrowed under the walls of the granaries, was eating and spoiling the grain needed for the next winter and seed to plant in the spring. The canines were too big and the humans too slow to eliminate them. Once again, it looked like civilization and mankind, along with domesticated dogs, were doomed to final extinction.

On the same ridge, two felines sat watching the village. "They'll never catch those little rodents."

The other nodded and said, "Look at those big stupid people and their big stupid canines. They'll all be starving by winter, and we'll have plenty of rodents to hunt this winter. Life is looking up."

"Do people have any value?" the first inquired.

"Very little, but they are clever. See how they built their village with comfortable warm houses for the winter and how they store food? Why, they even tamed our natural enemy, the canine!"

"Hmmm." They both sat in silent thought.

"What do you say? Let's go down there and see if we can work out a deal to our advantage."

So the two felines went down to the village and approached the humans with their dogs, ever on guard, miserable and dejected and scattered around the fire. Most of their food had all been spoiled by the rodents. What little was left wouldn't keep them alive through the winter, and the canines were talking about leaving the village.

"Hello, camp," the first feline said to the people, "protect us from your dogs, and we'll come in and talk with you." The humans gave appropriate commands and invited them to approach. "Why are you so miserable?"

Looking at the two sleek, well-fed felines, the headman said, "We have been invaded by little rodents. They are eating and fouling our reserve of grain, and we can't stop them. They are too small and fast for our dogs. We fear that we will all die of starvation this winter."

"Oh really?" one feline said after he dropped a dead mouse at the feet of the headman. "They don't look that fast to us."

"You can hunt and kill them." Now the entire crowd of humans was interested and passing the dead creature among them.

"Sure, if we had a reason. But it takes an effort to kill the little creatures and guard the supply of grain. We don't really like to exert ourselves that much. We prefer a comfortable life."

The humans quickly gathered out of earshot from the felines and discussed the matter. Once the agreement was reached, they turned to the two and the headman said, "You would be welcome to stay here and hunt the little creatures and even sleep inside our homes where it is dry and warm. We can have dogs living with some and cats another."

"Well, that's fine, as far as it goes," one said, "but we are looking for guarantees. We need to be fed daily and given a warm, comfortable place to sleep."

"That can be arranged," said the headman. "We can even treat you as we do our dogs. We can hug and pet you and rub your bellies."

"Only when we ask for it," said the feline. "Some of us may not object to being petted and stroked once in a while, but it must be on our terms. And no giving us orders like you do to the dogs. We are not canines. And don't think you can take us on walks with ropes tied about our necks. We need our independence for this arrangement to work."

The humans gathered together to discuss the offer. It was more difficult dealing with these creatures than the canines. After some discussion, the headman agreed to the terms on behalf of the village.

"Just one more issue," said the feline, winking to its mate as it licked its whiskers, "we also will be entitled to take a crap in our new homes any time we want. We don't like going outside at night."

The humans were shocked. The humans and the canines had to go outside to do their business. But they had no choice but to agree to this final term.

"All right," the headman said, "but only if you bury it in a box filled with dirt or sand." Finally, all the terms to this sacred contract were agreed to, and the felines began the job of clearing the rodents from the village.

The canines, not fully domesticated, were met with a dilemma for they really hated felines and enjoyed chasing them up trees. But realizing that the felines had also reached an agreement with the humans, an agreement that was beneficial to all parties, they reluctantly agreed to a truce of sorts; and thus they all coexisted and prospered, albeit with an unsteady alliance that often broke down.

That is the story of how our domesticated friends saved civilization. Today, dogs and cats still provide valuable service to mankind. With mouse and rattraps, poisons and pellet guns, you may be able to do without a cat. With security systems and fortified structures, you may be able to do without a dog; but I wouldn't want to try.

CHAPTER 22

Dual Life

1976 to 2001

My boss—and yes, my mentor and patron—Mrs. Marilyn Lundy retired as president of Matrix Human Services in Detroit in 2001. I had worked directly for her for twenty-three years. She had my personal loyalty, and yes, I would have taken a bullet for her. She asked me to remain for six months as legal counsel and administrator to help with the transition. Unfortunately, the new president and I didn't see eye to eye. I was told that a new broom sweeps clean and was soon also out the door.

It had been a pleasure to work for Mrs. Lundy. She would see a need and develop a narrative to understand and resolve the problem; and then I would be tasked to find a way to implement a solution. She was the brains and vision; I was the bronze and muscle.

In the early eighties, Mrs. Lundy and some of her friends became interested in saving Detroit's old Orchestra Hall from the wrecking ball. Orchestra Hall was reputed to be one of the finest acoustical auditoriums in the world. I was told by her that in the old days, engineers would come from around the world to study its form and shape. It was an acoustic marvel destined to soon be demolished. The orchestra had abandoned it for the modern Ford Auditorium on the riverfront, and after years of mixed use, it had fallen into decay and been abandoned.

Mrs. Lundy said she and her committee of suburban ladies and musicians wanted to view it from the inside. After several days of trying, without success, to get official permission to enter the facility, I decided I had to use a little "self-help."

On a cold snowy day in mid-December, we met on Parsons Street near a padlocked stage door. I brought my trusty bolt cutter and an extra lock. A quick snip and we were in. It was a surreal sight. Most of the seats had been torn out, and piles of litter and debris were everywhere. A large hole in the ceiling allowed dim winter light and snow to enter.

Near the stage, a derelict had found another entrance and had set up a bedroll on the cold floor. He had a small cook fire going, and on a spit, he was roasting what appeared to be a pigeon.

Mrs. Lundy and her friends stood in amazement, looking about at the structure, and began telling stories of visits during its glory days. Upon exiting the building, I used my lock to secure the chain.

Later, Mrs. Lundy instructed me to draft and file the documents for a new nonprofit, Orchestra Place Development Corporation. I was then assigned to be its secretary and told to organize any and all businesses and institutions in the area in this great cause: to save one of Detroit's gems. Soon we were off and running in saving the building, restoration, and the return of the Detroit Symphony. Today, Orchestra Hall is a world-class venue for classical music and performances thanks, in large part, to the vision and dedication of Mrs. Lundy. We made a great team. She thought the grand ideas and the needs of society; I dealt with the nuts and bolts of administration (e.g., she pushed for charter schools in Michigan, and I wrote the charter for the first charter school, Casa Maria Academy).

As I briefly mentioned earlier, one of our projects was the total gut-rehab of the eight-story red brick headquarters on Parsons Street. It was renovated into premier section 8 housing for seniors and folks with disabilities. In return for the asset of Casgrain Hall (Its 1927 construction was in sad shape and in need of major systems' overhaul.), the League of Catholic Women received a thirty-year rental lease for the first two levels for one dollar per year plus utilities with free parking in a lot across the street.

Mrs. Lundy dedicated her life and fortune to help the less fortunate. She reached out to young women and men—black, white, and Hispanic—and mentored and promoted from within. She was loved by all who met her.

Early on in this position, I secured a job with the US Department of Education as a grant reader. I would be sent to Washington, DC, on the government's dime and booked into a nice hotel along with scores of other readers. We would read, evaluate, and rank educational proposals throughout the country for funding. In this way, I learned the vocabulary and techniques of grantsmanship. Soon, the majority of my proposals were being funded. I was then able to hire and train a professional grant writer, and I moved more into contract compliance and oversight. It was a great and exciting job.

Mrs. Lundy was concerned when the Archdiocese of Detroit pulled the plug on its Head Start programs, and I was tasked to write the proposal that was funded to become Vistas Nuevas's Head Start in Southwest Detroit. I had also written CETA grants that were funded for job-training programs and a proposal that resulted in the funding for homes for runaway youth in Detroit. Soon we were administering everything from pre-release programs for female offenders to community centers for blacks and Hispanic youth. I built a percentage of my salary, roughly equal with the percentage of time I actually spent monitoring that project, into each budget. Soon my entire salary was being picked up by various funding sources: city, county, state, and federal. I always saved a percentage of time for research and development of new areas that caught Mrs. Lundy's attention. I worked to set up the first unemployment insurance and workers' compensation self-insurance pools for nonprofit corporations in the state. This entailed sitting on the boards, which met monthly in Lansing at the University Club.

Not only did Mrs. Lundy encourage and help me to get my law degree by allowing a flexible work schedule in which to take classes (even during the day, when necessary) but I was also allowed to make up the time during evenings or weekends. How many established administrators are willing today to take young employees in tow and help set their course on the right track? She was very special, and I often raise a glass in a toast to Mrs. Lundy.

During this period, I began teaching, first at the Detroit College of Business, which merged into Davenport University. Thinking I would love to teach at Wayne State University, only a few blocks from my office, I accepted a position in their accounting department, teaching a legal survey course in preparation for their CPA exams. I had sixty-three students enrolled that semester, and I saw my department head once. At the end of the semester, I went back to Davenport, hat in hand, and was lucky enough to get my old position back (average class size of twenty students with an office desk near my department head).

During this period, Erma and I were living in two distinct worlds. One world was of business luncheons, black-tie events, charitable events (I actually had two tuxedos at once), plays, operas, world travel, and dinner invites to homes of rich folks in Grosse Pointe. On the other hand, we still lived in the same house in the old run-down Woodbridge and dealt with crime on a daily basis.

We accepted invitations from acquaintances in the affluent suburbs, but it was a rare event when anyone would accept our return invitation, that is with the exception of Mrs. Lundy. Erma taught computers at that time, and after one of her home-cooked meals, she would help Mrs. Lundy on a computer problem. It was a new skill, and we were all learning.

We were often questioned why we lived in the city. We knew we were not cut out for the affluent suburban lifestyle, so we never tried out for it. I could not—or I should say, would not—accept gifts or favors or even a free lunch without making sure I returned one of equal or greater value. I issued guidelines that all gifts received from the many vendors doing business with our family of social-service agencies were to be logged in and turned over to the Christmas committee to be raffled at our annual holiday party. Staff morale was never better. Strange, but I felt a closer kinship with the maintenance crew than with the elite. When our son was born, I had taught during the day and, in order to pay the medical bill, did janitorial and maintenance work at the school in the evenings. I loved being with the counselors and teachers, directly interacting with the problems and clients, than I did with the elite board members.

Erma and I stayed small and low profile, avoiding political factions and groups. At that time, Erma was still a blue-collar Democrat while I had morphed from an antiwar liberal into a moderate Republican.

CHAPTER 23

Benedictine High

2001–2004

I wandered around a bit aimlessly and in a daze for several weeks after leaving my position with Matrix. I had to decide if I wanted to pursue a career in nonprofit law (where I already had over two decades of experience) or concentrate on teaching at the college level (which I still enjoyed after teaching for two decades) or something else. The old saying "When one door closes, another opens" is true.

I had spent the last twenty-three years working directly for Mrs. Lundy. I didn't make any of the big decisions, only implementations. Once she approved a project, I would work out the minutiae and get the job done. I wanted to know if I could use her ideas and methods (i.e., think in terms of the big picture) by bringing folks onboard and motivating the stakeholders to change physical reality for the better. In other words, I wanted to be responsible for all the decisions, big and small. I wanted to be the boss.

During this period, I met lots of people and sought their advice and guidance. Of course, I met with Mrs. Lundy (Erma and I would often take her to lunch after her retirement). She listened to my quandary and advised me to go back into education (Mrs. Lundy sat not only on the board of education for the Archdiocese of Detroit but was also a member of the Michigan Department of Education, an elected position). She knew of a particularly challenging situation that had developed in Detroit. Benedictine High School had fallen on hard times. It had had several principals during the prior year, and the facility, once an exemplar in educational circles, was now graffiti-ridden and in danger of closing. The wonderful parish priest, a Benedictine abbot, was in his nineties and had to decide the fate of this once-glorious institution.

The large Italian Catholic neighborhood had moved to the suburbs. The student population was now 100 percent black and, as far as anyone knew, non-Catholic. How long could the Benedictines afford to keep up a failing school delivering an inferior education?

Benedictine High had recently lost its academic accreditation, all its sports teams were under suspension for one reason or another, and the computer classes had to be taught without the aid of even one operating computer. All the computers had been vandalized or stolen.

Across the freeway from the high school was the parish grade school that was also running a deficit. The grade school had once been the feeder school for Benedictine High, but now its parents thought better and were sending their children to other high schools. Who could blame them? Tuition had gone up and quality had gone down at the high school. What a mess!

After meeting with the abbot and discussing the pros and cons of just closing the doors, he suggested that I go over and observe and then tell him if the school could be salvaged. The prior principal had recently left under unknown circumstances, and the bookkeeper informed me that the budget was a disaster and funds unaccounted for.

The grade-school principal was doing double duty, trying to maintain both schools until the abbot made a final decision. Both schools were owned by the Benedictine Order, not the Archdiocese of Detroit, so his was the final decision.

After three days of observations and discussions with staff, parents, and students, I identified strengths and weaknesses and developed a flowchart to help in the decision. Some staff had given up on the students and would have to go. Others were demoralized, but in a proper environment, they could again become excellent teachers.

They cared about the students and used their own money to purchase materials. I was crazy to think I could affect a positive change. I should tell the abbot to lock the doors and try to sell the facility (but the bottom had fallen out of the real estate market in Detroit).

Erma was in a good professional position. She was the head administrator of a school in Ferndale, Michigan, a suburb just north of Detroit; so I could take the chance. After much soul-searching and prayer, I told the abbot that I would be willing to make a two-year commitment if he would give me his complete confidence and support when requested.

I developed a plan of action involving parent meetings, staff evaluations, and in several cases, terminations and reorganization. I contacted a nearby Air Force base, and through a Dads' Club member (more about that later), we were able to bring in a full classroom of older but very usable "scrubbed" desktop computers, monitors, and keyboards.

The parents were informed that a new sheriff was in town and that the student dress code, which had fallen into disuse, would be strictly enforced the next year and grades would depend on academic success (I had discovered that, with the loss of its counselor, grades were altered after the fact).

It was interesting being a white male principal in an all-black school. During the first semester, I often heard the term *white devil* applied to me by both students and the teachers, but I loved the challenge.

The first changes dealt with the physical appearance of the facility. The janitor and I met regularly to discuss troubled areas, graffiti, chewing gum, and girls' bathrooms. For too long, the students had run the institution. That was about to change.

During the first week of school, the janitor again came to complain about the ninth-grade girls putting on their lipstick in the bathrooms and kissing the mirrors, leaving him a difficult cleaning job. I told him that I had heard of a surefire method to resolve the problem, and the next day the ninth-grade girls were brought to their bathroom in groups by their teachers. After a brief admonition not to smear up the mirror, I informed them of the time and effort that the janitor had to expend in cleaning the mirrors. I told the janitor to show the girls what he had to do. He took a big mop from a bucket, dunked it in the nearest toilet, then put it back in the bucket, and with the push of the lever, squeezed it. He then mopped down the mirror where the lipstick kisses had been. Next, using a squeegee and a rag, he cleaned the mirror's surface. Several of the girls made strange gagging sounds as they turned away in disgust. We never had a problem with the girls' bathroom mirrors again.

Unfortunately, disgruntled former employees no longer had access to the facility (i.e., they could no longer carry out food from the freezers or supplies from the office or janitor's closet), so they decided to carry out a major late-night B&E and loot the facility.

Unbeknownst to them, I had recently upgraded the security system and had the call center direct all after-hours alerts directly to my home phone. Early one morning, during the first week of school, I received a call that the alarms in the cafeteria had been activated. I quickly dressed and grabbed a German P38 9 mm pistol I had just cleaned, and with Gunner, my Rottweiler, I quickly drove to the school and entered through the front door. I could hear the alarm ringing and the smashing and tearing of metal on metal coming from a rear corridor. It sounded like the gang was having a field day.

I took Gunner's leash off and yelled at the top of my voice, "Sic 'em! Go now," and such commands. Gunner looked at me once for confirmation and then tore down the hallway, his barks ringing through the building like gunshots. I had previously changed the locks on the metal gate that separated the back corridor from the cafeteria and knew that Gunner could not get at them until I arrived, but he could scare the hell out of anyone back there. The ripping noises stopped, tools were dropped, and screams and yells echoed down the halls as people made for the exit as if their lives depended on it. They jumped into vehicles and gunned engines in their get-aways out of the rear parking lot. I saw piles of loot stacked near the exits, ready to be transferred into vehicles. Several old vending machines belonging to the Dads' Club had been vandalized and the doors pried open.

Once I was sure all had gone, I called the security company and informed them that I had arrived at the building and all was clear. I placed Gunner in my office at the other end of the building and told him to be quiet. I had finished returning items back to storage and almost finished pushing the vending machines' damaged fronts toward the wall when the police arrived. I didn't have to worry about contaminating the crime scene. The police didn't bother to take any prints. I gave the officer my name, birth date, and position, as evidenced by my ID. They looked around and soon left. I secured the building and reset the alarm, and then Gunner and I drove back home in time to feed Gunner his breakfast, clean up, and put on a suit for the new school day. Over the next month, there were three other attempts at night to raid the facility. We (Gunner and I) arrived each time before the police. None were successful. Soon they just quit coming, and the Dads' Club upgraded the vending machines and put in healthier options, like water and nutrition bars. All life is a compromise. You can either sleep or get up and do your duty.

During this period, we also had the 9/11 terrorist attack on the World Trade Center in New York. Soon our phone lines were jammed. I informed parents that their children were safe, but if they felt insecure, they could come by and remove them for the remainder of the day. It took a few days to get the school back to normal, whatever that means. I soon developed the policy of opening the school an hour early and keeping it open an hour or more later in the evenings for the convenience of working parents. It was free babysitting, and they began to love me.

I got to know the students, especially the troublemakers, on a first-name basis. I soon developed my list of secret agents and spies among the student body. It was easier to recruit than one might think. With a promise of absolute confidentiality, I soon became privy to every prank and act of vandalism planned by the students—e.g., at a neighboring black high school, students had pressed molding clay into the locks around the building and caused shutdown for a day. I was informed that this was planned for the next day at our facility. The following morning, I witnessed two students rolling the clay to warm it in their hands prior to pressing it into a lock. I caught them red-handed; and as a punishment, they had to clean the school, under my supervision, for the next four weeks. They met with me on Saturday at 9:00 a.m. for gum scrapping and toilet detail. A principal in a Catholic School is like a medieval lord in his manor. Only the king can overrule him.

One senior girl (whose father was a well-to-do auto dealer) decided to play a prank on the school. During lunch one day, she started screaming that there were rats running loose in the cafeteria. Pandemonium broke out, food was thrown, tables were overturned, and kids ran screaming and laughing into the hallways. The assistant principal and I were on lunchroom duty so the teachers could have a break together, and I spotted a little white mouse scurrying under the tables and around overturned chairs. The little guy was frightened and cowered and trembled in a corner. I reached down and picked him up by his tail and realized it looked just like one of the mice kept in the biology room. I contacted the biology teacher, but after a quick visit to her room, we found all her creatures accounted for. I then gave her a new one for her habitat.

Later that evening, after order was finally restored and several calls returned to irate parents and PTA members who questioned the sanitary conditions of our kitchen and cafeteria (I assured them that our kitchen facilities were spotless and invited them to do an inspection with me. None accepted my invitation.) I sat in my office with the photos of all the students at or near the tables where the mouse was first spotted. All were senior girls.

I had previously instituted a photo ID (the pictures could also be used to get to know the students for identification and also for the yearbook). I took the photos of the suspected girls to the pet stores in the area. Sure enough, at the second store, the senior girl who had screamed first was identified as having purchased two white mice the previous week.

Calling the girl in question into my office, I questioned her, but she steadfastly refused to confess or give additional information. She didn't deny that she had purchased two mice but insisted that the one I had caught was not hers. I told her that we were going to check her locker. With this, she panicked as I contacted the janitor to bring a set of bolt cutters to the office. She frantically called her father with her cell phone, crying and calling for his help. He soon arrived and indignantly told me I had no authority to invade his daughter's privacy. I, in turn, quickly informed him that he had signed a letter of agreement in which it was explicitly stated that the lockers were the property of the school and could be inspected with or without cause by the principal—that was me. Students had no expectation of privacy in the lockers. All locks used had to be approved or else they were subject to being cut.

Then, in front of the angry father and his sobbing daughter, I had the janitor cut off the lock and open the door to find a small metal cage containing a dead mouse. It had died of neglect. I immediately suspended the girl for three days pending a hearing before the PTA board. Her father began to bully and scream that I couldn't do that. He then stormed out with his daughter in tow and went to complain to the abbot without success. He then filed a complaint against me with the Archdiocese of Detroit superintendent's office, but after sending in a written explanation, the complaint was dismissed (I had a fair number of complaints filed against me during the early period for wrongful termination from disgruntled staff whose contracts had not been renewed. I responded to the charges myself without going through the Archdiocese's lawyers and defended myself successively at all the hearings. The Archdiocese's lawyers were not happy with me). I again met with the father and his daughter with members of the PTA and gave the girl a chance to explain her behavior; but she refused to own up to the prank, and rather than taking the suspension, her father withdrew her from the school. Word soon got around that even a graduating senior with a well-connected father was not immune from punishment.

In another case, I was informed that students were planning on smearing Vaseline on the handrail of the major stairwell after lunch on Friday. Again, they were caught red-handed. They were free labor for Saturday morning detentions. Soon the facility was spotless, and we were moving outside—first around our facility and then into the neighboring area—on clean-up missions. I wasn't getting much sleep, but life was sure fun. I began meeting with parents before and after classes, calling and visiting homes in the evenings. I received a great deal of parental support; after all, they were paying high tuition.

The school bell system had not worked for years. I got it repaired and the school was running on strict times. I would be in the hallways during classroom changes and developed a system of demerits for the slightest infractions. I've always believed that you are going to fight with high school students on some level. I would rather have it on dress code, dropped papers, and chewing gum rather than guns, knives, drugs, and assaults.

It was a slow process, but soon, the students learned that the result of five or more demerits resulted in an early Saturday morning detention with the Man. The janitor and I would take crews around the building and scrape chewing gum from the floors and under desks, clean toilets, wash windows, and pick up trash in and around the facility. Uniforms began to be worn properly and ties properly tied (I even conducted classes in how to tie a perfect full Windsor knot). Trash and chewing gum were soon deposited in trash cans found around the building, not on the highly polished floors or under desks. During the holidays, improvements were made and rooms thoroughly cleaned and painted. The arts and crafts room was placed back in operation, and a teacher was hired for that class. Music, band, and choir again became part of the curriculum.

I found my biggest problems in high school sports. The only sport not suspended was track-and-field, so we emphasized that first. The Dads' Club operated the sporting events and managed all concessions, but since the suspensions in football and basketball, revenue had fallen and facilities had been neglected. The Dads' Club was composed of great men, pillars of their community; most were retired and committed to the community. Many had children and grandchildren who had graduated from "Benny" years before. They were angry and disappointed with the church, and it was easy to see why. As white flight eliminated the Catholic communities in Detroit, the church no longer had an interest in maintaining facilities for non-Catholic populations. Lucky for us, the Benedictine monastery was committed to remaining put, and after discussion, the abbot was willing to invest real dollars into the maintenance and improvements of the facilities.

As for the Dads' Club, I attended a meeting, listened, took notes, and at the end, asked if I could host a "thank-you" event where they would be my honored guests for grilled bratwurst and knackwurst with German potato salad, sauerkraut, German beer, and a little something stronger on the side. I knew I could not compete with their ribs and barbecues, so why try? I was of German ancestry, so I went with what I knew. I had become a grillmeister and was asked by the German Consulate to man the grills at the annual garden party held at the counsel general's suburban estate for all foreign dignitaries, business, and political types. I was ready.

The Dads' Club members, after being served food and drink, agreed to back me 100 percent; and with their leadership, we began a program of redemption and rebuilding our major sports: boys' and girls' basketball, boys' football, and girls' cheerleading (we never were really able to generate interest in boys' baseball).

Nothing came easily, but the girls' basketball team caught fire and was soon undefeated in its bid for state championship. This raised school morale, and soon we had the funds to repair the vandalized locker rooms, ceiling lights, and smashed glass blocks (where students took pride in being able to smash with hard-thrown baseballs). Soon a refinished floor brought the old auditorium back to life, and we were welcomed back into the Catholic High School League. Our games were sellouts. One of our students sang the national anthem, and a member of the Dads' Club led in the recital of the Lord's Prayer.

I also required everyone going out for any sport to take a mandatory course in weight lifting, bodybuilding, and nutrition. Biology and health teachers became involved and encouraged good nutrition and sleep habits. During our second year of operation, our girls' basketball team won the state championship (with every girl on the varsity team being offered a scholarship to different colleges and universities).

Unfortunately, we were faced with a serious health problem at home. Erma was a building manager for an alternative education school in Ferndale when a non-student entered the building and assaulted one of her students. Erma immediately came to the aid of the victim but was shoved backward, hitting her head hard against a wall; she then fell to the floor, smacking her head again. She wound up with stitches and a serious closed-head injury. She was viewed as damaged goods by the school and never brought back to work.

After a period of rehab, I became concerned that she was losing interest in life and sleeping excessive hours and really not caring much about anything. On walks, she would become dizzy and confused. She needed structure and a purpose in life.

What better way than becoming a full-time unpaid volunteer at Benedictine High? She first became an unlimited substitute, pressed into service whenever a teacher called in sick or we needed an extra body to supervise. We would go to work together before dawn and come home late after dark. Most weekends were spent on office work at the school. We grew closer and happier. In time, she recovered from her injuries and became a regular teacher at Benny.

In sports, we were on a roll, but we didn't have a deep bench to win the top honors in boys' basketball. Our boys on varsity and junior varsity were literally worn out with play. Each student-athlete had to participate in a minimum of two sports and keep a C+, or better, average. Racking up detentions or violent outbursts would result in students being benched for games to the consternation of coaches, parents, and fans; but I held firm. I can't tell you the number of times coaches and Dads' Club members came to pressure me to allow a young man to play when his grades had sunk below the requisite level or he had gotten into a fight or violated too many rules. But the most hated and despised man in Detroit made no exceptions.

Each and every sport had its own unique problems but at the heart were the twin problems of excessive egos of coaches and poor bookkeeping for revenue. At the end of the second year, our track-and-field team had scored major victories and set a few new records in Michigan events. Our boys' football team had become district champions in Michigan (not a mean title for a small private school). I ordered both Erma and myself a beautiful black with white team letter jacket (mine had the word *principal* emblazoned in big letters on the back). We were having a ball.

At the same time, I had to concentrate on getting the school back in the good graces of the accreditation agency. This was a major step involving a commitment from all stakeholders, staff, students, parents, and the abbot. I was lucky in discovering Mr. Newkirk, the capable teacher who became an administrator par excellent. With his help as a newly minted assistant principal, we were able to cover both the parking lot before and after school and also sit in on the all-important teacher/parent meetings. Somehow, with the grace of God and the hard work of the staff, we gained our accreditation and were in good standing with the powers that be.

Another major emphasis was the contractual requirement with all teachers and administrators (including me) to prepare and teach an after-school SAT preparation class for juniors and seniors. It wasn't long before our students' grades went up along with their SAT scores. Soon major colleges and universities were knocking on our doors to recruit our students.

I was already into the third year of my two-year commitment with the abbot and was busy trying to work out a plan to take the high school public as a charter school, thus providing the parish with a stream of rental income that could be used to subsidize the grade school (where the parish's commitment still lay). Several educational organizations were interested, with one willing to sign a lease for the following year with the condition being that I had to be there during the summer to provide oversight and continuity for the charter school. All the returning students would be automatically accepted into the new school (without any tuition), and the staff would be employed by the charter school. The charter school wanted me to commit for one additional year; but I had not yet signed an employment agreement when in June of '04, I suffered a massive heart attack while mowing my backyard.

Plans change overnight.

CHAPTER 24

Social Security and Opportunity

Detroit, Michigan
Summer of 2004

In June of 2004, I suffered a major heart attack and had a qua-
druple bypass, followed by months of rehab. At that point,
I knew it was the end of my days as principal at Benedictine
High, and I decided to hang up my spurs. I went down to the social
security office on Michigan Avenue and, after taking a number, settled in with a good book. I always travel with reading material, so I
didn't mind the wait.

When my number was finally called, I explained to a matured
black lady behind the counter that I wanted to apply for early social
security. She gave me several pamphlets and some forms to fill out,
and then she asked why I was taking early retirement. I told her
about my heart attack and rehabilitation. She suggested that I apply
for disability and explained that I would get more money than early
retirement.

I explained to her that I wasn't totally disabled and could work,
but at age sixty-two, I just chose to retire while I had some time left
to enjoy. Most of the men in my father's family had died of heart
attacks during middle age. My father had retired at age sixty-five and,
shortly thereafter, died of a heart attack. Dad had talked about retirement and how he and Mom were going to travel and spend time

working in his garden. I didn't want that to happen to me. Besides, I couldn't claim, under oath, to be totally disabled. Under the early retirement rules, I could still work a part-time job and receive my social security benefits. In addition, I had vested in a defined benefits pension plan and could collect.

The lady leaned back in her chair and smiled. She shook her head in disbelief, not understanding why someone would willingly leave money on the table. I explained to her again about the early deaths of my uncles and how my dad made it to sixty-five years and that I wanted to beat his record. Besides, I wasn't physically disabled and couldn't bring myself to say I was for some extra money.

It was simple really. I was taught never to take something that didn't belong to me but to fight for what was mine. Next, she asked if I had thought about filing for unemployment benefits since I had lost the position of principal. I had thought about it and downloaded and reviewed the forms and began to fill them out, but for the same reason, I couldn't bring myself to take a benefit I didn't deserve (to receive UI benefits in Michigan, one must be ready, willing, and able to work, which I wasn't).

I remembered a television episode I had seen years ago (was it in *Twilight Zone?*) about a man who pretended to be disabled from an accident. It was an insurance scam, but he couldn't get away from the observing eyes of an insurance agent who followed him and would have denied the claim if he saw him without the neck brace and the crutch. The con was brilliant in its simplicity. The man, pretending to be disabled, was going to visit a religious site, like Lourdes, where miracles were reported daily. He would be cured and walk away. The insurance company would not be able to prove it was a scam. The next morning, he lined up with the other disabled folks and went forward for the cure. He received the blessing, turned, but instead of tossing aside his crutch and brace, he turned and hobbled away. Not only did he not receive a cure but he was also disabled from that moment on. What comes around goes around.

Besides, Erma had continued teaching at the charter school where I had been principal, so I spent most of the time reading or walking our dog, Gunner. Each morning I spent time opening e-mails and looking at videos sent by friends. This morning, the e-mail was entitled "The 10 Poorest Cities in the United States."

Because she was working full-time and I was just lounging about, I told Erma I would take over all the housework, cooking, shopping, laundry (except ironing), plus continue with the outside work and maintenance. Erma would often come in late, very tired and frustrated. The least I could do was have a nice meal prepared and the table set, often with an arrangement of seasonal flowers.

That evening I asked Erma to guess which city in the United States was the poorest. She thought about it and said, "It's got to be a Southern city, maybe..." She then named a few poor cities we had visited in the past.

"No, according to this report, it's good old Detroit with a poverty rate of 32.5 percent of people living below the poverty level." The doorbell rang, and a volunteer was handing out newsletters entitled the *Woodbridge Watcher*. It cautioned residents to be on their guard against a recent crime wave and recited the latest crimes in the area.

Our zip code, 48208, simply known as 08, had a reputation for two things: violence and poverty. And yet it was snugly ensconced between the Wayne State University and Corktown, the old Irish residential area in Detroit.

Our neighborhood, Woodbridge, was created from the Woodbridge Farms in the late nineteenth century. A lot of folks in Detroit get confused because there is a street on the east side near the river also called Woodbridge. Back in the eighties it had a popular restaurant called the Woodbridge Tavern. Nearby was a restaurant named the Soup Kitchen; but they are all gone now, and only the name confusion lives on. Now our neighborhood has a restaurant called the Woodbridge Pub on Trumbull Avenue.

Detroit was in a depression even before the latest great recession. It has a population of urban blacks, some white liberal Democrats, seniors, veterans, and welfare recipients, and then there's us. We stayed because we love this old neighborhood and its mixture of peoples, poverty and all.

In the wake of the recent economic fiasco, corrupt politicians, downturn in the economy, financial scandals, foreclosures, and abandoned properties, Detroit's middle-class tax base was destroyed; and whites and well-to-do blacks stumbled over one another trying to get out first. The saying "the last one out, turn off the lights" became all too real.

The city needs residents. Yes, that's right; it needs middle-class, taxpaying, law-abiding residents. We've got all the welfare recipients and impoverished seniors, political activists, cheats, frauds, thugs, and victims we can support. Young blacks with talent and education have moved out in droves, following the whites to the suburbs ringing Detroit—they won't come back until the situation improves, especially the schools. And who can blame them? But young folks (white, black, Hispanic, and oriental) with a history and tradition of risk-taking, hard work, and confronting hostile environments will never find a better opportunity to acquire property and wealth as it now exists in the inner city.

You'll have to work for it, sure, and be willing to fight, of course, and sweat and maybe bleed a little, yes; but this is a once-in-a-lifetime opportunity to acquire property and have a shot at a secure and comfortable life.

Erma and I were having breakfast in a newly reopened restaurant on Michigan Avenue. The owners, a young white couple, came over to introduce themselves. They were from Canada, and their menu featured poutine as its special. (It's a meat or mushroom sauce poured over french fries, popular in Canada and very good.) I asked how a nice-looking couple from Canada had wound up in Downtown Detroit. The wife explained that they were both in the hospitality industry in Toronto and realized that they would have to work most of their lives to own their own restaurant. Here in Detroit, they had found an abandoned restaurant; secured a loan to renovate; and a year later, after much blood sweat and tears, they opened to rave reviews.

There is so much available land and abandoned buildings with the utility infrastructure in place. Those who can acquire property, defend it, and develop it will prosper. An absentee landlord situation will not work in Detroit. You have to be willing to live in the community, be a good citizen, keep your property up, defend it, and be a valuable member of the neighborhood—not simply acquire it and sit on it! We have too many speculators buying up parcels of prime land and sitting on them waiting for a major development to buy them out. I can feel it in my bones. Good things are going to happen here.

CHAPTER 25

Public Flyers and Trash Cans

Woodbridge
2005–2008

As Erma and I were returning to our car from lunch with some friends at the Woodbridge Pub (an upscale metro-restaurant catering to the younger crowd), I noticed a flyer under our car's wiper. Taking a look at it, I noted that it was loaded with useful information. Let's go over it from a Detroiter's point of view (remember, this flyer was distributed to a target population of mainly suburban patrons and students—usually not Detroiters).

The first advice to program emergency numbers in your cell phone is a good idea. But just remember, in the event of a real emergency, there is no one you can call who can get there before the muggers or thugs you just noted.

The second bit of advice, regarding leaving items in your vehicle, is practical. I remember when the president of Matrix Human Services, Mrs. Marilyn Lundy (from Grosse Pointe of the Fisher family fame), placed her kitchen refuse in a box and slipped it into a plastic shopping bag—probably from some upscale store. Her thought was that once she was at her office, she would ask a janitor to drop the box into our garbage receptacle; but she got busy and forgot and left it in the back seat in public view.

Unfortunately, when Marilyn came out to go to a luncheon meeting, she found that someone had smashed the rear window and stolen her box of trash. Can you imagine the consternation of the thief in going through the effort to break into a car and find a box from an upscale store only to open it and discover old banana peels, carrot shavings, and old tea bags? It's enough to make a grown thief cry. The moral of the story is "out of sight, out of mind."

The next bit of advice is interesting. "Keep your head up, and don't be afraid to make eye contact with people." Good advice. Too many students are mugged while walking down the street late at night listening to their headphones or distracted by an electronic device. Music and conversation are good, but walking to your car in the dead of the night is not the time or place to be distracted. Keep the cell phone in one hand and the keys in the other—that is if that's all you got. Notice that nowhere in the flyer does it talk about carrying a "big stick." Remember, this was written by Wayne State University. They are concerned with their liability as much as the safety of the students.

The other side of the flyer also had a valuable piece of information: get the glass on your vehicle etched with the VIN number. A friend told me that a car door with glass from a popular vehicle is worth fifty dollars to a thief from a chop shop. He also said that the same door with the VIN (vehicle identification number) etched into the glass is almost worthless—maybe five dollars. The chop shop must first take the glass out and replace it.

Another trick I still use, though not as important now with many cop cars carrying functioning computers, is to take a pocket-knife and mark an X on the tab that we adhere to our license plates. The tab has the expiration date of the plate. A few years ago, there was a brisk underground business in peeling off new tabs and placing them on plates of vehicles with an expired plate. This is a serious problem in Detroit and probably Wayne County (i.e., people driving on expired plates, many without insurance or even a valid driver's license).

A cop friend told me that when he is patrolling in a police vehicle with a working computer, he could arrest a dozen residents within an hour or so for the illegal plate, expired license, and/or lapsed insurance; but he has been told that there is no room in the jail, so he can only write them a civil ticket and send them on their way.

It's hard to believe that Detroit could get any worse, but it did. Folks seemed to give up or just not give a damn. Telephone poles, trees, public art, and those huge commercial flower pots were targeted by drivers of stolen vehicles. They seemed to enjoy ramming things and leaving a scene of chaos in their wake. If the car became inoperative, it was simply abandoned. Suburbanites were rear-ended, then when they got out to exchange insurance information and examine the damage to their vehicle, they were robbed, if lucky. Often they were beaten and carjacked. PSAs (public service announcements) advised drivers to remain in their vehicle and go to a safe, well-lit area (e.g., a police station parking lot) to exchange information. The city, day by day, was becoming more beaten and neglected. Streetlights didn't work, trash often wasn't picked up, and it was seldom we saw a police officer on patrol.

Each day, trash blew in from Grand River Avenue and kids to and from school, or wherever they were going, casually dropped trash in the street without thinking. The city had become a third-world nation.

The Serenity Prayer kept coming to mind (I think it was by Reinhold Niebuhr, but may have been based on earlier prayers):

> God grant me the serenity
> To accept the things I cannot change;
> Courage to change the things I can;
> And the wisdom to know the difference.

The prayer is based on an active-stoic philosophy of acceptance and action. I can't change the political corruption, crime, fear, and racism all around me; but I do my part to help others, patrol the community, and clean up the trash in and around my property. I can help my neighbors and make this place a little better for everyone.

I asked Erma what she thought about my placing a garbage can at the corner of our streets. I told her I could fence in the small area, plant flowers, and place a nice trash can atop a utility cover. She said the outside was my domain and, if it pleased me, to do it.

During the first storm, my trash can blew away. The second one was stolen and used to carry away a neighbor's lawn tools that he had left in his yard while he ran in to take a telephone call. The third one has been in place for several years and is used mainly for dog waste but, on occasion, a kid will drop trash in it. In the past, cars would pull up to the curb to dump ashtrays and toss fast-food bags onto the street. This seems to have ended. Folks seem to be using the can without prompting.

I also decided over the next few years to settle in and make basic improvements inside and outside of my houses. I painted and spruced up the houses and stained the fences with honey gold and renewed my effort to have the nicest lawn in the neighborhood. Our little corner began to glow.

Forces were underway to make positive changes in the neighborhood. Ten of the old Jeffries high-rise apartment buildings had been imploded and replaced with senior housing. This removal of many dangerous people was especially felt in our neighboring community. For years we had been lobbying Wayne State University (with twenty-seven thousand students) to get them to expand their boundaries to include policing of the Woodbridge community.

Finally, they agreed to extend their boundaries to include our neighborhood. The WSU area is one of the safest communities in North America. It has its own sworn police department, and we loved them. When called, they immediately come. During this period, I continued working part-time and taking care of the house while Erma taught computers at a charter school. On a personal level, things began to improve.

CHAPTER 26

Tricks of the Trade

Detroit, Michigan
Winter 2008–2009

T hings were getting worse. Street crime in our neighborhood was out of control. I know that with each new downturn of the economy, crime would spike throughout the city. As the easy federal and state money programs for the indigent dried up, the thugs and predatory gangs looked for easy pickings in the neighborhoods. Cars were being broken into, wheels were stolen. (A resident came home from work, parked and locked his car, and went in for the night. The next morning, he came out to go back to work but instead found his vehicle neatly sitting on cement blocks with the lug nuts scattered nearby and all four wheels gone.) Students, seniors, and women were being mugged, and in one recent case, we had a female student kidnapped and raped. Many of the crimes were now being committed with impunity during broad daylight. It was beginning to be like the bad old days.

Seniors again hid behind locked doors, and residents once again formed safety committees to patrol their neighborhoods. The organization, Safe in Woodbridge, was begun and held regular community meetings at the Fredrick Douglass Library. A committee of the best liberal residents decided to try to resurrect the old citizens CB patrol, but they never could get it off the ground. No one would go out on patrol.

This had been a popular program back in the early eighties to address a spike in street crime. Back then, Erma and I ran the base station out of our house and switched on and off, patrolling the streets in a vehicle with magnetic "CB Patrol" signs on the doors and a battery-operated amber light flashing from the top. We carried heavy flashlights but had to sign a statement that we would not carry weapons for liability reasons.

By the way, the CB patrol was an effective tool in combating street crime; but it required manpower, discipline, and organization—things that today's liberals seem to have in short supply. Neither Erma nor I joined this time. I was convinced that I could do more good armed with a .357 S&W and a Rottweiler patrolling the streets and alleys in the neighborhood.

The streets were becoming more dangerous; and like most good intentions, after a few preliminary meetings, the safety committee faded into inaction. People screamed about the need for more police protection, but the City administration was so corrupt and inept that the screaming did little good. Streetlights didn't work, and once again, people hid from crime.

A few of us old-timers were still out walking our dogs. A few of us with big-breed dogs still went out to walk the neighborhood early in the morning (when folks were going to work) and after dark (when people were returning home).

I paid particular attention to the alleys and streets hit hardest by street crime. I was not a part of any committee or organization, so the "do not carry" rule didn't apply to me. I had no organizational structure, no chain of command, and no group or association to sue. I was on my own. Each morning and many evenings, my dog and I went walking and let the chips fall where they may.

I loved the dawn patrol, and it's still my favorite. My Rottweiler, Gunner, and I would leave the house early—before dawn. I would carry a pistol in my right coat pocket where my fingers could easily wrap around the fat Hogue aftermarket grip that I had installed. I wore an old coat—if I had to shoot through the material, so be it. It would be no great loss. I never carried anything in my right pocket except the weapon. Keys, pocketknife, comb, change, etc. all went into the left-hand pocket. My flip phone went in my left shirt pocket.

I'm of the school that you don't announce your intentions. I don't believe in open carry. I know it's a hot topic among gun rights advocates, but why give the bad guy an advantage? First, he doesn't know whether or not you are carrying, and if so, where it is located.

I believe that you just stand your ground and be ready to defend it. My hero growing up was Teddy Roosevelt, and like Teddy, I believe that you walk quietly through this valley of death (I added that part) and carry a big stick. My stick of choice then was an S&W .357 J frame (that's a five-shot revolver for those of you not into weapons) with the first round loaded with bird shot followed by four very deadly hollow points.

Why bird shot, you ask? Because, over the years, I've had to deal with packs of feral dogs on more than one occasion. Nothing stops and scatters a pack of dogs like a taste of bird shot (Napoleon's whiff of grapeshot comes to mind). After that first round, all bets are off.

With Gunner's leash in my left hand, we would walk north on Avery through the residential neighborhood up to the freeway then over to Trumbull Avenue (a commercial street that is the easterly north-south boundary of the neighborhood) then south to Grand River, through Scripps Park (a run-down hangout for derelicts and drug addicts), and then home. The walk took about an hour and a quarter at a fast pace. I usually would vary the streets and walk through different alleys, but we covered the entire neighborhood.

During the walks, I always greeted neighbors and strangers alike with "Good morning," and I would study their response. I would always greet them from afar to let them know I was approaching.

"Good morning," I'd sing out so as not to startle anyone getting into their cars on the way to work.

When you greet someone, you can look him in the eyes, study his behavior, and look at his build, the color of his skin, and his clothing. From a little distance, you can check out his posture, hands, and whether or not he is alone or have an accomplice. Often, a suspicious individual would grunt something and quickly turn and walk the other direction toward one of the commercial streets.

If you just walk by with eyes down, absorbed in your own thoughts or listening to earphones, you lose a lot of information about your environment—information that could prove vital to your ability to return safely home. Some suspicious-looking folks, when greeted by me, become nervous and are eager to walk away or get back into their vehicles and drive off, especially when I made a show of taking out a pad and pen to note the license plate and make of vehicle.

For a while, a white panel work van, parked at different spots in the area, would speed off anytime I came into its view; and I never did get its plate number. I also used my notepad to jot down the location, makes, and models of abandoned cars; sinkholes; downed power lines; abandoned buildings; and other dangerous points of interest.

Gunner and I often walked to a corner, crossed the street, and then walked back toward the suspicious individuals, keeping an eye on them. If a person is up to no good, he'll move on.

I got to know my neighbors pretty well; many of the women who worked the early shift came to their doors and watched for us before going to their vehicles. They were reluctant to leave the safety of their homes until we came by. I would wave an acknowledgment, and my Rottweiler and I would wait until they got safely into their vehicles and drove off.

Sometimes we would stop and ask if we could assist in cleaning the ice or snow from the windshield and glass. Believe it or not, some folks tried to give me a tip. I told the neighbor that I did it because I could and didn't mind at all. Besides, it was a good way to get to know the neighbors. My first rule of city living is "never leave your vehicle parked on the street."

But some of the apartment dwellers had no choice. The landlord didn't have enough garage space. If so, always keep your vehicle clear of personal items and put a club on the steering wheel and have the wheels turned in toward the curb. Put wheel locks on, if you have them, though it won't prevent theft if someone really wants your wheels; it may just slow them down enough for someone to intervene.

Gerry, an old-timer on Commonwealth, recently heard a noise on the street and came out armed with a baseball bat. Gerry is a brave man. If I had a medal for valor, I'd award him one. He chased off three guys taking the wheels off a neighbor's car. If you have a garage, always park it inside. Not only will it keep your vehicle safe but it will also be easier to start up and get going on a cold morning. Another big reason to park in the garage is that no one will know if you are home or not. Thieves want to break into a home when it's empty; there's less chance of getting shot. They really don't care so much about an alarm system. They go off so often in the city that people have grown immune to them. I make a real effort to get up and go check when I hear an alarm, even to the point of walking around the house or vehicle. In truth, they were all false alarms; but one day, who knows?

So why do we stay? I could have retired again, but Erma was still working. Besides, I don't like being pushed around and told where I can't live.

CHAPTER 27

Calling Neighbors

Wisconsin
Spring of 2009

Erma and I love to travel. We visit relatives and friends or just go sightseeing around the United States. Typically, we leave our dog Sasha at home (she does provide a layer of defense). A neighbor comes in to let her out, feed her, fill up her water bowls, and bring her in at night. The neighbor also picks up the circulars and flyers. I, in turn, do the same for him when he's out of town. This way it is difficult for someone to know if we are home. We don't park the vehicles on the street (They are always safer in the garage at night.), so it's hard to know if we are home.

Once, we were traveling to the Wisconsin Dells for a little trip; we were just a bit north of Chicago when my cell phone rang with a call from a neighbor's wife.

"Help!" she cried.

I asked her to take it easy and tell Erma what was happening. I handed the phone over to Erma, who put the speaker on.

"Dave please come quick and bring your gun," she cried out in panic. "There is a crazy man on our porch, and he's killing a woman. I've yelled at him and told him I'd let my dog loose if he didn't stop. He said he would kill me and my dog if I opened the door. Help! Please come quick."

"I'm sorry," Erma replied, "we're north of Chicago right now, and Dave can't come. Call the Wayne State Police." Wayne State University has a fully functioning police department, and if called, they would now come into our neighborhood.

"Do you have their number?" she begged.

Both Erma and I have Wayne's emergency number on our cell phones. Erma gave her the number and told her to also call 911. There was no one else to call. Most of our neighbors were die-hard liberals who didn't believe in guns and lived to see all weapons banned. The only other person in the area who also carried was a former cop named Chuck, but there was real tension between the two neighbors. A year earlier Chuck's dogs, unfortunately not on a leash, killed her dog, also not on a leash. Her dog had come off her porch, and the two had fought to the death on the sidewalk. It happened so fast they couldn't separate them.

Bad blood had existed between them ever since. It got to the point that I would invite one to a backyard cookout only if the other was not coming. It was like juggling live hand grenades.

Hanging up, Erma and I looked at each other and deeply sighed. "All we can do now is pray." We both made the sign of the cross and silently prayed for the safety and well-being of our neighbors and the woman being killed on the porch. If you can't do anything else, you can always pray.

After a wonderful vacation in the Wisconsin Dells (a vacation in which we didn't hear one curse word or have to deal with any acts of violence), we returned to Detroit, in truth, a little anxious as to the condition of our neighbors.

All looked quiet as we circled the block and entered the garage (we always circle the block to check out the neighborhood and alleys). The next day, while working in the front yard, I had several neighbors come over to tell me of the strange happenings on my neighbors' front porch.

As I pieced the story together, it seemed as if a man and woman, both black, parked their car at our corner filling station and then got into a terrific verbal alteration. Loud curses, shouts, screams, and slamming car doors led several neighbors to their windows to watch. But no one went out to offer assistance.

The woman was seen to slap the man and then to run up our street. A few seconds later, he came after her. At our corner, she stopped, looked both ways, and then looked back at him. He was not approaching fast. She then ran up onto my neighbors' front porch and began banging on the door and crying for help.

The story gets a little vague because no one had a good vantage point; but my friend Chuck, the retired cop I spoke about, just happened to be driving by and heard the ruckus and pulled up in front of our neighbors' house (and who says prayers aren't answered?). Chuck is a good six-foot-three muscular middle-aged black man, but he has a bad back. He carries his .40 Glock at all times.

I talked to Chuck later, and he picked up the story at this point. "My helper Carl called to tell me that a dude was chasing this woman up the street. Carl said he saw him run up on the porch and smack this lady who was pounding on the door. I got out and approached with caution. Carl followed at a distance."

Chuck motioned with his head toward my neighbors' home and continued, "I heard her banging on the door and saw him pick up a rock from the front porch. Her face was all cut up and blood was streaming from her mouth, but she was still screaming and cussing at him and trying to defend herself.

"He had raised his arm high with the rock in his hand, ready to strike her in the head, when I said, 'Hit her again and I'll drop you.' This stopped him cold. I don't think he knew anyone was behind him. I was pointing my pistol at him. But his back was to me, and I didn't want to shoot a brother in the back, you can see that?" I nodded agreement and asked him to continue. He then said, "'You can't shoot me. I ain't got no gun.'" I thought about the double negative and then asked Chuck what happened next.

Chuck continued, "I told him, 'If you hit her, I'll drop you.' He dropped the rock and jumped off the porch and ran back to the gas station. Next, I heard a car burn rubber as it pulled out. I waited to see if he was coming back with a gun or was circling the block, so I hung around a while. He didn't, so Carl and I left."

"How was the woman who was attacked?" I asked.

"The woman said she didn't want an EMS and was on her cell phone to someone named Jerome, telling him about the happening. She said there was no reason to call the police and that they would take care of the problem themselves. About ten or fifteen minutes later, a car pulled up, she jumped in and takes off, and that was the end of that," Chuck said, finishing his narrative.

I soon learned from another neighbor that the police had arrived about a half hour after the incident, but everyone had gone back inside and there was nothing to see and no witnesses to give statements. He said that he didn't want to get involved and had gone inside himself and closed his door. He said that the police knocked on several doors but no one answered. The woman was gone; the man and his car were gone. The lady where the incident occurred had come out, turned on her garden hose, and sprayed the blood drops from the porch and sidewalk before the police arrived. She then dropped one of her favorite rocks from her porch into the trash container and went back inside. It was just another little non-incident in the neighborhood.

I can't tell you how many times the gas station has been the center of violence in our community, but people need to gas up their vehicles and buy snacks and a newspaper. We'll discuss urban hot spots later and what to look out for.

As for my neighbors whose porch was invaded, they still live here. I'll give them credit for that. He did come over after the incident and ask me about the steps necessary to get a permit to own and carry. I said, "It is better to have it and not need it than to need it and not have it." Sound advice. I hope it takes.

Home on the Range

Summer of 2010

I finished my burger and fries and pushed the empty platter to the side of the table and asked, "Can I run something by you?"

Erma looked up and smiled. Still munching on a french fry, she assented with a "Sure."

"I was working in the alley yesterday and came up with the first chapter of a cowboy story I've been mentally playing around with. Can I run the storyline by you...get your honest opinion? It's just a concept and a bit rough."

"Sure, let's hear it," she answered.

"All right, now picture a Western cattle range in the 1880s. You see a lone cowboy bending at work next to a fence post. His large brown horse, reins tied to a fence post, slowly chomps the dry grass along its base. It's a hot day..."

The cowboy removed an iron staple from his mouth with his left hand and carefully positioned it just so, then using his right hand, he hammered it over a strand of barbwire on to the post, careful not to hit his fingers. He then proceeded to hammer another staple on to another strand. The hammer blows rang out over the quiet afternoon—almost like a church bell calling folks to prayer.

The cowboy straightened up. He was a large man, over six feet in height, dressed in faded jeans held in place with a large leather belt with a military belt buckle on which is inscribed "the USA." He was conspicuous for not having a gun belted to it. His feet were shod in worn, dusty square-toed work boots; and his broad shoulders and thick chest were covered with a sweat-stained blue checkered shirt. His dark-brown eyes matched the color of his hair, which was collar length and escaping around a broad-brimmed high-crowned hat with a stampede strap loose at his chin. His brown mustache covered his upper lips and curved down on either side of his mouth.

Glancing toward a small rise to the far east, he saw the heads and then the bodies of a trio of men ride up to the top and pause, each studying the range. The lead man had a large square-jawed unshaven face, an unkempt appearance, and hard gray eyes. He had a rifle in his scabbard at the ready and carried two six-guns strapped to his waist. He looked relaxed and confident as he carefully studied the man at the fence. He pulled his hat brim down to shade his eyes and slowly walked the horse forward.

Following close behind, on either side, rode two of the hardest men the cowboy had ever seen. One, a mid-sized Mexican, was wearing a black flat-topped hat with fancy embroidering. Across his chest the man wore crossed bandoliers filled to capacity with stubby-heavy cartridges. He was mounted on a beautiful full-blooded black and sat high on a fancy California saddle with silver inlays.

The cowboy noticed his ivory-handled six-shooter, probably a Colt, in a black tie-down holster. He looked fast. He also carried a Winchester rifle in his right hand with its butt resting casually on the saddle in front of his leg. The cowboy studied the weapon, and from the hex barrel, it looked like an 1873 model. Might be a .38-40 Winchester. A black mustache drooped on either side of Mexican's hard mouth. Then, flashing beautiful white teeth, the Mexican smiled and said something to the leader, who smiled and nodded.

The third man, an Indian or perhaps a half-breed, was dressed in leather britches and rode shirtless. A large wicked-looking knife, known in these parts as an Arkansas toothpick, was strapped to his side. He was lean with hard muscles exposed to the sun. His black braids hung down on either side of his clean face. He carried a carbine rifle in his right hand held at the ready. His finger was on its trigger and his thumb on its hammer. His left hand lightly held the reins.

The trio paused, surveying the range. The Indian sat still on his pony and then suddenly stood up high in the stirrups of an old Army saddle and turned to scan the back trail. He nodded assent, and the three rode slow and easy over the rise.

Removing the last staples from his mouth, the cowboy walked to his horse and dropped his hammer and the staples into his saddlebag. He then slowly removed a large red bandanna from his hip pocket and, removing his battered Stetson, wiped its band and then his face (careful to make sure he got no sweat in his eyes) and awaited their approach.

"Afternoon," the cowboy said in greeting. "Mighty hot weather we're having. Something I can help you'ns with?"

The big square-jawed man walked his horse a few feet in front of his two companions, a position of leadership; and rising from the saddle, he flexed his body and rolled his large shoulders and stated, "You live around here?"

"Yes, sir, we got a small ranch over the next rise—run a few head a cattle and put in some fodder crops." His voice trailed off.

The square-jawed man nodded toward the rise behind the cowboy's back and asked, "Over yonder?"

"Yes, sir, just me and the misses and our youngster. She's thirteen and going on thirty...a real handful living out here. It's pretty lonely for a kid. We don't have much, but I'm sure the misses can rustle up some grub for you'ns."

The square-jawed man studied the fence, and rising in his saddle to follow its line, he said, "I hate barbed wire. I don't like hemming critters or people in. It ain't natural."

"Well, sir," replied the cowboy, "I ain't parcel to it myself, but the agreement I have with the big ranch to the north is that I keep it mended...you know...it's an agreement."

"Fernando...Lobo...either you like barbwire?" The Mexican shook his head in the negative while the Indian continued scanning the horizons.

"Well, sir," said the cowboy, again slowly removing the red bandanna from his hip pocket, mopping his face, and then returning it to his hip pocket. "Sure is a hot 'ne today. I got a pump at the house and can sure give you some sweet cold water and refill your canteens."

"How do you know our canteens need filling?" the square-jawed man demanded.

"I was just guessing by the looks of your mounts. They've been rode hard," the cowboy responded. And then he added, "Didn't mean nothing by it."

"Didn't mean nothing by it," Square Jaw mocked. "Either you boys hear such a thing? He didn't mean nothing by it." Fernando flashed an evil grin as Lobo's darting eyes continued to dart around the range.

Square Jaw smiled and said, "Now tell me about that farm of yours and your nice little family."

"Like I said, mister, it's a small ranch. And me and the misses and our youngin, we works it. The wife likes to put out a garden and me—"

"Now tell me about your misses. Fernando here would like to meet her. And Lobo there, now granted, he ain't much to look at, but he sure does like to play with little girls, don't you, Lobo?" The Indian nodded with no change in his facial expression.

"Now, farmer"—Square Jaw addressed the cowboy with the ultimate insult—"I understand that your youngster is thirteen... hmm...maybe a little old for Lobo, but I guess he'll have to make do. Now tell me about that misses of yours."

The cowboy stood in place, gathering his thoughts, then responded, "Please, mister, we're peaceable folks, Christians. I'm unarmed 'cepting for that old Sharps rifle there"—he nodded toward his horse—"I use it to bring down an occasional elk. We don't want no trouble."

"Well, now"—Square Jaw sadly shook his head—"Fernando, did you hear that? He don't want no trouble. What do you think we should do? Just ride away 'cause he's so Christian and white?"

"No, senor, I think it might be fun to play a little game with this hombre. I rope him and pull him home to his little Christian family. Give him a free ride behind…it'll make him nice and, how do you say, tender. Then I'd like to meet his wife. After you, of course, senor."

Square Jaw rubbed the stubble on his chin as if thinking and said, "Sounds like a good plan, Fernando. You rope him, and then we'll all go pay a visit to his little Christian family." Fernando smoothly placed his rifle in its saddle scabbard and leaned forward for his lariat. At that moment, the cowboy reached back again for his bandanna, for what appeared to be a final wipe of the sweat from his face.

But instead, the trio watched the bandanna fall to the ground. The cowboy's right hand came up fast from his back with a short-barreled .45 Colt, and his left hand went to work fanning its hammer.

The earsplitting explosions spewed a cloud of acrid smoke and spit lightning flashes of lead from its muzzle. The first rounds hit Fernando in the throat, pitching him backward and off his horse, then without a second's pause, the flames spit lead into the Indian's chest, tearing huge tunnels through his body.

The Indian had vainly tried to move his horse out of the line of fire and had kicked the sides of his horse once before dropping his rifle and tumbling to the ground. His horse broke into a gallop and disappeared over the rise in the direction they had come.

The thunderous roar of the six-shot revolver, which, in truth, sounded like one mighty roar, faded away. The gray smoke cloud curled around the scene and slowly dissipated as the cowboy leveled his pistol toward the chest of the square-jawed man who sat frozen in surprise. It was cocked and aimed for the center of his chest.

"Now it's your turn, you son of a bitch." The cowboy's words were hard as flint.

The square-jawed man had never seen such fancy gun work, but he had heard of it. Where? "Wait." He cleared his mind. "Look here, we were only funning you. We weren't actually going to do anything, just having a little joke." Now the square-jawed man's face began to perspire, and his eyes began to sting from the beads of sweat that were playing havoc with his vision. He didn't move a muscle.

"Funning, was it?" answered the cowboy. "A joke? My ass. You were playing with me the way a cat plays with a mouse. I'll tell you what, mister, now I'm going to have a little fun with you.

"You know what I told you about having a family and a ranch over the next rise? That was just bullshit. I ride for the Little R brand, work for Mr. Kincaid. He's the biggest cattleman in these parts and a law unto himself. We've got no sheriff or marshal hereabouts. Now listen and listen good 'cause your life depends on your answer and I don't have time to jaw with you. Mr. Kincaid is one of those men who runs his ranch like a king of old in England. He's a hard man, but a fair one. He believes in what he calls rehabilitation. Do you know what that word means?"

The square-jawed man nodded that he had heard the term; his breathing began to relax a little, and his eyes shifted around to the bodies of his companions sprawled out on the ground with their blood soaking into the thirsty ground.

He looked at the muzzle of the short-barreled .45 leveled at this chest. Squinting hard, he saw the visible chambers looked empty, but the one under the hammer was covered by the barrel. Had the cowboy fired five or six shots? It had all happened so fast. Could he pull leather first or run him down? "Ya, I know what it means."

"Good," continued the cowboy, "because Mr. Kincaid believes that there is something good in each man and, if given the opportunity to see the errors of his way, he can change. Take me for instance. I was caught relieving Mr. Kincaid of a few head of cattle—almost five years ago. They caught us fair and square. And after my partners, Lefty and McAllen, got shot to pieces, I surrendered. The old man Kincaid gave me a choice: stand trial before him as the lawgiver, like some king from the Old Testament, or be hung on the spot." The square-jawed man began to listen with interest.

"Well, you can see I'm still here, and I had to admit every mean and ornery thing I'd ever done during that trial. When it was over and I had said my piece and begged for mercy, Mr. Kincaid pronounced sentence. I was given a one-year sentence of hard labor on the ranch—just like a convict or a slave.

"At the end of that year, I was given another choice. I could have my horse, saddle, gun, and the clothes on my back and ride away as a free man, or I could swear an oath of loyalty to Mr. Kincaid as a hired hand and get $100 a month plus room and board."

The square-jawed man leaned forward with real interest and said, "A hundred a month? Why that's twice the going wage."

"True," said the cowboy, "but you see, I have special talents. I'm fast, as you saw yourself, and I don't miss. A hundred dollars is what I said, and a hundred dollars is what I get. And I'm worth every cent of it to Mr. Kincaid."

A hundred dollars a month, thought Square Jaw. When all was said and done, he didn't make that much in rustling and robbing small ranches; but still, there were other side benefits that money couldn't buy.

"Now you have a choice, mister. Either go for your irons or unbuckle your holster and drop it. Either way makes no difference to me. I'm just following orders. What'll it be?" The cowboy extended his arm and lined up his shot, but it really wasn't much of a shot at that distance.

"Hold on a second," uttered Square Jaw. With all his attention, he focused on the big barreled gun palmed in the cowboy's right hand. Had he fired five or six shots? With all his squinting, he couldn't tell if a live round was under the hammer.

He stated, "I think you fired all six rounds when you fast-fanned on my compadres. I think you are holding a losing hand." Square Jaw studied the cowboy's face, looking for some tell, a reaction. He saw no change, but then a brief smile played about the cowboy's lips.

"You willing to call my hand? I've counted my shots since I was knee-high to a grasshopper. Any man who don't count is a fool, and I can't abide a fool. So try me. Mr. Kincaid said I can kill in self-defense and I can kill in resisting arrest. I just can't kill an unarmed man. You've got your pistols hanging at your hip, so let's get on with it. Dinner'll soon be waiting."

"You going to give me a chance, ain't you? At least put your gun at your side." Square Jaw sweated out his decision.

The cowboy's pistol remained aimed at his chest center, and a .45 makes a big hole at that range. How had he palmed it so fast? He must have had it hidden at his back, near the red bandanna that the square-jawed man saw still lying on the ground. A back belt holster explained why he hadn't seen the cowboy going for it. *I thought he was just going to mop the sweat from his face again.*

Now Square Jaw was sweating with the sun beating down on him. His eyes smarted as he tried to blink away the sting. Square Jaw played enough poker to know when a man showed fear or excitement. You had to know when to call a bet and when to fold.

"What'll it be? I can't just stand here all day, but I can only kill you if you draw on me or resist arrest. So I'm arresting you on the count of three. Drop your belt or I'll kill you. One."

A drop of sweat hung on Square Jaw's eyelid, and he tried to blink it away. He tried to swallow, but his parched throat cried out for some of the cold water he'd heard about. He moved his trigger finger in anticipation. The cowboy stood stock still with his pistol pointing directly at Square-jaw's heart and said, "Two."

"All right, you win." Square Jaw raised his hands in surrender, then lowering his right hand, he began to unbuckle his gun belt, hesitating for a last glance at the .45 pointing straight at his heart; but with no satisfaction, he let the holster and its guns drop to the ground at the cowboy's feet. The cowboy's eyes never left his target.

"Now, off your horse. Easy now." The cowboy scooped up Square Jaw's holsters and weapons and moved back so he could cover his dismount.

"The cowboy hoisted the gun belt over his right shoulder and removed one of Square Jaw's .44 Remingtons with his left hand. He twirled it a few times to feel its balance. It felt good and he smiled. Though he was a Colt man himself, the cowboy liked it. He checked the .44's cylinders and listened to its music as he rolled the cylinder along his right sleeve. It was a long barrel with a factory hammer, not any good for fanning, but it had a nice weight and good balance.

"You carry all six rounds, one even under the hammer," the cowboy commented aloud. "Dangerous! Now drop your holdout. Come on," he commanded.

"I ain't got no holdout."

"Sure you do, and if you don't drop it now, I'll put one between your eyes with your own pistol."

Square Jaw's shoulders drooped. He heaved and slowly removed a small two-round derringer from a vest pocket and let it fall to the ground.

The Remington's mechanism was as smooth as silk, and the cowboy enjoyed cocking and releasing the hammer with his thumb. The cowboy motioned for Square Jaw to move back against the barbed-wire fence where he could easily cover him. "If you move, I'll kill you."

He then retrieved the sidearms and rifles belonging to Square Jaw's deceased companions and searched each body for holdouts and knives and money.

Only finding a few silver dollars, the cowboy slipped them into his vest pocket and mused at how little crime paid. He walked over to his horse and dropped the knives and pistols, both of which were well-worn and covered with trail dust, into his saddlebag.

"Now go over nice and slow and put your two friends over these mounts. Tie 'em down underneath, nice and tight." The cowboy slipped his .45 into his back holster and buckled on Square Jaw's gun belt. The sight of him doing this caused Square-Jaw to grimace in pain and mutter curses under his breath.

"I bet she's got a hair trigger."

Square Jaw grunted an assent as he checked to make sure the knots holding Fernando and Lobo were tight and then asked, "At the end of the year or so, do they give you back your own guns?"

"Can't say," answered the cowboy, leaving Square Jaw a bit puzzled.

"Well, did they give you back your own guns?"

"Said I can't say." The cowboy snatched and replaced the Remington several times from the left holster then did the same with the weapon on his right hip. His movements were so fast they seemed a blur.

After emptying the Winchesters and returning them to their saddle scabbards, he faced Square-Jaw, who had just finished his task and was asking, "Can I get a drink from the canteen there?"

"Sure," the cowboy tossed him the canteen and said, "a condemned man gets a final request."

"Huh?" Square Jaw looked confused. "What do you mean 'condemned man'? I did everything you asked. Now take me to Mr. Kincaid for my trial."

"Well, you see," answered the cowboy, "what I'm aiming to tell you is that there ain't no Mr. Kincaid, ain't going to be no trial, no spread over the rise. You got any last words?"

"You can't just kill me. You said that…" Square Jaw's voice trailed off as it finally registered on him that he had been cleaned out in the highest-stake game of his life. He had been bluffed, and holding the winning hand, he had folded.

"Your short gun was empty, wasn't it?"

The cowboy just nodded and smiled.

"You don't work for no ranch neither. Then who are you? A bounty hunter?"

The cowboy nodded again and said, "You and your partners are worth money dead or alive. I don't take killers back alive. I've trailed you boys across two states from the Indian territories. It was simple enough. I just followed your trail of burned cabins and butchered bodies. I rode wide around your camp last night after I was sure you were headed this way. I picked the hammer and staples up from the last cabin you burned. The rancher won't need it anymore."

Square Jaw shook his head in disbelief from side to side and said, "You can't—"

The cowboy's hand, quick as a snake bite, pulled the pistol from its leather and shot Square Jaw in the center of his chest. The .44 drove deep into its target, driving the man back into the barbed wire where it snagged and held him upright in death. The cowboy then spun the revolver, made sure the empty round was under the hammer, and holstered it, leaving the reeking acidic smoke to drift over the range.

The cowboy removed his short-barreled .45 and ejected the five spent rounds and slowly reloaded it from a vest pocket. He never kept one under the hammer. Spinning the cylinder and cocking it, he released the hammer carefully and slid it in his back holster, hidden under the back of his vest.

After finding Lobo's horse over the rise, he lifted and pulled Square Jaw off the wire and heaved him across the horse's saddle. Then he tied the man's wrists and feet securely under the mount. He then attached Lobo's horse to Fernando's black and it to Square Jaw's and then tied it to his mare. He formed a nice little pack train.

Before mounting, the cowboy retrieved a stack of wanted posters from his saddlebag and smiled as he added up the amounts. Returning the posters, he mounted and, lead rope in hand, moseyed his little pack train toward the nearest town with a telegraph, a train, and a bath.

"Well, what do you think of it?" I asked Erma and said, "Remember, it's just a rough cut."

"Wow," Erma exclaimed, "you've sure been reading a lot of cowboy books recently. But what's the underlying message? Are you saying that when things get so bad you can lie and kill without the benefit of trial—what, all in the name of justice?"

"Not sure about all that. Let's just say that you need to fight fire with fire."

CHAPTER 29

A Long Walk around a Small Island

Detroit
Early March 2011

My friend Aaron and I walked Belle Isle on most Saturday mornings (good days and bad). We've known each other since the mid-1970s and even practiced law together for a time. We rounded the northern end of Belle Isle, the once-beautiful jewel of a park set in the middle of the Detroit River (by the way, the Detroit River really isn't a river at all. It's more of a strait or channel emptying Lake Saint Clair and Lake Huron on down to Lake Erie).

Huffing and puffing, we rapidly moved toward the wooded part of the island. The wind coming off the water was biting cold and stung my eyes. I blinked repeatedly as we turned onto a narrow road through the wooded interior of the island. With the wind no longer coming face-on, we could again talk.

We were in the midst of another recession (the big one this time), but things were so bad no one noticed. "Things are getting worse. Hardly a day goes by when someone isn't mugged or a car or house robbed. It's beginning to again look like the bad old days." Aaron didn't reply. He lived in a luxury high-rise condo on the riverfront with its premises patrolled by armed guards. He had moved farther politically to the left and was becoming an entrenched progressive, but I loved him like a misguided and wayward brother.

By the way, I believe that this country is like a huge jet airplane. Look at it head-on, and it has a big curve in the middle and then the wings taper off on the right and left. We need the majority of people in the middle and the wings balanced in order to fly properly. Unfortunately, we have become bimodal in shape. Folks are moving further to the right and left. Our plane wobbles when it flies. We need more folks in the middle, both right and left; but the more each party moves away from the middle, the more unstable our flight becomes.

"So let me ask you," I asked him, "would you walk the island with us on Saturday mornings if I didn't carry a weapon and have a Rottweiler?"

"I don't like guns, but I can see they have a place in our history. I'd like to have them in museums and view them as historical oddities that once plagued man."

"Sure," I agreed. "I'd also like to live in utopia, but this is Detroit. You come armed or you don't come at all."

We were deep in the wooded part of the island that once, not many years ago, sheltered a herd of miniature deer. Erma and I would come on the island with a bag of apples and carrots, and the miniature deer would come up to her window and receive food from her hand. But for some unexplained reason, they had been rounded up and had disappeared from the island.

"So answer me. Would you walk the island without me and my guns, say, during the summer when it's crowded with folk?"

"Sure I would. I don't depend on you and your guns. Do you really carry more than one? I come because of Sasha. You were the one who said that if you had a choice between a gun and your dog, you'd take the dog."

"Well said, and yes, I do carry two weapons. Does that make me paranoid?"

"Perhaps," he answered.

"I tell you, without an equalizer, I wouldn't be out and about as much as I am. There isn't any part of the city we won't travel in—well, with the exception of certain sections on the east side." We both laughed. Aaron lived on the east side of Jefferson, one of the safest neighborhoods in Detroit; but we both knew I wasn't talking about his neighborhood.

I thought of all the times during the summer when we walked the island and passed through the crowds of young folks gathered at a point on the island's east side to party. With loud rap and R & B music booming from sound systems mounted in the trunks of vehicles, the young people danced, drank, and grilled.

It's like Moses parting the Red Sea, I thought as we approached the gathering. As if on cue, they began to separate and open a path, lining each side to watch two old white men walking a huge Rottweiler through their midst. Detroiters love and fear the Rottweiler; therefore, anyone who commands one or more immediately has street creds (credentials).

From the crowd good-natured comments and questions followed.

"Beautiful dog."

"Do you have any pups?"

"How old is she?"

"Is she pure-blooded?"

And "Does she bite?"

I answered with a smile and a friendly wave of the hand as we kept walking. As soon as we passed through, the party resumed.

CHAPTER 30

Memories of Detroit's Chinatown and the Grand Ole Opry

October 2011

When you think things couldn't get any worse, the bottom falls out of the auto market. Thousands of Detroiters with good jobs and mortgages were suddenly unemployed and soon-to-be homeless. The current recession had knocked the props out from under the few middle-class residents in our community, and the neighborhood had scores of abandoned homes. Folks, unable to make payments, would drop the keys in the mailbox and abandon their homes. Soon crews of wreckers would appear to strip the house of anything of value and leave a shell.

Why did we remain in a failing community? Maybe it was just pure stubbornness. We weren't going to abandon our community we knew so well. Maybe I was still trying to prove to myself that I really wasn't a coward for not volunteering to go to Vietnam, as so many of my friends and family members had gone (including my brother-in-law who volunteered to do a second tour manning radar equipment at distant firebases).

Our community didn't collapse all at once, but things kept going downhill. It seemed as if each day, a new crisis would hit. I am not one to get depressed or easily give up, but I needed a change of scenery.

I called my brother, Danny Mac, and his wife, J. K., to see if they wanted to go on a joint vacation.

It took a while to talk them into coming to Detroit (J. K's first visit, even though we had been trying to get her to come for years). I learned from J. K. that one reason for her reluctance was her impression that Detroiters were anti-Japanese and violent. I assured her that both Erma and I were well armed and that we would only travel in a pack. Plus, we had a state-of-the-art security system, dogs, and layers of defense (including iron bars on windows and steel doors with extra-secure dead bolts). Somehow, we won her over and had a great time visiting museums, restaurants, and Windsor, Canada.

J. K. acknowledged that Detroiters were not as bad as she had supposed, and upon questioning her as to how she had formed her opinion, she said "Vincent Chin." I remember well the sad case of his being killed on the streets of Detroit back in June of 1982. He was just twenty-seven years old at the time and was celebrating his bachelor's party with friends at a strip club where he was mistaken for Japanese by two out-of-work auto workers. Detroit's auto industry was in a deep recession at that time, largely due to inferior domestic production and increased competition from Japanese and German auto manufacturers.

I remember hearing that the assailants were ejected from the club but that they got a baseball bat from their vehicle and proceeded to chase Vincent Chin down the street. They caught him, and as one held him down, the other smashed his skull in with the bat. The assault took place right outside McDonald's on Woodward Avenue, our main drag, yet no one intervened. After a trial where the two assailants were found guilty of manslaughter, they had to pay a fine ($3,000) and received probation. They never went to prison. I've always wondered where Vincent's friends were hiding during the assault. One good man or woman with a gun might have prevented his killing.

At that time, my boss, Mrs. Marilyn Lundy, had assigned me to work with the City on a project to revitalize the Woodward Corridor.

She remembered Detroit's glory days and wanted to see revitalization during her lifetime. A block off Woodward Avenue was the abandoned buildings that had one been Detroit's Chinatown. She had "volunteered" me to host a team of Chinese money men from Hong Kong (the British colony was to be returned to Communist China in 1997). The rich Chinese citizens were concerned about their wealth being expropriated by the new masters. They were traveling the world to find safe areas to fund and relocate. I thought we had a natural here and spent several days chauffeuring them around and, with the aid of a translator, showing off the benefits of relocating in Detroit where land could be had at rock-bottom prices. Things could only get better, or so I thought.

Then, in the middle of their visit, the two thugs killed Vincent Chin; and my plans for a new Chinatown went to hell in a handbasket. The few remaining Chinese restaurants soon closed, and the boarded-up buildings became shooting galleries for drug addicts and homeless squatters.

That was then; this was now, twenty-nine years later. It didn't seem possible for the city to get any worse, but it had. The city and county governments were corrupt. Kickbacks and bribes were part of everyday ordinance compliance. We were spiraling down for a hard landing to the economic bottom.

I really needed our road trip to Pigeon Forge and neighboring Gatlinburg and the Smoky Mountains in Tennessee. We hiked mountain trails; went to musicals, restaurants, and plays; and had a great time. I didn't think about Detroit once during the visit.

One funny thing did happen in Gatlinburg. We were walking up the main drag to our car when we passed a Western-wear shop. Both Erma and I are addicted to wearing cowboy boots (the most comfortable footwear in the world). I love Dan Post while Erma buys a variety of boots for comfort and fashion statements.

J. K. asked Danny Mac if she could go in and look at some boots displayed in a store window. Danny said that no one in Spokane wore Western clothes and boots and they might send a wrong message.

J. K. reminded him that his brother and sister-in-law wore them and said that they were comfortable. Besides, she had said please.

You have to remember that J. K. was raised in a traditional Japanese-American family where the man of the house is highly respected and his opinion catered to by the women.

At this point, Erma said she wanted to look at a new pair and grabbed J. K.'s arm and entered the store. Dan and I wandered around the store, looking at leather goods, but neither of us bought anything. We soon left the store and sat on a sidewalk bench and people-watched.

About forty-five minutes later, Erma and J. K. emerged, both wearing new high-heeled Western boots. J. K., with her back held straight, styled on the sidewalk for Danny Mac. He confessed he liked them on her. J. K. said they made her feel taller (true, with three-inch heels) and gave her more confidence. Her personality seemed to change from a quiet and retiring housewife into a modern self-reliant lady who knew what she wanted and knew how to get it.

All joking aside, J. K. is one of the sweetest ladies I've ever met. Once, when I was visiting them, I went to bed in their guest bedroom with nothing but a reading lamp on the bedside table. I woke up to the fragrance of fresh-cut flowers to find memorabilia from my father (watch, key chain, and photos) tastefully arranged on the table. With the passing of my father and all my uncles, I was the oldest male member of the family. I suppose she thought I deserved special treatment.

Next, we drove to Nashville and stayed at a nice hotel downtown. Neither Dan nor J. K. had ever been to the Grand Ole Opry, either at the old Ryman Auditorium downtown or the new auditorium at Opryland, so we went to both plus did a riverboat dinner cruise on General Jackson, a paddle-wheel showboat.

The next morning, I got up and, as was my custom, took a walk. This was when the Occupy Wall Street movement had fanned out across the United States. In the plaza, in front of the government building, about fifty tents were set up; and scrubby hippy types were waking up, stretching, and putting on coffee. I wandered over and asked a young bearded man with a knit cap pulled low over his ears what it was about. He began by giving me some pseudo-Marxist mumbo jumbo about the evils of the banking system and how we needed to bring the greedy capitalist system to its knees. It seemed as if Wall Street—with its greedy, war-mongering profit motive—was grinding the other 99 percent of the Americans into the dust.

"What do you replace it with, after you get rid of the capitalists?" I asked, thinking he would offer some benevolent all-powerful government; but no, he sought true anarchy. He advocated the elimination of all laws and governments.

"People can then be truly free," he said.

But I asked, "Free to do what?" Others around us listened as we engaged in a lively discussion. They expressed their fear and distrust of the current system (I can understand why a generation of pampered kids, indebted to the banking system because of excessive college loans, might be bitter and angry).

"But you are living off the system you hate so much," I pointed out. "Look at the tents and sleeping bags you just crawled out of. Someone manufactured them with resources gathered by others and sold them to you."

"Oh, no." I was informed that they were donated to the movement by friends who saw the system as evil.

"Okay," I said, "how many of you panhandle and beg for money? I saw several of you down on Broadway last night among the crowds of tourists, begging. Someone had to earn that money that you were given, didn't they?"

We discussed human greed and the damage it causes when unregulated. I agreed that we needed checks and balances and reasonable regulations; but we must have, like Goldilocks's request from the bears, just the right amount: not too many, not too few. Have you ever thought about that child's story? It can be seen as an analogy about our economy.

At that moment, a cry was heard and repeated around the plaza: "Doughnuts and muffins have arrived, coffee too. Come and get them."

"And where is this coming from?" I asked.

"One of the local Christian women's groups provides us with breakfast each morning. They are allied with our cause."

"But don't you see they are part of the system that you hate and want to bring down? If you destroy the free enterprise system, who will bring you bran muffins with blueberries and coffee in the morning?"

Most of the group began quickly moving to the tables where coffee urns and boxes of pastries were being set up by church volunteers. "I was told that you have to get there before the bums and street people move in," one said by way of explanation for the abrupt departure; but the young bearded man with the knit cap stayed to continue the conversation.

"I can tell you are committed to your cause," I said, "and nothing I can say will change your mind. I don't want you to miss your breakfast. Let me just say this in parting. Stuff some padding under your knit cap and protect your head because, at some point, probably sooner rather than later, those in power will tire of your presence and find an excuse to come in and remove you. I've seen Detroit mounted police with nightsticks breaking up an antiwar protest by breaking heads. Take my advice and get a helmet. You are going to need it."

Not long after our return to Detroit, I read of how police in several cities, including Nashville, had removed the protestors, often by force, for any one of a number of reasons (e.g., lack of camping permits, poor sanitation, the safety of citizens, impeding traffic, etc.). Frankly, the system just got tired of them.

By the way, in Detroit, the City leaders simply allowed the weather to freeze out the protesters. A news reporter broke the story that most of the tents were actually empty at night as the protesters sought warmth in the homes of friends, family, and supporters. The protest in Detroit had just fizzled out.

CHAPTER 31

Tricks of the Trade
(the Turnaround)

Detroit, Michigan
Winter 2001

Over the years I've developed a few little nervous traits. I hate visiting friends in the suburbs and sitting in front of a picture window at night, backlit and framed in a window. It's like I have a tag on me saying, "Shoot me, I'm a sitting duck." I also hate sitting in a restaurant with my back to the public or the door. I like a table or booth where I can sit with my back against a solid wall and watch the comings and goings of the patrons.

When we go to Windsor (just across the river from Detroit) for dinner, I go "naked." Well, not literally, but I feel naked because I don't carry. They are very strict about that in Canada. Folks still talk about the time when the Southern Baptist ministers had a convention in Detroit; and about a dozen different cars headed over the bridge to Canada, loaded with fine Southern preachers and their wives, only to get arrested and have their cars impounded for carrying guns into Canada. It almost became an international event when folks from Washington, DC, were able to resolve the situation and get the hostages home and their vehicles restored.

I remember the time I was shot at once through a backlit window and have been cautious ever since. Some valuable lessons came out of that experience. I'll tell you about it later. When someone rings the doorbell at night, the front porch light goes on automatically as I switch off the interior hall light before asking who they are and what they want. I want the person on my porch to be backlit and feeling like a target is hanging around his neck.

Another little nervous tic I have acquired is to do a quick look-see when I pass anyone on the street. This trait I didn't acquire in Detroit. I had a bad experience when I was a kid. My parents allowed me to go to a Catholic seminary boarding school in Jefferson City, Missouri, for the ninth grade.

Home for the summer vacation that year, I wore my good sports jacket with school crest, slacks, and polished shoes and went to the county fair (that would be the Butler County Fair in Poplar Bluff, Missouri), and I stood out like a sore thumb.

While walking around the midway, three white boys (about my age and size) stopped me, asking for cigarettes. After informing them that I didn't smoke, they then asked for money. One demanded, "Borrow me a dollar."

Laughing to myself, but without answering them, I simply turned around and walked off with their taunts following me. Later, near the rides, I saw the same three walking toward me. I just looked straight forward and kept walking. The boys stepped out of my way as I passed; and I was feeling pretty good about myself when, suddenly, the last boy, as soon as I passed, pivoted and swung a Coke bottle, hitting me in the back of my head with a solid blow.

I went down in the sawdust like a sack of potatoes, and they went after my wallet and watch; but I rolled on my back and managed to get in two or three good kicks (I then knew firsthand how the term "to roll someone" came about.). Several fairgoers saw the commotion and rushed over and chased the boys off.

"You're not from around here, are you?" one man asked.

"No, sir." I admitted that I was home from boarding school as I struggled, still a bit dazed, to get upright. A man helped me up, and I dusted the sawdust from my slacks and jacket.

"Boy," he said, "we got a lot of white trash and riffraff around these parts. You shouldn't stand out so much. You look like you got a little money on you. Be careful. And you may want to get some ice on that spot or you'll have a goose egg there tomorrow."

I thanked him and the others; assured them that I was fine and didn't need medical assistance. (I had a lump on the back of my head and a splitting headache, but luckily, the bottle hadn't broken the skin.) Then I went off to buy my own bottle of soda.

No one even thought about calling the cops, least of all me. After taking a swig from the Coke bottle, I then poured the remaining contents on the ground behind a tent. I then tested the weight of the bottle by slapping it a few times into my left palm. I was ready and went looking for the three punks. It's probably good for all of us that I never found them, but I did learn a valuable life lesson from the three punks from Poplar Bluff, Missouri.

Travel with a friend, blend in, don't stand out, and not only keep your eyes open but also pass on the right. Drop your chin and look back when you pass a person on the street. Make sure that they don't turn on you. You can block with your left arm and do what you have to do with the right.

In my Detroit neighborhood, I became known as the "the man with the Rottweiler." When I pass someone on the sidewalk, I automatically say hello and, once passed, tuck my head down and glance to the side as he passes by. I don't want to ever be sucker punched again, and thus far I have not.

If he is walking on, it's cool. If he is turning back around toward me, I say, "You want something?" They have always turned back and moved on. Best to keep your eyes open.

Any time, day or night, I can be found walking in the neighborhood. As others began to walk their dogs, crime began to decrease. Today, unless it's the dead of winter, you can't go outside without meeting a neighbor—men and women—walking dogs (by the way, even on the coldest mornings, we are still out before dawn—it's become a habit and my Rottweiler, named Sasha, becomes cranky if she doesn't get an early morning walk).

Citizens taking back their neighborhood have gone a long way to reducing crime and bringing the community together. For example, this morning I met a young woman taking her trash can to the sidewalk for pickup. She introduced herself, and after exchanging brief synopsis of our lives in the neighborhood (she and her husband were new arrivals), we parted with a friendly wave.

Frankly, if you don't have the guts or the inclination to walk the streets of your own neighborhood and take the time and effort to get to know your neighbors, you might as well stay in the suburbs! Why don't you lock yourself in your apartment and call 911 when you have an emergency? Good luck with that!

CHAPTER 32

Winter Ice and a Life Lesson

February 2012

Lest I give the wrong impression, it doesn't take a gung-ho type A personality to survive in the new urban frontier; in fact, I dare say that type of person will be short-lived. No, it's not a matter of being the toughest and meanest s.o.b., but one who can adapt best to the environment has the best chance of survival.

It takes a person who is thoughtful, plans ahead, and is careful about his surroundings. For example, last night, Erma and I went to Nancy Whiskey's, a neighborhood watering hole, to watch the Super Bowl game. We enjoyed the first half and the half-time performance, and I don't even care for Madonna; but at the beginning of the third quarter, we paid our bill, said our goodbyes, and slid out. Why? Because we know through long years of experience that the most dangerous time to be out is when the bars close. If you leave a bar, nightclub, or saloon sober and alert, you will avoid many pitfalls.

We were safely at home, snuggled up on the couch with our Rottweiler between us, when other folks are out there dealing with stickup men, police, snow, cold weather, and black ice (This is when snow and ice melt during the day and freeze again at night, often forming a black superslick, almost-invisible surface near doors and on sidewalks, especially near downspouts. It is a very nasty and dangerous, especially for older folks). A little stiffness is all I had the next day.

I understand that the single greatest cause of injury among older folks is a slip and fall, and I believe it. You see, not all the dangers are from punks and thugs. I've found that the chance of a slip and fall on an early morning winter's walk is especially great. I've taken a few hard falls in my time and have learned not to try to break the fall with hands and elbows but to keep them tucked, get hit on your shoulder, and roll as much as possible before you pop back up.

I'll pass on a little trick I learned years ago. The soles of most winter boots and shoes become hard and don't provide much traction on ice. They are designed for snow. On ice, I've found it's best to wear two pairs of socks and put a good insert in a pair of rubber totes—don't wear shoes. Your feet can flex and grip and help keep balance, even if you slip a little. Thus far, knock on wood, I've never had a slip and fall while wearing my rubber totes.

A person must use his head while living in the city. Don't crowd others or look for a fight because you'll surely find one. If I learned anything from my father, it was how to spot and avoid trouble before it happened. It doesn't mean that you have to back down or be a victim, but it does mean that you can't be part of the problem. You have to be the solution!

When I was in the seventh grade, we lived on Grand Avenue in the little southeast Missouri town of Poplar Bluff, about a mile and a half from our school, which was on the other side of town. On several occasions, walking home the most direct route, I was confronted by a group of early teens (about my age) who claimed that they controlled the street and I would have to pay a toll.

That was my first experience with foulmouthed cursing and swearing. As I easily jogged past, I heard insults that I had no idea what they meant, but I knew it was bad.

"Run, you little m—f—er" rang in my ears then other curse words, followed by howls of delight and laughter. I had already heard some curse words, and my buddies and I had practiced them; but this was a whole new level. That night I told my mother about the incidents and the demand for money. I made my money delivering papers, turning over neighbors' gardens, and generally doing any odd job I could get. I wasn't about to give up my hard-earned money.

The next day, after school, I stopped by 303 Liquor and Sporting Goods on Main Street. I quickly walked past the rows of adult (we called them "girly") magazines and went to gaze at the rotating selection of knives. The clerk showed me a beautiful imitation pearl-handled folding knife with an eight-inch blade that had a button on the side. Depress it, and with a light flick of the wrist, the blade snapped open and locked into place. It was called a kingfisher and cost a dollar plus tax. I called it my Young Sword.

That afternoon, I walked home feeling safe in the knowledge that I had my kingfisher with me, ready to spring into action with the push of a button. Now I would show those punks who the "m—f—" was.

Lucky for them, they were not on patrol that afternoon. That evening, after dinner, I was in my room looking at a *Hot Rod* magazine when my dad opened my door and stepped in. I had hung my jacket on the hook on the back of the door, and when he closed it, the jacket fell, hitting the floor with a thud. He stopped and turned, picking up the jacket and measuring the weight in his hand. He pulled the knife out from the pocket, opened the blade, studied it for a second before closing it, and then replacing it in the pocket.

"Where did you get the knife?"

I told him I'd bought it at 303 Liquor.

"I don't want you hanging around that place. You know, Son," he said, "in this state, if you carry a knife with a blade longer than three inches, it is considered a dangerous weapon. Just like carrying a gun. You can go to prison for it. You know, we have never had a Suttner go to jail, much less prison. Why do you think you've got to carry it?"

I told Dad about the incident and how I had purchased the knife, with my own money, for my protection.

"It's about principle," I said.

"Son, let me ask you a question. Let's say it's a beautiful sunny day, and you are walking down a sidewalk. You've got every right to walk down that sidewalk. And then you see—right in front of you—a big pile of dog crap. If you keep walking, you are going step right in it. Remember, you've got every right to walk on that sidewalk. What do you do?"

"Well, Dad, I'm not stupid. I'm going to walk around it."

"Son, I know you're not stupid. But you are hardheaded, so believe me. Some people are dog crap. You've got to learn to walk around them. If you get in a fight with them, it's just like stepping in dog crap. You get it all over you, and you stink as bad as they do. The law won't be able to tell the difference. Do I make myself clear?"

"Yes, Dad, you're telling me that those boys are crap and I've got to learn to walk around them and not look for a fight. But, Dad," I inquired, "what if I can't get away? If they gang up on me?"

"Now, Son, it's true that once in a great while, you won't be able to walk around. At that point, you must deal with the situation like a man—in any way you can. Look for an equalizer. I myself like a nice ax handle, a bottle, or a two-by-four, if one is handy. But each man must make that choice. Son, usually, if you are thinking right, you can talk your way out of a problem. The situation where you have to fight doesn't come up that often in life. Do I make myself clear?"

I nodded.

"Look, Son, odds are you are going to get into more trouble carrying an illegal knife or pistol. That's why I don't have any pistols. They are no good for hunting and just get someone killed. If it's legal, that's different. Just make sure that you walk around trouble if you can. If you can't, then you may have to fight. If you have to fight, use every means, fair and foul, to survive."

Dad made himself very clear. I kept that knife for years, using it to clean fish and play splits with my little brother—a game I don't recommend. It involves two contestants facing each other armed with knives. First, one throws his knife into the ground within a few inches of his opponent's foot. If the blade sticks perfectly in the soil, the opponent will have to stretch his foot to the knife and keep stretching through successive plays until the opponent's blade doesn't stick. Then it's the other's turn. First, he will stick the knife between the other's feet, but often, he's stretched out and off-balance. If he is successful, he brings his feet back to normal position (shoulder width) and his feet together. His body is now balanced, and it's his turn to make the other do the split. My brother and I whiled away hours in this game.

But I stopped carrying the knife around town and never had to open it in anger. I took up baseball after school, though I was never really that good at it; but it gave me an excuse to carry a bat and glove around town. I would fantasize about being jumped by a gang and defending myself, or some other victim, with my trusty Louisville Slugger.

In fact, I found that I could walk a few blocks out of the way and avoid the gang of toughs entirely. That next fall, Mom and Dad moved the family to a house on the other side of the town near our church and school.

CHAPTER 33

Just Walking in the Rain

Detroit, Michigan
Spring 2012

I began the first week of April with a determination to accomplish all the open items on my to-do list. I had retired-retired (for the third and last time) on January 1, 2012, and was determined to get it right. Up early, I finished two full sets of exercises, followed by a tumbler of water. After feeding Sasha and leaving a note for Erma on the kitchen whiteboard ("Gone for a walk, love Dave, 7:40 a.m."), we headed out (Erma has a rule that all absenteeism from the house must be documented with dates and times leaving and purpose on the kitchen whiteboard).

The heavy rain that had fallen during the night had subsided to drizzle and mist. A blanket of fog swirled close to the ground, but I was as snug as that proverbial bug in a rug. I wore my long hooded East German Army poncho that I had purchased for five marks from an East German soldier in Berlin after the wall had come down. I pulled my felt fedora down on my head, and we set out.

I began my morning prayers and rosary while Sasha examined every bush and object for new odors, but unfortunately, they had been all washed away. She contented herself with briskly walking at my side, eyes open and ears working, ever alert. My early morning world was very quiet and peaceful.

Thirty minutes later, we turned south on Trumbull Avenue and continued a circuit for home. The rains began again with sudden downpours followed by constant pelting rain. At the busy intersection of Warren and Trumbull, we had the green light. But first I put Sasha on a sit command and checked out the situation before proceeding south on Trumbull Avenue.

The City had recently installed a button for the pedestrians to push to gain a "walk" signal before crossing. Pushing the button, we waited at the corner for the signal to recycle. Sasha sat in a pool of water looking mildly irritated. She was definitely not a water dog, but I had trained her to sit at every corner and wait for my command to walk.

The rains had caused delays, and the splashing traffic was fast as people hurried to work. We moved back a few feet as a truck's tires splashed waves of water toward us. I heard a low growl as Sasha glared at the receding taillights.

The "walk" signal appeared quickly, and I glanced around, checking to make sure that we were clear. No one was in the right-hand lane behind us to turn right in front of us, and that was good. Glancing ahead and to the sides, all looked clear. We stepped into the crosswalk, and suddenly, I saw a car approaching on Trumbull Avenue going north. It was traveling much too fast for the road conditions; but it was parallel to us, and it had no left-turn blinkers on to signal a turn into our crosswalk. There should be no danger. The light was green for his as well, and he should pass by us going north on Trumbull as we walked south.

We were just into the crosswalk when the car, without signaling, suddenly began to make a hard turn into our crosswalk. We had the green walk sign and the legal right away, but soon we'd be "dead" right. I had just finished my last Hail Mary when I felt, more than heard, the sound of its engine and the slush of its wheels on the wet pavement as it turned toward us to avoid an oncoming car going south on Trumbull. He didn't see us until his vehicle was on top of us.

I thought of jumping back to the curb, but I knew we'd never make it. A dog on a leash doesn't execute an about-face pivot with grace. I yelled, "Jump," to Sasha and pulled her leash hard as I sprinted forward away from the oncoming path of the car. Suddenly, I knew I'd never make it clear of the vehicle. It was too close. Jumping just out of the car's path, Sasha slipped on the pavement. She almost went under its wheels but gained enough purchase on the wet pavement to leap out of the way with the assistance of a good hard pull on her leash.

Relying on instinct more than thought, I smacked the flat of my palm against the side of the moving vehicle and used its energy to push off away from its mass. Looking into the driver's window, I saw in a flash the face of a young black man in a business suit and tie. His eyes were as big as saucers as he realized his situation. His mouth opened to yell something as he grabbed the steering wheel, turning the wheel away from us just enough. He slammed hard on the brakes. The car came to a screeching halt and skidded through the intersection, missing us by mere inches.

I slammed my fist down hard on the car's rear trunk lid, denting its surface as I screamed something, though I can't remember what. There is a time for justifiable anger, and this was it. The driver turned his head back to look at us. He still held a cell phone in his hand pressed against an ear. In a panic, he glanced around and then accelerated. His car sped through the intersection, doing a nice fishtail as he overcorrected and disappeared down Warren Avenue. I briefly saw his license plate but didn't bother to remember it. We had survived, and I couldn't blame him for hightailing out of a dangerous situation. After all, he had almost run over a crazy old white man, who had pounded on his car while screaming insults at him, dressed in a German military cape with a Rottweiler.

In similar circumstances, I would also have had the urge to run away, but I hoped I would have pulled to the side to see if there were any injuries and to apologize. Sasha and I looked at each other.

"Are you okay?" I asked. She replied by pulling on her leash to get us moving out of the intersection. It was over, and dogs live in the moment. The signal was still counting down as we sprinted across the street; and we only had six, five, four, three, two, one seconds to make it to the other curb. Cars sped by, and a few drivers looking our way. Sasha was not in the least bit concerned. That was then; this is now. So we continued our walk.

"Thank you, God," I silently whispered. "That was a close call."

On the way home, I thought about Detroit and its drivers. We have some of the world's worst, and thankfully, some of the best. At any given time, we have drunks and drug addicts in stolen cars tearing around the community looking for crimes of opportunity. In addition, we have the millennials, white and black, impatient and thoughtless with eyes glued to their electronic devices, in a hurry to get to where they are going.

With the free Obama phones, now every nitwit has one, or more, and is constantly on it in the most inappropriate situations. We have so many drivers without auto insurance that one must carry, at a prohibitive premium, uninsured and underinsured coverages. Detroiters who have insurance coverage pay the nation's highest rates.

Over and over again, I've witnessed drivers involved in accidents flee the scene. The kids who run from the cops grow up to be adults who flee from the scene of an accident (more likely than not, one they caused), and we are left to clean up and pay the price.

If you are going to live in the city, you must be alert and not be on your cell phone or listening to music on headphones. Keep your eyes and ears open; and you just might, with the help of God, make it home safely.

CHAPTER 34

The Old Curiosity Shop
on Michigan Avenue

Detroit, Michigan
May 2012

I was comfortably reclining in the padded barber's chair at my barbershop on Michigan Avenue. My eyelids were closed, and I was beginning to droop into that pleasant state of semiconsciousness as the barber, Old Lopez, applied fresh hot towels to my face already covered in soapy foam he had whipped up in an old ceramic shaving mug. I listened to the rhythm of steady strokes as he sharpened the straight-edge razor on the long leather strap. If you've had a shave by a professional barber, you know the state I was in. If you've never had one, well, it's your loss. It's a throwback to the nineteenth century and one of life's little pleasures.

The barber was an older Mexican gentleman who had worked at Ford's and, after retirement, had taken up the razor in lieu of idleness. He lived in a small bungalow in Southwest Detroit's Mexicantown with his wife and an extended family. It was easy to understand why he preferred the male world of his barbershop. I heard his voice, but the words didn't register in my semi-stupor until I heard him ask, "Are you still a collector of weapons?"

"Yes." I came fully awake and answered, "I've acquired several classic weapons over the years." I had concentrated on the late nineteenth century and World War I era weapons with a fondness for the various Mauser rifles. I had to be cautious talking while receiving a shave. During a pause, I inquired, "Why do you ask?"

"*Sí*, I remember our past conversations. You know Senor Goldblum (not his real name) from the antique shop down the street?" I was afraid to nod an assent with a razor at work on my neck, so I grunted an affirmative.

"I cut his hair this morning," Old Lopez continued. "He tells me that he has two important pistols for sale. They come from the estate of a famous Catholic priest, a Father... I no remember his name, but a very famous person in Detroit."

"The estate of a famous priest," I repeated. My mind turned to the only famous priest I could think of—the "radio priest."

"Could it have been Father Coughlin of the Shrine of the Little Flower?"

"*Sí*, I believe that was his name. You know of him? Senor Goldblum said he has the two pistols he carried."

Father Coughlin, I thought. *The "radio priest" of the 1930s carrying not just one gun but two. Who knew?*

Father Charles Edward Coughlin had indeed been famous in the 1930s, not just in Detroit but across the country and Canada. He was the pastor of the Shrine of the Little Flower (or as commonly called, Shrine of the Silver Dollar), a parish north of Detroit on Woodward Avenue in Royal Oak.

I had first heard of him in an undergrad American history class at Southeast Missouri College in Cape Girardeau, Missouri, where I got my BS degree. He also headed a political organization, something or other for Social Justice. I remembered from my class notes that he had become involved in banking reform during the depth of the Great Depression and had become a thorn in the side of FDR; and this led him to anti-Semitism. My professor reported that he had also broadcast *The Protocols of the Elders of Zion* on his radio show. They were fraudulent accounts, allegedly exposing a Jewish plot to seize control of the world.

He also expressed open sympathy for Mussolini on his radio program for the aid Italy was providing in its fight against the Republican-elected government in Spain (which was anti-Catholic). Later he became more anti-Semitic and a supporter of Hitler's forces fighting to support General Franco in Spain. The exploits of the Condor Legion are well-known. According to my professor, this small war gave both Italy and Germany an opportunity to test new military tactics and hardware in actual combat situations. He had called it a "dress rehearsal" for World War II.

I also had another contact with Father Coughlin when we purchased the house next door in 1973 for $1,500. The house had suffered a fire on the second floor, caused by a tenant smoking in bed, and the owner said he was going to tear it down. I asked how much it would cost to tear it down and fill in the hole where the structure had been. He said about four thousand dollars (a huge sum in those days). I then offered him $1,500 cash money for it "as is," contents and all.

We had a deal and shook hands. He drew up a simple quit-claim deed. I looted our savings account, and we owned a slightly damaged house stuffed with contents. One of the portmanteaus in the basement was loaded with suits and personal effects of a dapper petite Italian wine merchant. He had traveled extensively through Europe, the US, and Canada and had a large collection of pamphlets and materials on Father Coughlin. Going through the information, I realized it was very pro-fascist and anti-Jewish.

My first thought was to burn it, but the love of history forbade it. We must learn from the past. If we destroy the past history that offends us, we lose its meaning. I soon contacted the Walter Ruther Archives at Wayne State University, where Erma and I had both used to write papers in a class we had taken on labor law. In looking up Father Coughlin, it seemed as if, due to the violent anti-Jewish content of his radio program, he was taken off the air by Pope Pius XII and, obeying, had removed himself from public life. He died in 1979 and was buried in Holy Sepulchre Cemetery in Southfield, Michigan.

After my haircut and shave, I walked down Michigan Avenue to the corner antique shop and was announced by an old-fashioned bell mounted to the doorframe. The owner, a large grizzled man of uncertain age, came to the front of the shop and inquired as to what I was looking for.

"Oh, just looking around," I replied. I was never too willing to show interest in any specific items.

He watched me as I walked leisurely up and down the narrow aisles crammed with tons of items from past generations. With hands clasped firmly behind my back, I would occasionally stop and observe some item then move on.

"Anything, in particular you are looking for?"

"No, just looking." This went on for another five minutes with the proprietor becoming more agitated by the second, so I asked, "Any knives, swords, or weapons of historic interest? I do a bit of collecting."

"Weapons, you say? You also interested in guns?"

"Perhaps, but not normally. But I do have a concealed-carry permit, so I am allowed to legally purchase and carry any gun in Michigan."

"Here, come and sit." He pointed at an old oak swivel office chair opposite him at a desk cluttered with toy train cars and tracks. "So you collect?"

"Edged weapons, swords, bayonets, and knives," I answered. I did have several swords hanging on my wall with an assortment of WWI bayonets lying about. My desk letter opener was an early MI bayonet. I tried never to lie. "Do you have anything interesting?"

"I might have something of interest, but not an edged weapon. Have you ever heard of Father Coughlin?"

I nodded in the affirmative, and he said that he had the two .38 caliber pistols that the priest carried for personal protection.

"Really?" I said. "I didn't know that priests were allowed to carry weapons. How do you know they were his? What sort of provenance do you have?"

"I have a copy of his signed application and his permit to carry, which describes the guns. Seems as if the KKK burned a cross at his parish and there were several death threats. Hard to figure. You'd think they were on the same team—after all, he was a Nazi priest. I also have a photo of him holding his pistols."

"True, but the Klan hated Catholics almost as much as Jews, second only to African Americans," I commented and asked to see the pistols and the provenance.

"Sure, you can see them, but I have them at another location."

I handed him my card and told him I would be interested in meeting with him again.

"By the way," I asked, "why do you call him a Nazi priest? He may have been Pro-fascist, but this was before the world knew of the horrors of the Nazis. I don't think he was as much a Nazi as he was Pro-fascist during the Spanish Civil War."

He cut me off with a swift retort. "He was a f—ing Nazi pig. Are you carrying?"

"Ah, yes, why?"

"Let's see it."

I slipped a small .380 semiautomatic from my coat pocket and placed it in front of me on the cluttered desk.

He smiled and pulled a Colt 1911 .45 caliber from under his jacket and also laid it on the table. It dwarfed my little gun.

"Your right," I said. "He was a f—ing Nazi."

Both smiling, we retrieved our weapons and agreed he would call me as to when I could view the guns and the documentation. He stated that he was looking for $6,000 for them. This was the opening bid. I would have to be careful with my counter. I didn't want to use up the funds for our next trip planned to Europe.

I never received his call, so a few days later, I stopped by to find the shop closed with police crime-scene tape across the entrance. I went to the barbershop and learned that someone had entered the antique shop and, when Mr. Goldblum had turned his back, had crushed his head by what the police believed to be a baseball bat. His wallet was missing, but the barber didn't know anything about his .45 Colt I knew he carried.

Hard to believe that Mr. Goldblum would have turned his back on someone he didn't know. Street folks in Detroit were getting desperate. I decided at that moment to let my mustache grow and ended the pleasure of a professional shave. I couldn't afford to be inattentive and half asleep while sitting in public in a barber's chair. That was my last professional shave. When and if things get better in Detroit, I'll go back to barbershop shaves, if I can find one.

CHAPTER 35

House Party

Woodbridge
October 2012

Ensconced in a neighbors' kitchen for the duration of the house party, I was taking pulls from an imported IPA while using my thumbnail to pry open and enjoy pistachio nuts. India Pale Ale was not my first choice in beer (I'm a PBR man, union made in the good old US of A.); and what's not to like about pistachios? That is after checking to make sure they are not imported from Iran. I have some deep negative feelings about Iran dating back to the Carter years. The most miserable time of my life was spent during that period, trying to get a high-interest loan that I needed. Times were really tough back then. Now I was in my own little world, minding my own business, when the hostess, with a young man trailing behind, entered. After smiles and handshakes, she continued with greetings.

She sized me up and stated, "We're the Millers, Catherine, and Bill (not their real names). And you are Mr. Suttner, Sasha's Dad?" She smiled, obviously in on the joke; for Sasha, my best friend and constant companion, was a hundred-pound Rottweiler with an attitude. She is well-known in the neighborhood and has her own Facebook page with a large following.

"Yes. I'm Dave, and Sasha is my girl," I answered and asked, "How long have you folks been in the neighborhood?" I had no idea who these people were. So many new residents were moving in to take advantage of the low prices due to the housing crisis. My wife had received the invitation via e-mail and placed it on the calendar. Once something is on the calendar, I simply go.

The young woman, nodding toward a young man standing quietly next to her and using her fingers to indicate they were a couple, replied, "We just moved in October. We so wanted to meet you. We met your lovely wife—Erma, isn't it? Is that with an *I* or an *E*?"

"It's Erma with an *E*," I replied. "You know, like Erma Bombeck."

"Who?" she asked. "Does she also live in Woodbridge?"

Oh, Lord, I thought, *I've gotten old.*

"Oh, it's with an *E*," I said.

She nodded. "We wanted to meet you. We've heard about you."

Wondering what was being said, I replied, "Not all bad, I hope."

Ignoring my quip, she continued, "You've been here a long time. I understand that you and Sasha patrol the neighborhood daily. Is that true?"

"Yes and no. Sasha and I go on daily walks around the neighborhood. It's a good exercise for us, and we try to keep an eye on things. But we don't really patrol." Sasha was our fifth Rottweiler since we'd lived in Detroit, and she loved her walks.

"That's good because we don't want an incident here like the George Zimmerman situation in Florida. That poor young man, Trevon Martin—dead, and for what? Racism and violence." She answered her own question.

I really wanted to answer, but I thought of Erma's admonitions; and besides, if it was a question, it really wasn't directed to me. So I didn't bother to respond. I took another pull from the very good craft beer.

"Everyone says that it's getting better around here, do you think so?" That was a question, so I just smiled and nodded in the affirmative.

"Yes, things are certainly improving, and it is young folks like you that are helping to make the difference." That was a nice statement. Erma had already warned me about getting into arguments with the neighbors and not to call anyone a pinko bleeding-heart leftist liberal.

"My parents" she continued, "at first, were concerned about us moving down here, you know, in the city. But I told them that it's much safer now. Don't you agree?"

How do you explain to a couple of nice wholesome white-bread kids from the affluent suburbs that, even though it's better than the "bad old days" when we had open gun battles in the streets, it's still Detroit—the murder capital of America? I thought of ways to explain how residents needed to be cautious; to keep doors dead-bolted; to be alert; to keep their vehicle parked in a garage; to have a good security system; to get a dog, preferably a big dog; and to carry a weapon.

"Well, if you are interested and have the time, we can sit down, and I'd be happy to point out some dos and don'ts." My statement was ignored.

"It's so exciting, isn't it?" I was not sure if it was a statement or a question, so I just nodded as she continued, "It's like being a part of an exciting adventure, you know. It's like being a part of some wonderful novel." More conversation flooded in on me. My secret spot had been discovered as a crowd moved into the kitchen.

I finished the beer and, looking around the living room, found Erma and nodded that we should make our goodbyes. We left shortly thereafter.

"Wonderful adventure," I thought aloud to myself and Erma as we walked home that cool October night.

"Erma," I asked, "were we ever that young or that naive?"

"I think I can remember being young once." She sighed. "But it seems like now we are the oldest at every party or gathering. Every time we enter a room, we raise the average age by decades. As to being naive, I don't think all these kids are naive. Most are bright, hardworking, and idealistic. A lot like we were at their age when we moved in after the riots. They have fresh ideas and dreams and want to live in a really cool neighborhood. That's what Woodbridge is becoming, a cool neighborhood. For the young people, it's a very hip place to live." Erma always thought the best of people. Maybe that's why everyone loves her, me especially.

We walked along the silent street, relaxed yet alert. A sudden noise down a side street alerted us. I quickly identified it as a car door slamming, causing us both to stop and peer into the gloom.

The streetlights were out again. Copper thieves had vandalized the street lighting, often with tragic consequences. The price of copper was on the increase, and the scrappers would go after copper wiring. Every so often, DTE Energy, our energy monopoly, would find human remains fried to a crisp in an attempt to steal high-voltage copper wire.

Erma asked, "Do you have your friend with you?"

"Sure do. Never leave home without it." I patted my coat pocket where a small but deadly efficient Kel-Tec .380 semiautomatic lay snugly in its little holster along with a second clip of hollow point ammo.

"I also brought my little guy to accompany us this evening." Erma placed her hand in her right coat pocket. We stopped, looked, and listened until we heard a house door open and close. It was just a neighbor coming home on a chilly fall night. We both chuckled and walked the remaining blocks to our home.

The little guy was traditionally my backup piece; but not wanting to take too much iron on me into a new neighbor's house, I left my favorite piece, affectionately named the Big Guy, at home. I hold good thoughts about my favorite weapon.

The Big Guy was a heavy stainless steel .357 S&W six-shot revolver, a real cop's gun, literally. A friend, who was a Detroit cop, had been assigned to the Warehouse District in the late eighties. He had the S&W revolver's guts reworked to a smooth hair trigger and put on better sits. He and his partner were responding to a burglary alarm at a warehouse where the door had been pried open. His partner called for backup; and my cop friend, gun in hand, went in to investigate. Suddenly, out of nowhere, a figure dove toward him, slicing his leather police jacket with a knife. His weapon responded and kept responding until he had emptied the cylinder into the would-be assailant. The cop got a three-day suspension and was ordered to get rid of the unauthorized weapon. It was a violation of police policy. He had to go back to a standard .38 special. I was the beneficiary of the decision and purchased the retooled revolver, holster, and a hundred rounds of very hot .357 ammo for $300.

I keep the first chamber loaded with a .38 special containing bird shot; the other five chambers house deadly .357 hollow points. Normally, I carried it in a shoulder holster under the left arm, but many neighbors object to big weapons making observable bulges being brought into their homes. No one said anything about nice little streamlined semiauto hidden deep in a pocket.

CHAPTER 36

New Neighbors

Early November 2012

The weather was great. We call it an Indian summer, a brief repeat of summer's warmth prior to the chill of winter. Several neighbors were also in their yards cleaning up the leaves and the trash that continually blew in from Grand River Avenue and enjoying the day.

"Hello, neighbor." A middle-aged couple came across the street to introduce themselves. They had just finished unloading a moving van and were taking a break from the unpacking and organizing after their move from California.

We chatted about the high taxes in California, natural disasters, their trip across the country, and her new job offered at a local college. In the first few minutes, they identified themselves as leftist progressives. I told them how in the eighties I had been a Johnson and Johnson Fellow and, on my first trip to Los Angeles, had experienced an earthquake. On my second trip, there were forest fires and mudslides; and on my last trip, I got caught up in the Rodney King riots. I was bad luck for Los Angeles and had no plans to return.

They informed me that their garage had to undergo major repairs before they could use it for parking, so they were going to spend their time on the interior of a beautiful Victorian home they had purchased at a bargain-basement price.

They inquired about crime and street parking for their vehicle. "Do you use a club?" I inquired.

"A club?" the man repeated and hesitated for a moment in thought. "No, but I have a baseball bat that I can keep in the car."

"No, not that kind of a club I'm talking about. You know, a club for your steering wheel to protect you from car thieves. It has limited value but is worth having and using." I then told him that I had heard about a neighbor a block away that came home last week, parked in front of her house, and after locking her car, ran in for a quick lunch. In less than an hour, she was back out of the house, careful to set her alarm and lock and dead-bolt her house. She got into her car and started its engine, but the roar was so terrific she got out to check. Several neighbors had come out on their porches to see that the noise was all about and saw her get out of her car and stoop to look under it. After a look-see, she went back inside to call the police.

During that short period, some brazen crooks had pulled up next to her vehicle and one had crawled under her vehicle with a battery-operated electric saw and, zip, zip, cut out her catalytic converter and driven away without anyone getting the make, model, and license number. It is a very expensive item to replace and worth almost as much as most vehicles parked in the neighborhood. To think, this had occurred in the middle of a workday. I explained how a club wouldn't have helped in this situation and stressed the need to place the priority on the garage. Later, several neighbors admitted to hearing the rip of a saw but simply thought someone was doing house repairs and didn't think much about it, at least not enough to investigate.

Over the decades, there have been perhaps a dozen times when I've failed to put my car in the garage and left it outside, but unless parked in my garage, I always attached the club. It was second nature. Once, in the late sixties, I came out to find my battery was gone. Another time, in the seventies, someone snapped the radio antenna off; and once, in the late eighties, someone stole my little Buick Century.

Our garage was built in an era of smaller vehicles. Most big American cars and trucks will not fit. When shopping for a new vehicle, we tell the dealer that it must fit in our garage and take it by the house on the test drive. On at least two occasions over the decades, we have had to take the vehicle back because the garage door would not close with it in the garage. We look forward to the day when the neighborhood is safe enough so we can own a four-wheel drive pickup truck and leave it safely parked on the street. But those days are years away

I loved that little Buick Century and never bothered to lock it. This was before I used a club. I kept a few dollar bills in the ashtray thinking that someone would take the money and leave the car alone. Unfortunately, the thief who stole it punched the lock anyway and broke the ignition collar and hot-wired it. It was used in a robbery downriver and abandoned with some of the loot still in the trunk. The little car was never the same after that. It had been violated. That's when I began to lock up my cars and religiously put clubs on the steering wheels. Since then we've not had any cars stolen, knock on wood.

I told the newcomers where they could buy a discounted club and went back to work knowing that the pleasant weather would not last.

CHAPTER 37

Election Day

Detroit, Michigan
November 2013

The morning of Election Day dawned gray, overcast, and cold with a biting north wind—normal for November. By midmorning, the rain clouds blew across the river into Canada and the sun broke through the cloud layer. It was a good omen for Detroit.

This election was filled with drama and hijinks that just couldn't be made up. Mike Duggan had resigned from his position at the Detroit Medical Center to begin a run for mayor of Detroit. The crime rate in Detroit was high. As we say, it was "off the hook." The FBI again listed us as one of the most dangerous cities in the country.

Most streetlights in our neighborhood were out (due to scrappers stealing the copper wires, or some said the City was just turning off the lights to save the expense). Arson and neglect had left whole neighborhoods abandoned and littered with dangerous open and abandoned buildings. They had become magnets for drug dealers, squatters, and criminal lowlives. Our neighborhood was hard hit with abandoned houses on each block. This posed a problem for the remaining neighbors who had to patrol and keep the properties up to avoid vandalism and scrapping.

Our Republican governor had appointed an emergency manager who took the city into bankruptcy. Some talked about having a fire sale of the masterpieces at the Detroit Institute of Arts; and others couldn't wait to sell our most beloved park, Belle Isle, to developers. Things were crazy. City services were crumbling; the bus drivers went out on strike. Why? Because so many had been robbed and beaten by gangs of hoodlums posing as riders. Any Good Samaritan standing up to these punks was put down without mercy. The city was in chaos. Gangs of young punks operated as if they had a license to beat, maim, and often kill with impunity. The police response was slow to no show.

The people were scared and angry. The newspapers headlines screamed "Can a White Man Win in Detroit?"

Mike Duggan was the white man in question. He was the self-styled "turnaround" king at the Detroit Medical Center and was busy organizing community groups. He got his needed signatures on the petitions completed early and turned them in only to find that a strict reading of the city charter resulted in his name being slapped off the ballot. Why? Because he filed early? Detroit was a black city with a black Democratic machine. He might upset the apple cart and actually bring change.

Defeated and dejected, he told his supporters that he was finished; but the grassroots crowds of whites and supportive blacks shouted back, "Hell no," and initiated a write-in campaign. It was such a long shot that it was almost guaranteed to fail. Then the political machine found a black barber with a sound-alike name, and he was also entered as a write-in. Detroit's politics was at its dirtiest, but yet the good people rose up—black, white, and Hispanic—and went to the polls and voted.

Enough Detroiters learned to spell *Michal Duggan* correctly—I understand that many carefully spelled his name on their hands—to place him on the ballot instead of Benny Napoleon who, as the son of a Baptist minister, a former chief of police, and sheriff of Wayne County, was logically the candidate to receive the majority of the black vote.

You have to understand that I am the only registered Republican in my precinct; so I vote for the person, not the party. If I voted for the party, my vote would have no effect. Benny and I had been in law school together. He was a year behind; but we had several classes together and I had grown to like and respect him.

In law school, we were both in the same decedent's estate class. The professor was known to assign an avalanche of cases each class and bury the unprepared students when called on to answer questions about a particular case. If called on to answer questions on a case that you had not briefed, it could mean failure.

The cases were not difficult; there were just so many of them. During the first class, I tried to identify the best students, one of whom was Benny. At the time, I was working full-time; active in my fraternity, Sigma Nu Phi; and trying to be a first-rate law student, plus carry on some form of family life.

After the first class, I asked the chosen students, five in addition to Benny, to meet me in the library. I proposed that we form a study group with each briefing a number of the cases assigned by the professor for that week. I encouraged each to read the remainder on their own but to do an excellent job of briefing the ones I assigned.

We would each brief our share of cases and have them typed up and run off for the other members of the group prior to class. In the event you got called on a case you had not briefed yourself, at least you had a fighting chance to answer the professor's questions.

Study groups of this sort were a common practice, and when time allowed, we would meet before class and review the cases. It was a real time-saver and gave our study group an advantage.

The group listened to my proposal, and all but Benny agreed. He said that he wanted to brief all his cases himself but thanked me for the offer. I also tried to brief all the cases, but in truth, some I skimmed; but I was older with four other degrees under my belt and had a gift for gab.

I gained a lot of respect for Benny that semester. He was always prepared and spoke up with authority and exactness. He would have made a great mayor. By the way, everyone in my study group received an A that semester; and as I found out later, so did Benny.

During the years as legal counsel working with Detroit's social service programs, I had, on several occasions, gone to Benny to ask for his assistance in solving a criminal problem near one of our programs. He was always professional and responsive.

So, back during that primary election, I supported him against the white candidate. It's strange how that worked out. I even put up a "Vote for Benny" yard sign.

Then I learned from Erma, during a mutual confession of honesty, that she had voted for Mike Duggan in the primary. She had canceled out my vote for my friend Benny! We decided that from then on we would coordinate our votes so as not to cancel each other out. My wife, along with thousands of other Detroiters, had voted for Mike during the primary out of a sense of fairness and decency.

"It just isn't right that he was taken off the ballot," Erma confessed. "Detroiters, black and white, have a strong sense of what's fair and what isn't." So I took down my "Benny for Mayor" sign, and Erma and I also both voted for Mike during the general election. Mike won as mayor during the difficult bankruptcy and financial crisis, but it wasn't long before things began to improve for all Detroiters.

CHAPTER 38

Criminal Enterprises

Woodbridge
Late November 2013

My longtime friend Tom comes by most Thursday mornings for a brisk walk with Sasha, followed by coffee and conversation, before he goes to his office or court. Rain or shine, hot or cold, we do a fast tour of the neighborhood, up to the university, and back. The average time is one hour and fifteen minutes. As we approached Commonwealth and Merrick on that beautiful cold morning, we saw a new ultra white SUV up on cement blocks. All four wheels were gone!

"I thought we got rid of those guys a few years ago," I said. "They pull up, usually in a van, and the crew jumps out, leaving a driver with the motor running. One guy jacks the car wheel clear while another, with an electric drill, takes the lugs off and drops them in the street. See?" I point out the shiny lug nuts scattered around the hubs. "Then a third man slips the wheel off and rolls it to the back of the van and then places a cement block under the hub. The jack is lowered and moved on, even taking the spare. They are all very professional, very slick."

"Why do you say you thought you got rid of them a few years ago?" Tom inquired as we walked by. I took a photo with my new cell phone with a camera, but there was nothing for us to do. We were too late to be of any assistance. When the owner would come out to go to work or class, he'd find his new SUV up on blocks. He would get mad and swear a blue streak (I didn't want to be around for that), then he would make a police report and he'd contact his insurance agent. All the clubs in the world would not protect him from this kind of thief.

"An old-timer, Gerry by name, who lives a block or so down on Commonwealth became a local hero a few years ago. He came out early one morning and caught a crew stealing the wheels of a neighbor's car. This was the summer before last. Well, he grabbed a baseball bat he kept next to the front door for just such a situation and charged them screaming like a madman. He said he got a good hit on one guy as he was jumping into the van and smacked their van a time or two as he chased after it. He told me it was a white delivery van and gave it a good dent on the left rear sliding door. They left their tools as they escaped. Gerry now has an electric drill and a jack that he uses every time he changes the oil in his truck."

"He was lucky." Tom continued, "What if they had guns?"

"Sure, he could have been killed. But most of these criminal enterprises aren't thugs. These are semi-professional criminals. It's their job, and they are good at it. They are in it for the money. They don't want action."

"It looks like they are back," he said.

"Yes," I agreed, "or maybe someone has recruited a new crew. It doesn't take a lot of skill or capital to train and equip a crew for this type of work."

I looked at Sasha. "We'll have to get out even earlier for our walks. Lots of students live in these apartments, and there are no garages provided." I gave Sasha a firm head rub, and we continued our walk. Our conversation moved on the politics and the culture wars. It would be interesting to see how this worked out.

Over the next few weeks, Sasha and I patrolled early in the morning, but the crew switched to nights. Over a dozen cars were hit by this gang in a two-week period from midnight to three in the morning. Being a thief in Detroit is hard work.

So many calls went into the Detroit Police Department, WSU's police department, and various political offices that a bait car was finally placed in the area. I understand that it had a transmitter that led the police to a chop-shop operation that was busted. The crew is now serving various jail terms and probation depending upon priors and deals. Unfortunately, it won't be long before some are released and the trouble will begin again.

CHAPTER 39

Electrical Problems

Woodbridge
Early December 2013

On a beautiful Saturday afternoon, I was working with Jim, our electrician, on some "current" electrical projects around the house. I make a list of electrical and plumbing issues that needed attention then, once or twice a year, bring in a professional on layoff to work on the problems. We had just finished correcting an outdoor lighting problem and were running new wire in steel conduit into my new workshop (what I mean to say is that Jim was doing the work while I handed tools when requested).

"Got a question for you," Jim asked. "You're still a lawyer, aren't you?"

"I'm retired as of January 1, 2012. But sure, I was a lawyer for many years." Then I explained that I am what they call an emeritus attorney (i.e., retired after having made it into my seventies in good standing with the Michigan Bar). "I'm inactive and no longer practice law or carry malpractice insurance, but I can still teach law if I want. Go ahead and ask your question, but I can't give legal advice"

Jim paused to put his thoughts in order. "It's about porn—you know, dirty pictures. Is it legal to look at it on the computer?"

"Interesting question," I continued. "The short answer is yes. As long as you are not breaking any laws, it's okay—legally that is, not talking about morally."

"Huh…" he mused.

"Under our current law," I continued, "an adult can look at adult porn without too many legal concerns. But one is running a risk with a website containing rape, bestiality, sadism, or child pornography. I don't see how anyone can get any pleasure out of watching another person suffer, but the reality is that many do. You see, it's mainly child porn that's uniformly illegal. It's the forbidden fruit, so to speak, of our society."

"Even for looking at it on the computer and you don't even buy it?" Jim seemed puzzled.

"Yeah, it could get you into big trouble with the feds, and it's a violation of state law too. It's not just the purchase of porn. It's downloading and opening the stuff up that can get you into big trouble. I understand that the police operate phony websites that advertise minors. If you open one and communicate, let's say to trade pictures of underaged kids or to hook up with a minor, you are subject to arrest and prosecution. They could get you for possession of child porn. It carries a huge fine, potential jail sentence, and the risk of being placed on the sexual offenders list."

"Wow. Isn't that entrapment or something?" Jim asked.

"Sounds like it might be, but I wouldn't want to test it. I had reason to look up the laws recently. And I can tell you, it's a wide net designed to catch a lot of little fish. Let's say you look at some nudies, and unbeknownst to you, some photos of underage girls are slipped in. You got a problem if they get a warrant and take your computer in for analysis. Of course, they would have to have probable cause and a warrant to conduct a search, but if you had your computer with you, say when you entered an airport terminal, they could make a valid argument. If they conduct a forensic search and find inappropriate materials—for example, child porn—by using…I think they call it cookies and icons."

"Can't I delete them?"

"Sure, you can try to clean your computer. But even if you take it to a computer service for cleaning, you might get reported. I understand they can reconstruct every site visited and every keystroke entered. You have to be careful when you get rid of an old computer that the deleted information can't be retrieved."

"It really is complicated."

"As I say, I went through some websites that were attached to cartoons and jokes that buddies e-mailed me and found several pictures that were questionable. That's when I began to look into the problem. Then there is also the problem of computer programs that regress a person's appearance. The program makes an adult appear to be a minor. Could it also be a crime for looking at those enhanced pictures if they are ruled to be obscene?"

"You mean like a dirty picture as opposed to, say, art?"

"Yeah, you got it. It's the same problem with adult cartoons. Just open a page of adult cartoons online, and you'll probably find all kinds of drawings of young-appearing characters engaged in sexual acts. Are they obscene and illegal? They may well be, of course, depending on the cartoon. If Goldilocks is doing it with the three bears, you may have a problem if she looks like a minor and the relations are explicit. And then there is the issue of bestiality, rape, child abuse. I could go on, but you see the problem. It can get complicated."

"Hmm...I never thought of that. I always just assumed that if it was on the computer, it was okay. You know, the girls were at least eighteen, but now I see it's not so simple. So what can I do?"

"Be cautious, leave it alone. Stay away from any sites that look inappropriate and the other stuff we mentioned. Or you can do what I did."

"Which is?"

"I installed good filters on our search engines to block porn. I tried it out, and it seems to works. I typed in 'adult cartoons' and just got a bunch of comic-book cartoons, nothing sexual. Prior to the filters, there would be tons of drawings, some very obscene, that would pop up. You may want to put a porn block on your computer. Some are better than others, many are free. And you may have to pay for the software, but it might be worth it."

I remembered the time, a few years ago, when a friend, who had a teenaged son, and I were talking about computers and the internet. He expressed concern that it would expose porn to his son. I had told him about porn blockers that had been developed, and after downloading, I encouraged him to type in a half-dozen inappropriate terms and hit Enter. The computer scanned sites and blocked many, but a few got through. It was an inexact science a few years ago, but it has since gotten better.

"It's hard to leave it alone. You're married, but I'm divorced. It's different."

We finished the project and moved on to another topic of conversation, but it caused me to think. I know that our society is awash with porn. It's so available even the free stuff is hard-core. In life, thorns are planted in with the wheat by evil people. If you try to dig them out, you'll damage the crop. So you let God sort it out in the next life. It's going to take folks with brains and authority to figure out how to balance, in a free society, the First Amendment rights to publish with the need to protect the family and society. This is just one more problem in living in the modern world that we must each come to grips with.

CHAPTER 40

Investigation

Woodbridge
Mid-December 2013

I received a text from Ed, a Detroit cop who lived across the street, that he wasn't sure if his garage door went down and asked us to check. I know that horrible feeling of uncertainty. "Did it go down and lock?" I can't tell you how many times I've circled the block to check on the garage doors.

I texted him, "Sure, no problem."

I said to Sasha, "Let's go, girl. We've got work to do." I got up from my desk and clicked her leash to her collar. One thing that neighbors do around here is look out after one another and their homes. We exchange phone numbers at our block club meetings, and for several neighbors, we have exchanged keys and house codes. Ed and I looked after each other's property and, from time to time, fed each other's dogs. You are not going to survive in the city on your own. You must identify good folks in your neighborhood and develop trust. Now that I've retired, I have more time to help my neighbors.

"I'm going with you," Erma said in a matter-of-fact manner; and I knew enough not to argue with her.

We quickly crossed the street and went to the alley behind Ed's house. His garage faced his alley, as did most of the neighbors. I had one of the few garages in the area that opened to the side street rather than an alley.

I can't tell you all the trouble we've had over the years from our alleys. I hate alleys, but due to the layout of the city in the late nineteenth century, I guess they are necessary.

"Look at that." I pointed to the ruts made by tires of a vehicle that had jumped the curb and had torn across the grass divider between the street and the sidewalk. The vehicle had left two deep impressions where the tires had cut deep furrows in the wet grass. They looked fresh. It had rained the night before, and the soil was saturated. Clumps of sod had been thrown by the tires.

"The driver just missed the telephone pole, and it looks like he blew a tire as his wheels cut back on to the street. Wow, this must have just happened. It wasn't there earlier when I had walked Sasha."

Erma noted that Ed's garage door was down and sent him a quick note to that effect and asked if he knew about a car jumping the curb near his alley. We walked over to Commonwealth Street to check out the progress of the mysterious vehicle. At the corner, we met another neighbor also studying the tire tracks and skid marks.

"Yep," he said, "that son of a bitch hit two cars parked further up on Commonwealth, then he hit the curb here." He pointed to the black imprint of rubber against the curb. "Look, there are no skid marks. He then fishtailed around the corner and headed down toward Grand River Avenue. The son of a bitch was drunk or high and didn't give a shit. He could have killed someone. The car was probably stolen."

I expressed my sympathy and nodded in agreement. Erma stood back and listened.

"Yes," I sympathized, "it's dangerous to park a car on the street in Detroit. It might just as likely not be there when you come out in the morning. You've got to have a garage to live around here and even then…" I trailed off as I remembered the time, not too many years ago, when a guy, high as a kite, clipped the bumper of Erma's van and hit my little Volkswagen, shoving it through my garage, followed by the big sedan the punk was driving. My garage happened to be filled with construction materials, cabinets, vanities, pipes, and lumber as I was getting ready for a remodeling job in the kitchen and bathrooms. It was all ruined.

It came back to me. I remembered I had been taking a nap when I heard a loud *boom*. The house shook, and the windows rattled from the impact. I jumped up and ran outside to find my little world in chaos. A cop car had been chasing the s—head down Grand River when he tried to get away by turning onto my side street. He didn't make it. After sending my little bug into my garage, his car tore through the corner of the garage, collapsing the roof, and finally smashing against the building on the other side of the alley. Smoke and steam billowed out from under his hood, and the s—head was still trying to start the car!

Erma had followed me out of the house, and before I knew it, she had reached in through the open driver's window and snatched the keys from the ignition. He started screaming at her and came out of the vehicle. Erma backed away with the keys tightly held behind her back. He screamed that he wanted his "f—keys."

At this point, I stepped in as he took a swing at Erma. Easily blocking the slow punch with my left forearm, I shoved him back into his vehicle and cocked my arm, ready to pop him in the jaw; but I didn't. His eyes were glazed and hollow. Nothing was there. He was no longer a threat, so I just shoved him back into the car where he remained until the police pulled up. The last I saw of him, he was handcuffed and being hauled away.

What a mess, oh my goodness. We've all been there, I thought.

"Goddamned punks and junkies. You know, we'd have a pretty good neighborhood if it wasn't for the damned s—heads plowing through." The neighbor took a breath and continued, "The police don't respond." He continued complaining and grumbling to another neighbor who had walked up.

We moved along to the next site. By this time, we had about a dozen neighbors who were on the street looking around. Several carried baseball bats. We greeted many on a first-name basis; others we only knew by sight. Everyone seemed to know Sasha and came over to pet and stroke her.

No one was hurt, and they caught the jerk on Grand River with two flat tires trying to flee the scene of the accident with sparks flying from two rims. This was just another day in Detroit.

CHAPTER 41

Community Gatherings, the Rights of Spring

Woodbridge
Spring 2014

T he *V* people (i.e., vegans and vegetarians) were clustered around a pasta (non-gluten) and kale dish. It was sort of an off-colored noodle sprinkled with green flakes and some other ingredients I didn't recognize.

"It looks good?" I tried to sound sincere. Chuckling, I continued, "It has green stuff on it."

The vegans turned away in disgust as I forked an all-beef knackwurst sausage and piled it high with sauerkraut topped off with a dash of brown spicy mustard.

"Nothing wrong with vegetarian food that a little meat won't fix," I said to no one in particular and, grabbing a beer from the ice cooler, began to eat. The vegan crowd moved away from the food table and, as a group, toward the patio, leaving me in peace.

"How are you doing?" A young man approached and extended a hand to shake. But both hands being somewhat busy, I extended my fist, still grasping the bottle of a longneck beer, for a quick fist bump. This is a great alternative to the handshake, and it's approved by the millennials.

"Great, great, but I don't remember your name."

"George. We met last winter at Bruce and Sue's big New Year's party." Erma and I had been the token Republicans invited to a gathering of progressives.

"Right, now I remember." I didn't know him from Adam, but upon Erma's advice, I'm trying to show more interest and understanding about our new neighbors. "You had just moved into the neighborhood." That's always a good guess with all the newcomers flooding into the community.

"I'm an engineer at Ford's. We bought the old Emerson House on Commonwealth."

"That's right." I began to actually remember him. "You were interested in doing some pistol shooting. Did you ever get your concealed-carry permit?" I resumed my meal between sips of beer.

"Well, you see," he continued, obviously embarrassed, "it's a bit complicated. My girlfriend, uh, that's her. Hey, baby." He called and waved. "Come here and say hi to Mr. Suttner. You remember him."

A petite blond turned and approached. A full glass of wine in her hands, she was careful not to spill any. "Mr. Suttner, this is Judy," he introduced.

"Nice to see you again." I smiled. "I see you survived your first winter in Detroit."

George continued, "I was just telling Dave why I don't have my concealed permit yet." Her expression suddenly changed, and her smile disappeared.

"Not again," she said under her breath. "We don't believe in private ownership of guns, and we don't associate with those who do."

After an awkward moment of silence, I said, "I think you're right. Not everyone should carry. Some will only hurt themselves or someone else. It's a lot of responsibility. So any new projects planned for your place?"

Turning, she saw some newly arriving friends and walked back toward the front door, careful not to spill a drop. George smiled and shrugged his shoulders and trailed behind. *Why didn't she just take a drink?* I thought. *Oh, well.* I took another bite of food and a long drink of beer.

"So you're Republican?" said a young super thin girl with tattoos covering her arms and throat. She was not much more than a kid, really. Then she smiled, helping herself to the food.

"Yep, that would be me." Neither of us made any attempt to shake hands or even fist bump. "I know you," I said. "You're Stacy, the dog whisperer, right?"

"I wouldn't go that far. I run the obedience school on Trumbull. I'm working with your neighbor's dog, John (not his real name). His dog is a mixed golden retriever named Rusty."

I didn't know the new neighbors' names, but I had been introduced to the handsome Rusty.

"He's a handful. How's it coming?" I inquired. Dog people communicate, no matter what their political differences.

"Oh boy, the stories I could tell. But it's coming along. How's Sasha?" For the next twenty minutes, we had our heads together discussing dogs. An old man and a tattooed young girl. It must have been an interesting sight.

"That's hardly enough to keep a bird alive," I said, pointing at her plate. "I brought some German brats, knocks, and sauerkraut. Want some?"

"Oh, no thanks. I'm vegan, but it does smell delicious."

"Do you still live in that hippy commune on Trumbull?" I inquired.

"Oh, you mean the Flex. It's not really a commune. I believe it once was, but it's evolved into more of a co-op."

She told me how she had run away from home at fifteen and wound up on the streets. Some old hippies had taken her in, and there she discovered that she had a talent with dogs. We discussed the organizational arrangement of the co-op, and I asked several questions about what happens if someone doesn't pull his or her fair share of work or help to pay the bills. It seems that it's very informal, but abuse of the system may result in a vote to remove.

Interesting life choices we make. We spent the next twenty minutes talking politics and philosophy; needless to say, the only thing we could agree on was the care and training of dogs. After a while, Erma came in and told me she was ready to leave. I gathered up the dishes we had brought. No one else had eaten our German brats. Good deal.

CHAPTER 42

Gassing Up in Detroit

Memorial Day 2014

The 2014 Memorial Day was bright and warm, a perfect Michigan day. We were invited up to Troy in Oakland County, north of Detroit, for a family outing at the Kuhns' home. Erma was still putzing around upstairs, and with time to kill, I called out, "I'll be back in about fifteen minutes...want to get some gas before we leave."

I'd been putting off gassing up for the past week (each day I watched the price for a gallon on unleaded 87 octane gas go from $3.45 to $3.55 to $3.68 per gallon, but now with the tank nearing empty, I had to gas up). The price now stood at $3.88 per gallon for regular.

Stupid to have put it off, I thought. *Oh, well.* "Come on, Sasha, let's go for a drive." Sasha is always ready and loves to look out of her back-seat window at the passing world. You can't help but wonder what she thinks about as we drive down a street passing everything in sight. We must seem like gods to our furry four-legged friends.

I pulled in position for pump number 2 and sat for a few moments, surveying the scene. I hit the button to control Sasha's window and lowered it enough for her to get her head out but not low enough to jump out.

I remembered that once, a few years ago, we had stopped for ice cream at a little stand on Drummond Island (the most easterly part of Michigan), and I had forgotten and left the van's window down. We went to the end of the line and stood examining the menu. There was a long line of folks ahead of us.

Suddenly there were screams, shouts, panic, and a scattering of people, many rushing to grab up children and run to the safety of their cars. I looked around in confusion and then saw Sasha, silently sitting quietly behind me, as if she was also studying the menu. Her great pink tongue came out, and she licked her muzzle in anticipation. Many apologies and a purchase of a free round of cones followed.

At the gas station, a car was pulling out, leaving only one scruffy-looking black guy loitering near the door. He seemed a bit nervous, head lowered with his eyes darting around. His right hand was at his right hip line, holding up his baggy pants. It looked like he was having a bad day.

First removing the money from my wallet while I sat in the car, I pocketed the keys (always left front) and exited the vehicle. As I approached the front door, I paused and waited. (No way was I going to get in front of him!)

Nodding, I paused and motioned with my head for him to go ahead.

He opened the door and entered the small convenience store and let the door swing back on me. But I was ready for it and caught the heavy door and followed him in. *No courtesy here,* I thought. *No holding the door open and allowing an older gentleman—that's me, in this case—to come in peacefully. Well, at least you know where you stand in the city. After all, this is Detroit. My granddaughter has a T-shirt that says, "I'm so tough that I vacation in Detroit."*

The attendant, a man of Middle Eastern extraction, stood impassively behind thick shatterproof glass walls, watching.

Mr. Droopy Pants stepped in and backed down the snack aisle but still facing forward. Strange! He was determined to get behind me. I saw his hand go from holding up his drooping pants to his right pocket. What was that bulge in there pulling down on his already-sagging pants? He motioned with his head for me to go ahead to the clerk, which would put him square at my back.

Slipping my right hand in my own pocket, I said, "No, you go ahead. You were here first." I looked straight into his hate-filled eyes. We both froze for a second. The attendant looked slightly annoyed at this unusual display of courtesy.

Did Mr. Baggy Pants have a gun, or was he just being polite? It was my experience that punks like to keep their shit, as they are apt to call a weapon, in their waistband rather than in a holster. I didn't know what he had in there, but I knew that my right fist was comfortably wrapped around my Little Guy, the .380 Kel-Tec, with my trigger finger safely alongside the frame. It would only take a heartbeat of time to curl my finger around the trigger and about 8.5 pounds of exertion to pull it. I hoped the explosion wouldn't burn my leg.

We had a high-profile case in Detroit a year or so ago where a SWAT-type cop was on a raid. He entered the house as a flash-bang grenade was tossed in. It went off, and in the confusion, he jerked and accidentally shot a little girl sleeping on a couch, killing her.

I know the cop didn't enter the house with the intention of killing a little sleeping girl. I don't know what his intentions were, and maybe he just wanted to be a hero because they had a reality television show crew with them, maybe not. But I do know that he had his finger on the trigger during a stressful situation. Not a wise thing to do.

Mr. Droopy stepped forward and asked for two single ciga-rettes. What's with that? The attendance shoved two individual cig-arettes through the slot in the glass, and Mr. Droopy Pants rattled some coins and turned to leave. I gave my best smile and nodded as I tracked his movement to the door and then he paused and turned.

I already had the money in my left hand and slid it into the slot and said, "Thirty dollars on pump two." I also put up two fingers of my left hand, seeing that my right hand was a little busy holding on to the Little Guy, in the old victory sign made famous by Winston Churchill or, more recently, the hippy peace sign, whichever. I never took my eyes off Mr. Droopy Pants as he stood by the door hesitating, trying to decide something.

Finally, he opened the door and exited with me falling in step behind with my hand still in my pocket. I made a mental note in the future to gas up with Erma as my spotter. Once again, I thanked the Good Lord that he hadn't pulled a weapon. It's my life's goal never to kill anyone but also, more important, never to have been killed by anyone.

CHAPTER 43

The People You Meet in Detroit

Sunday
June 1, 2014

S unday is our kick-back day. Erma and I usually go to the 8:30
a.m. service at Saint Anne Church. Mass is held in the small
chapel attached to the rear of the church. The chapel contains
the remains of the famous Father Gabriel Richard in a glass case off
to the left of the altar. Saint Anne's is the second-oldest parish in
North America, founded by Cadillac in 1701.

After church, we have a huge breakfast of bacon, eggs, hash
browns, toast, tomato slices, and hot pepper with coffee for me and
the same plus pancakes and a Diet Coke for Erma at one of our
favorite diners, usually Duly's Coney Island (inexpensive, great quality food, and efficient service). It's the gold standard for breakfast,
and one of the reasons we remained here during the bad days.

Sasha and I decided to take a walk around the neighborhood,
winding up at the old Scripps Park. I planned on reading, and Sasha
planned to lie in the grass and snooze. We had just entered the vacant
lots at Alexandrine and Grand River Avenue—I was waiting for Sasha
to do her business, or not. I turned my back to her—a lady likes to
have some privacy—and dug out a plastic bag, just in case. Besides,
it was good to have it in hand in case a neighbor happened to drive
by. I was one of the biggest advocates of responsible dog ownership

and did not want to give even the appearance of not cleaning up after my dog.

Detroiters just don't seem to care about their sidewalks. Most drive rather than walk, and when a Detroiter must walk (a true old-school Detroiter that is), one walks down the middle of a street, not on a sidewalk. Why, you ask? Much danger lurks in shadows. It's now part of our DNA. Our sidewalks, after a winter thaw, are literally a mess. I tell folks to be careful walking. "Watch your step—land mines."

I'm always preaching the importance of being a good master and keeping the dogs on a leash when walking. A well-trained dog, on a leash, can protect its master; and I've always said that if forced to choose, I would pick Sasha over carrying my 1911 .45 pistol. The stories I could tell about people allowing their dogs to get away off leash. But that is for another chapter.

Suddenly, a black minivan pulled off Grand River and came to a stop at the curb about twenty yards away. The driver, a petite Asian woman, lowered her window and politely asked if they could talk to us.

"May we speak with you, please?" Both Sasha, who had totally forgotten about her daily business, and I relaxed. I removed my hand from under my shirt and, smiling, nodded in the affirmative.

"We are from Japan and doing a story on the decline of a great American city. It will be shown in Japan. Do you live in Detroit?" Two Asian men, along with the lady driver, climbed out of the vehicle.

One man lifted a large shoulder-mounted camera; and the other, clearly the boss of the trio, held a microphone and carried a power pack or recording device on a shoulder strap. All three were Asian and short in stature with black hair and dark inquiring eyes. All were dressed in jeans, tennis shoes, and T-shirts with symbols and illustrations I did not understand. They did not ask for my name, and the cameraman immediately began panning the neighborhood and then focused on me.

As they approached, Sasha stood at rigid attention. She was unsure about all this. Her nubbin of a tail didn't wag, and a low guttural warning issued from her as they approached.

"Good girl. It's okay," I said, and Sasha relaxed and, after a few moments, slid to the earth and stretched out in the grass, alert and watchful.

Well, I thought, *if it's only shown in Japan, I guess it's okay.* I had made it a rule, decades before, never to become a public figure. There was little chance of that anyway, but I stayed away from journalists and cameras. I liked to live under the radar, so to speak.

The mike man said something to the lady, and she asked me again if I lived in Detroit and for how long.

"Yes." I pointed to our house across the street. I was pleased that the yards were manicured and the flowers in bloom. I didn't want the people in Japan to think that we were savages. "That's our home. My wife and I have lived there since the early seventies, and this is my companion, Ms. Sasha."

The cameraman focused on Sasha as the lady reporter translated for the mike man. He nodded his understanding and said something to her in Japanese.

The lady then asked my opinion about the recent bankruptcy. I replied something to the effect that we deserved it after years of political corruption, poor schools, graft, and crime. Most of the taxpayers had moved out, leaving the city broken and in debt. But we had a new mayor, and there was hope. The lady translated, but the mike man didn't seem to buy what she was saying.

After some more Japanese, she nodded and said, "We just visited the old train station, once so great. Now the area looks so dangerous, so neglected and unsafe." She smiled and waited for a reply. I didn't hear the question, so I just smiled and nodded agreement. Sasha stretched, sighed, and obviously found the whole affair a bore.

"Do you feel your area is safe? A city once so great, now so low and dangerous," she added.

I could see where this interview was going. "I love this town." I began by saying that we had traveled all over this country and had not found a better place to live. "Sure, there is crime and graffiti"—I pointed to some of the buildings on Grand River—"but it's home. We raised our family here and plan on spending the remainder of our days here. It's a great neighborhood." She again translated, and the mike man shook his head in the negative and told her something else to ask.

"But is it safe?"

"It's safe for us. We walk the streets when we choose. Now, remember, most Detroiters have dogs for warning and protection. And many have concealed-weapon permits. Yes, I'd say it's better now than when we first moved in." She translated, and the mike man looked confused and asked for clarification.

"How is it possible for it to be better now, as you say, when Detroit was once a great city?"

"In truth, there are sections of Detroit, much of the east side for example, that has been abandoned. It looks like a war zone, but this community is an oasis of sorts. We have a real neighborhood here. We know our neighbors and look out for each other. Years ago, when we first moved in as students at Wayne State University, there were packs of wild dogs running feral and gangs of armed thugs over at the projects. It's much better now. We are building a real community."

The lady translated, and the mike man said something in Japanese. They bowed goodbye and started to leave. I also bowed respectfully and smiled and waved goodbye as they piled into the van and pulled away. Obviously, my interview did not fit in their narrative of the decline and fall of a once-great city.

Sasha and I continued on our walk and thought about our reputation in the world press and remembered the T-shirts that my granddaughters had obtained after a visit. It pronounced, in bold print, "I'm so tough that I vacation in Detroit."

CHAPTER 44

A Kinder, Gentler Neighbor

Mid-July 2014

The early July weather in Detroit had been unusually warm and humid, so when a cold front came rolling in from the north, it brought the day-time highs down to the low seventies and quite enjoyable. Sasha and I were returning from our second neighborhood walk of the day.

"Did you have a nice walk?" Erma inquired as we entered.

Hanging up Sasha's pink leash, I answered, "Yes, well. It's really lovely out there."

We followed Erma back to the kitchen where she was busy setting the table and preparing the evening meal. I got a tumbler of water from the sink and, leaning against the doorframe, tried to stay out of the way. Our kitchen is too small. It's really a one-person operation.

Sasha went to her bowl and lapped up some water then collapsed on the floor with an audible thud. She placed one paw over the other and watched.

"You know the fellow who lives on Commonwealth, the one who has a black Labrador dog named Pete?" I asked.

Erma answered, "The one that Gunner had a problem with a few years ago?"

"Yeah, that the one."

Several years ago, while walking with our previous Rottweiler, Gunner (a big, very serious, no-nonsense dog), we passed on the other side of the street from where Pete lived. I was listening to a story on an old Walkman cassette player and not paying much attention to my surroundings when, suddenly, there was a yell from a fellow chasing a large black dog that was barking as it darted across the street toward us.

Suddenly, Gunner dropped his head and backed out of his collar, which is always loose; and in an instance, there was a blur of fur and a snap of teeth and a loud yelp. The black dog had its ear split open, and blood droplets were flying everywhere. It jumped back, howling in pain, then it turned tail and ran back across the street into the arms of the man following behind.

Gunner issued a few loud barks and a low growl but didn't give chase, which was good because I was holding his leash, which was attached to an empty collar. The man turned out to be a new neighbor. He grabbed the black's collar and began walking it across the street, but his dog broke free and disappeared into the open door of his house.

"Pete," he called after his dog, but Pete was having none of it. Turning back to us, he said, "Pete is young. We've only had him a year, and he's a little wild. Sorry about that."

"No problem," I said. Gunner then sat, and I had just replaced his collar and leash and was giving give him a few strokes. "But you know, you should keep your dog on a leash." Gunner was so well-behaved that I gave him some extra petting and several "Good boys."

I thought his dog had just got a street lesson in why he shouldn't run up on folks. "You may want to check his ear," I called out. "I think Gunner may have nipped him. Hope he's all right."

He turned back toward his house, calling "Pete, Pete, you okay, buddy?" We just walked on. After relaying that incident to Erma, she asked me if I was going to pay for Pete's vet bill. I laughed and said, "No way," and that I thought that the young dog just learned a valuable lesson.

"But what if he files a complaint against Gunner?" Erma expressed concern.

"Not to worry. Gunner was on a leash, licensed, with shots and tags up-to-date. The black lab was off leash with no tags, and it crossed the street and attacked us. Lucky for him that it was us. Anyone else would file a complaint against Pete. I wonder if his shots are up-to-date. I could really make trouble for him. But no harm, no foul." The affair thus ended.

Back to the present. "Go on, what happened?" Erma waited for the rest of the story.

"Okay, so he's there in his yard, and we stop just to be neighborly."

"This is the same man, Pete's owner?"

I nodded in the affirmative and continued. "First we talked about the weather. Then I ask him what happened to global warming seeing that it's only seventy degrees in the middle of July. 'It's kind of hard to still blame that on Bush,' I said, but he said that it's now called climate change and we need to be concerned about warming and cooling and he blamed it on Republicans and threw in the technique of fracking for natural gas. I told him I hadn't heard of any fracking problems in Michigan. He said I was uninformed. Soon we were into a big political discussion on the middle of the sidewalk."

"Oh no!" Erma stopped her food preparation and gave me her full attention. "Go on, what did you do?"

"Well, it's like this—"

She interrupted with "As my dad used to say, 'It's an awfully deep subject for such a shallow mind.' Just tell me what happened. Did anyone get hurt?"

"No, nothing like that." I ignored her comment and cleared my throat as I got my thoughts together. "We were simply talking first about one thing and then another, and before I knew it, we were in a heated debate about the problem with illegal aliens on our southern borders. Can you believe it? He claims that the border is just too long and it can't be patrolled and we need to welcome the illegals with open arms."

Taking a breath, I continued, "What are we supposed to do? I asked him if we are just supposed to accept busloads of illegals with open arms and open wallets and give them all the comforts of the

American dream. Instead of answering, he claimed that I was biased and unfair against Latinos. Imagine that! We go to a Hispanic parish each Sunday, and our granddaughters are half-Hispanic."

Erma just stood there and nodded for me to continue.

"So he said that I should use the politically correct term *undocumented immigrants*, not *illegal aliens*. Give me a break."

"What next?" Erma continued. "It didn't just end there, did it?"

"Well…ummm, next I called him a bleeding-heart liberal who towed the party line. Next, he got a little ticked off and said that he was not a liberal. It seems like no one wants to be called a liberal these days. I asked him who he voted for during the past two elections, that is, if he wasn't embarrassed to answer. He said that he was proud to have voted for Obama but that didn't make him a liberal. Then he said that Obama was a disappointment, too much of a centralist for him. He called himself a 'rational progressive.'"

His wife came out then and called him in, so we went on home.

CHAPTER 45

Don't Get Comfortable

Woodbridge
July 16, 2014

Sasha's urgent barks brought me to an instant state of being wide-awake. Glancing at the bedside clock, 1:05 a.m. registered in my brain. "Okay, Sasha," I called, "what is it, baby?" She barked again in an urgent "come quick" tone that only a Rottweiler can issue.

Turning to Erma's form in the bed, I said, "Something is going on. I'll go and check."

Grabbing my glasses, I descended the stairs to find Sasha at the front door, attempting to peer out. She was on full alert with her legs spread out. Her body was rigidity elongated. She issued another bark then moved back from the door for me to look.

Our neighbor's new van was parked in the entrance of their drive, blocking the sidewalk. I could hear the conversation from the other side of the van. *Just friends coming home late and talking,* I thought and went back to bed. But first I gave Sasha a "Good girl" and a pat on her head. She trotted back to her bed on the couch.

The next morning, as was my wont, with coffee in hand, I opened the front door to survey the neighborhood. The neighbor's van was in the same place, still blocking the sidewalk. I called out to

Erma, "The neighbors are going to get a ticket for blocking the walk. That's so strange. What do you make of it?"

Erma called me into her office. She was seated at her computer checking the e-mails. "My goodness," she said, "early this morning, at about 1:00 a.m., someone tried to steal our renters' van. They tore out the ignition system, but they didn't make it out of the driveway. That must have been what Sasha barked about when you got up."

"Oh no, son of a gun, they were stealing their van. Oh my goodness!" I was stunned. I had been lulled into a false sense of security by month after month of uneventful living.

"I could have...I should have...done something, gone out to investigate. I might have been able, you know, to stop..."

"It was stopped," Erma said. "Maybe it was Sasha's barking that scared them off, who knows?"

I reflected on the event and the fact that our young renters had just suffered a loss while on our property. I felt responsible, and I hadn't even bothered to go out and check.

I had broken the first rule of urban living. It's the 24-7 rule. Never be without a gun and extra ammo during the wee hours of the morning. I had also broken the second rule: always sleep ready to get up for an emergency. For years, I had slept in shorts and a shirt. When an incident occurred, I was up and in my shorts, pistol and flashlight in hand and ready to move. I can't tell you how many times I received a call in the middle of the night to respond to a burglar alarm at one of the sites I was responsible for or to assist a neighbor in distress.

I had gone to bed in my undershorts and a T-shirt, hardly attire fit to be out on a public street.

Again, with retirement, I no longer had any duty to investigate alarms going off in the middle of the night. It was wonderful just to be able to go to bed and sleep through the night. I was off my game. From then on, I went back to keeping the pistol and flashlight next to the bed.

Erma received another e-mail and said, "It seems as if they are targeting Dodge minivans." I thought of Erma's new vehicle, a

Chrysler Town and Country minivan, safely parked in the garage (we hoped). "Several have been recently stolen from the neighborhood."

"I wonder if they had a club on it," I mused. Erma shrugged her shoulders. For years we had both followed the rule to never leave our car parked without the club on the steering wheel and the alarm on. I had, once again, gotten lazy. Normally, I didn't bother with the club. I remembered back in the early nineties when our son, Bob, had bought Baby from me, a beautiful 1986 white Mustang convertible (kept in a garage, it had never been subjected to a snowflake or road salt), and drove it to his new posting in San Antonio, Texas.

He said that when he arrived home one evening, he had to parallel park in a narrow space a block or so from his unit. When he left the next morning for work, all the cars in front and behind him were gone—stolen.

The police said a criminal ring had targeted their neighborhood that night and taken multiple cars and driven them either to chop shops or into Mexico, where they would never be heard from again. Being from Detroit, Bob had dutifully attached the club to the steering wheel. His was the only car parked on the street the next morning.

Erma picked up her gym bag, kissed me goodbye, and left for the Y for swimming and classes in Zumba and Tai Chi. I continued to mentally kick myself around the block. Sasha had done everything right. I had done everything wrong.

Now the neighbors' van was sitting in their drive, blocking the sidewalk. It was probably going to be ticketed for illegal parking while waiting for a tow truck. I sat on my front porch, sipping coffee. The least I could do was to explain to the parking enforcement officer why their vehicle was illegally parked.

A few minutes later, the phone rang. I had a feeling it was Erma and picked up with a "Hello." I had just violated another rule. We never pick up the house phone unless and until we hear the answering machine record a voice of someone we actually want to speak with.

"I was just thinking, Why don't we install some lights on the side of the rental house with a motion detector? Something to think about."

"Good idea. There is an old light out there. It hasn't worked in years. We'll go and check on a new light fixture," I said and she hung up.

When something happens, we always spend time analyzing it and trying to do some prevention. That's why our house is like a fortified compound with an eight-foot double-planked fence and layers of defenses including iron bars in windows, a security system, and a Rottweiler standing guard.

After speaking with the neighbors and expressing my sympathy and anger against all thugs, punks, and gangbangers, the car hauler arrived. I helped push the van into the street and line it up for transportation.

The van's owner expressed anger and chagrin at forgetting to put the club on the steering wheel. His roommate had given him a club, but he hadn't yet opened the plastic and put it in the van.

I remembered that I was going to give my granddaughter one for her car. We thought she was coming up here this fall as a student at University of Michigan, but she selected a college in Texas instead. I was trying to remember if mine was still in the car. I hadn't used it in almost a year.

I planned on heading out the next day to a big-box hardware store to find a proper light fixture. In the meantime, I would start using my club again when I left the car parked without the garage. Things are getting better, but it's still a little dicey.

CHAPTER 46

Sasha's Last Walk

Woodbridge
Late July 2014

S asha's end came unexpectedly and quickly. Wednesday evening, she didn't feel well and asked not to go on a long walk; rather, she just wanted to go to the field across the street and do her business. Her stool looked black and watery.

That evening, as we sat on the front porch, I told Erma that I was going to take Sasha to the vet the next morning. The vet opens at 9:00 a.m.

I stroked Sasha's head and sides and talked to her gently. "Get to feeling better, and we'll go for a long walk tomorrow morning." She just looked up at me and then let her head fall to the porch.

The next morning, Sasha was breathing heavily, and her eyes had lost their luster and life. She had tried to make it to the door but had collapsed on the floor in a pool of bloody discharge from her anus.

I told her it was all right and not to worry. We had one of the best vets just around the corner.

How are we going to get her to the vets? I thought. She weighed about 110 pounds, and she couldn't walk. I suddenly thought of the wheelbarrow. *Yes,* I thought, *that might work. Put a blanket under her*

and lift her into the wheelbarrow and roll her to the animal hospital.
Erma had a better idea.

I talked to Sasha about nothing in particular as I gently lifted her onto an old gurney that Erma had retrieved from the basement. Erma and I then easily moved her to the front porch. I continued talking to her and petting her as Erma returned in a few minutes with the van and its seats lowered to easily convey Sasha to the animal hospital. I continued talking to Sasha and petting her and telling her if she would just get well we'd go on a nice walk. I told her how much we loved and needed her and how she just had to get well. Her breathing became more and more labored until, finally, she just gave up the ghost and passed on. It happened that fast.

Our friend Tom pulled up, and after a moment to confirm that she was indeed dead, he helped carry her to the van and then into the animal hospital. The only thing for them to do was to have her cremated.

On the mantel in Erma's office rested the urns from previous Rottweilers. Sasha would join good company. We had made arrangements with our son, Bob, that after our death, he would place their ashes in our burial plots. We had purchased three plots in the family area near Mom and Dad and other family members.

Even if Bob couldn't get permission from the pastor of the Catholic church, he promised to sneak in to the graveyard at night and dig small holes in our graves and place their ashes in and then pat the soil back down. Erma gets the males, and I get my girls. No muss, no fuss. Then we'll all be together for eternity.

Saturday morning, I was at the animal hospital waiting for the door to open. The doctor explained how Sasha's spleen had ruptured during the previous night and she had bled out internally. I was told that it was probably not painful and fairly fast. I thanked the doc and received a small urn with Sasha's remains. I placed it in a plastic bag I had in my back pocket. I always carried plastic bags on walks with Sasha to pick up her considerable deposits.

Upon leaving, I felt like she was still with me. "Well, Sasha," I said, "are you ready for your walk this morning?" I chatted with her as we walked along and told her to look at the beautiful day. We stopped to watch some small black squirrels chase and play around the trees in Scripps Park, and once we stopped to observe a stray dog. He saw us and ran away down the street. "You'd better run," I said aloud. "Sasha will get you."

I had promised Sasha a long walk, but it seemed to take hours. Every block, neighbors stopped and asked where Sasha was. I raised the plastic bag and told each in turn that we were going for our last walk together. I lost count of the number of folks who came out of their houses and talked about what a good dog she had been. Sasha had been with us for years, and we patrolled the neighborhood every morning on the dawn patrol.

Comments like "She was so well-behaved" and "She was a perfect lady and will be missed" and "I always felt safe when I saw you two coming down the street" were made. Folks I didn't even know stopped me to inquire and then express sympathy.

Almost every day, for the past five years, we had patrolled the neighborhood during some of the worse times in Detroit. In truth, she was better known than I was. She was the only dog I know of that had her own Facebook page with hundreds of friends. Finally, we made it back to the house and began the process of cleaning and organizing all the items that meant so much to Sasha. Her dog food was donated to an animal shelter, but her collar and leashes were boxed, awaiting future developments.

As I told Erma, "We'll go through yet another period of grieving, but the only way to get over the loss of a dog is to get another one." Erma posted a notice on Sasha's Facebook page about her passing, and the warm wishes and expressions of sympathy flooded in over the next week.

"It's funny," I told one neighbor. "Sasha was the meanest, hardest-headed dog we ever had. I told Erma that one of us was going to have to change and it wasn't going to be me. Our first six months together were horrible. She was just mean and ill-tempered. But one day, almost overnight, she changed. She began to love us and we loved her and she wound up being the sweetest, best dog we've ever had. Go figure."

CHAPTER 47

The World in Crisis

Woodbridge
Mid-August 2014

"What a week. What terrible times we live in," I commented to Erma while reading the morning paper at the kitchen table. The news channel, on only as background, caught my attention.

Ukraine was being torn apart by civil war and invasion by pro-Russian forces. A civilian jet had been shot down over the war zone with the loss of everyone onboard. (Who would fly over a war zone? Oh yes, the same country that had totally lost a plane earlier in the year, that's who!)

Iraq was again in flames as America watched the hard-won gains slipping between our fingers. Small Christian and non-Muslim enclaves in the mountains were being attacked. Their choice—convert to Islam or die! The civil war in Syria ground on.

The big news on television was the Ebola virus with claims that it could soon reach pandemic proportions in West Africa. The news was that several infected medical workers were being brought back to the US for treatment. America was on edge.

That evening, we retired to the entertainment room to watch a little television and relax. The show was entitled *The Last Ship*. It was set in the near future in a world in which a deadly infection had been unleashed, resulting in the loss of 80 percent of the world's population. The scientist aboard the American destroyer worked to find a cure while the captain and crew played a cat-and-mouse game with a Russian ship commanded by Mad Ivan. Holy Moly!

If things weren't bad enough, reports were pouring in about young people from Central and South America massing on our southern border and coming across in droves. Who was financing and planning this wave of young illegals? Is the whole world going nuts? Who is going to take care of and pay for these kids? Oh, that's right, the taxpayers.

Next, rockets, by the hundreds, started falling on Israeli towns and villages. Israel begins a determined and costly attack on the network, which serves as the terrorist pipeline into Israel. Administration and Democrat support for Israel began to falter. Many liberals questioned the wisdom of continued support for the Israeli state. Then we watched in awe as the new Israel Iron Dome missile defense system destroyed the incoming rockets high in the sky. Next, we saw the graphic photos of the dead and injured Palestinian civilians killed and wounded by the Israel attacks. I've figured it out. The difference between the Palestinian and Israel command systems is simple. The Arabs use their civilians to protect their rockets, while the Jews use their rockets to protect their civilians.

The next day we learned that our top comic was found dead. Yes, Robin Williams of *Mork and Mindy* fame had committed suicide. When our comedians can't take it anymore, what chance do the rest of us have? Oh, yes, I almost forgot—Ferguson, Missouri, was gripped by a series of civil disturbances and riots resulting from a police officer killing an unarmed black youth. On top of everything else, I missed my dog, Sasha.

Checking my .357 Smith and Wesson, I slipped it in my holster, and making sure my shirt covered the weapon, I went on a neighborhood walk to clear my head. We were being hammered by too much information, most of it bad. Folks were feeling anxious.

I walked the streets, waving and greeting neighbors; and along the way, I began to calm down. All was well in the neighborhood. Stopping to chat with some working in their yards, I forgot all about the national and international news. My little world was right here, in this old neighborhood. My mood improved, and I began to think about a new dog—a Rottweiler, of course. I was familiar with the breed and wanted a dog not only for companionship but also for security. This is the only breed I know of that will take a bullet intended for its master.

CHAPTER 48

Remembrance

Late August 2014

Erma and I were watching the news at the kitchen table. The big story was the riots in the Missouri town of Ferguson, which followed the shooting of an unarmed black youth by a white cop. The only thing I know is that you have to wait until the verdict is in. They were trying the cop in the press and on the news. The mainstream media wanted his head on a silver platter.

"You were caught up in a riot when we first moved into Detroit, weren't you?" Erma asked.

I thought of all the times I had been in near-riot situations with mobs running and howling for blood. Then I remembered that awful day.

"Yes. It was when I was subbing at a west side junior high. It happened that winter of 1970 and 1971. I had a homeroom first period. There was this heavyset black kid. He was the class clown, sort of fat and clumsy but funny with a great smile all the time. He was a real class cutup, and I liked him. He sat up front, on the front row, right in front of my desk. He would do some of the silliest things to get a laugh. Once he rolled out of his seat on the floor and stretched out in a pretend sleeping mode.

"I had been trying to counsel the kid about time and place appropriateness, but it never seemed to take. He was a real free spirit. He had great comic talent but had no checks or controls on his behavior. Everything was for a laugh. He just couldn't pass up a chance to give a wisecrack or a joke. I couldn't shut him up.

"Once, we were discussing American history, and I told him to put his hand down for the umpteenth time. He said, 'Ya, sir, Mr. Teacher. Please don't put me back in the fields picking cotton. I'll do better.' The class broke up in laughter, and the assistant principal stuck his head in to make sure all was copasetic."

Erma asked, "I thought we were talking about a riot?"

"Oh, yes, I got sidetracked."

The television then flashed to a new story of a young black American male who had converted from Christianity to Islam and been radicalized. He had gone to the Middle East and was killed fighting in Syria for the terrorists. His American family had been blindsided, according to the commenters. I turned off the set.

My memory went back to that day, one of the defining days of my life. I remembered that homeroom began like any other day, taking attendance and reading announcements. It was during homeroom that I saw the funny kid first get the shakes and have what looked like a seizure. Was he joking?

Together with a couple of kids, we pulled him from the desk. He had slid down and got himself caught up. He was really big, and we carefully laid his body on the floor and moved the desks away from him. I put his jacket under his head and noticed that he had a bottle of brightly colored pills in his jacket. I removed it and sadly shook my head.

His eyes had glazed over, and saliva had stopped bubbling at his mouth and ran down his face. I had called for a runner to go to the office with a quick message asking for help and to get an emergency unit here fast. I was holding the kid in my arms and when the assistant principal arrived to look in, he had already stopped moving. The students all backed away from me, forming a circle. They were standing in silence when some students from across the hall came pouring in, and one said, "He killed him. The white teacher killed him dead."

"No one killed him," I heard one of my students say. "He overdosed on some drugs he brought to school. The white teacher didn't kill him." The voice of the student defending me was drowned out by the screams and antics of other students who pushed and shoved their way into our classroom. They hooted and yelled and jumped onto desks, spilling books and school supplies onto the floor, which some proceeded to kick around with glee.

I sat in a circle of children. Some of the girls were quietly crying, and the guys were holding in their emotions. They all knew the class clown and liked him. Around school, the other students took advantage of the crisis by pushing and pulling on one another. Several fist fights broke out, and there was much pushing and shoving; but the ring of my students around me held the mob in check. I simply sat on the floor holding the black kid in my arms and rocked gently back and forth, telling him it would be all right.

The students were finally moved out of the room by the assistant principal and neighboring teachers. The ambulance arrived and the attendants, after checking for life and working for a while, placed the kid on a stretcher and pulled the blanket up over his face.

The world now knew he was dead. I gave the bottle of pills to the assistant principal, who had restored some order, and told him briefly what had happened. I looked around the room. My classroom was in shambles. I knew I would never be invited back. I was then ordered to the faculty lounge to await instructions.

I watched through an open window of the second-floor lounge as the kid's body was carried through a throng of students and adults milling around in the schoolyard. There was an angry buzz, and it was getting louder. Someone shouted, "There he is," and a bottle smashed into the window frame near my head, sending glass fragments showering down onto the crowd.

I ducked away from the window and waited. Over the next hour, the crowd grew in size and volume. A local television truck appeared, and a camera crew set up to record the event for the six-o'clock news. I could hear individual threats boom out above the general hubbub: "Let's get him," "He killed the n—er," and "Kill the white fu—er."

Soon the crowd took on an atmosphere of anticipation. I could feel the tension rising to a boiling point. I examined my conscience.

I could have done better. I should have done better. At that point, I made a commitment to learn first aid and be ready for the next medical challenge.

I had stood back from the window, watching the scene, when additional police cars arrived and the officers pushed the people back from the door.

A few minutes later, I heard them troop up the stairs and open the faculty room door.

"Do you want to make a statement here or down at the precinct?"

"I can make it here," I answered.

"Do you want a lawyer?"

"No. Why would I want a lawyer?"

"We talked to the assistant principal," said the officer. "He filled us in on what happened. Now let's hear your story."

I repeated the facts in as much detail as I could remember. I told him about the bottle of pills, which the assistant principal seemed to have forgotten to mention. A few minutes later, an officer was back with the bottle of pills and asked, "Is this the same bottle you confiscated from the deceased student?"

"Yes," I answered.

"Okay. Do you have anything in your classroom with your name or address on it?"

I thought before answering. "Yes. I bring in magazines from home, *Newsweek*, *Time*, and such. I use them for class projects. They have my name and mailing address on them. They are on my desk."

A few minutes later, an officer returned and watched me tear out the mailing labels from the various magazines. I was then escorted back to my classroom to collect my briefcase, hat, and coat and then walked to the front of the building. My car was parked on the adjacent fenced-in lot.

Standing at the door atop the stairs, flanked by five uniformed police on each side, I looked out into a sea of angry screaming black faces filled with hate and frustration. All the school teachers and administrators seemed to have vanished. I did not see one friendly face in the crowd. None of my students were visible. The crowd got larger by the minute, with many swearing and cursing with raised clenched fists. The neighborhood high school had emptied, its students making a field trip to protest the killing of a black kid by a white teacher.

The officer in charge asked if his men were ready. There was a quick nod, and I was suddenly literally swept forward and into the screaming mob. The mob parted. Some tried to get through the officers; and a few glancing blows hit my shoulder and back, almost knocking my hat off.

Two pop bottles flew in dangerously close, and I ducked as a rock hit a bystander in the face on the other side of me. She let out a howl of pain between bloody lips and broken teeth. I could hear her screams and curses as we pushed forward. I was spit upon and cursed at as we forced our way through the mob to the parking lot where the gate was guarded by several uniformed officers.

I was little battered and ruffled, but I made it through without injury or the need for medical assistance. The officer told me to be available if needed but to just go home for the time being. I got in my car just as a bottle hit the asphalt near my car. One shattered the windshield of a teacher's vehicle parked next to me.

I drove to our little apartment of Calumet and waited for Erma and Bobby to return home. I stayed off a few days before accepting an assignment at a different school. By then, the news cycle had moved on and Detroit had lost interest. The police never called me to the station for further questioning.

CHAPTER 19

Stand Tall

Woodbridge
Early October 2014

B asic services of all varieties are few and far between in the inner city. When we moved into Detroit in the late sixties, we had neighborhood mom-and-pop stores, hardware stores, and even a gun shop, dry cleaners, drugstores, banks, and a movie theater. These primarily white-owned stores, one by one, failed, moved out, or were put out of business with high insurance rates, robberies, and fear. A few are coming back, the restaurant and bar types, but you have to drive away to get your basics.

These dead and decayed buildings litter our commercial avenues. Often made of solid steel reinforced concrete or brick, their empty and open shells remain, waiting for some young developer with vision and drive. Many, but by no means all, are owned by greedy speculators who play the dog in the manger and hold on to make a killing when large tracts of vacant land are needed for a sports or entertainment complex. In our neighborhood, many are abandoned and owned by the city.

The stores that remain, few in number, have evolved in nature. They do more with less. The corner gas station is now also a convenience store, bank, coffee shop, and deli. The pharmacy is now a full-line mini grocery and department store selling all types of cheap personal and household goods as well as groceries, beer, and wine. The dollar store has replaced the department store.

Last week I drove out Michigan Avenue to the nearest CVS Drugstore for my annual flu shot. Turning the corner to the front of the building, I heard a commotion of loud-voiced oaths and angry threats. Two young men—one Hispanic, one black, both thin and in their early twenties—were squared off posturing, ready to fight. They circled each other, fists clenched. Both were determined and ready.

A young black lady with a cell phone at the ready told me they had been friends but had had a falling out.

"Over what?" I asked. She didn't know—maybe drugs, turf, or a girl. Who knows? They were both from this neighborhood and had grown up together.

An older Latina woman stood with her back pressed against the wall. With frightened eyes, she watched the little drama play out. Others stood watching or quickly slipped behind brick pillars, seeking safety in case shots were to ring out.

Watching them very closely and noting they weren't carrying guns, I commanded in my best teacher voice, "BREAK IT UP, YOU TWO," then added, "MOVE ALONG. YOU'RE BLOCKING TRAFFIC."

They froze and both turned to look at me, but they didn't move along. Heck, I'd have to use a different approach. I watched their hands very carefully, still no weapons yet.

"You." I pointed at the young black man, but before I could issue a directive, the young black woman leaned forward and whispered in my ear, "Be careful, mister, he's got a knife."

"Thanks," I said without letting my eyes leave his hands, carefully stealing glances at the young Hispanic who still stood in a threatening posture with fists clenched. Good, at least he wasn't going for a weapon.

"You, young man." I nodded toward the black man. "Don't even think of going for that knife or weapon. Now back up, both of you," I commanded. We now formed a tight triangle. I took a threatening step forward toward them and waited to see how it would play out. I always keep my hands atop each other, right on top of left, at belt-buckle level. My left hand was holding the front of my jacket while my right hand was at the ready. This was the climax coming up.

If they didn't back off and if there were still no weapons in play, I was planning my next move. I was going to tell them that they had better clear out before the police arrived. The cops had been called. I was saving that one for last. It was my tried-and-true method and had gotten me out of many a scrape.

As I stepped forward, both young men stepped back; and with a few choice insults muttered at each other and a few directed at me, they retreated and exited the area. People stepped out and returned to their business. The older Latina woman who was pressed against the wall behind me came up and thanked me, saying how afraid she was to go to the store.

The young black lady said she had already called the police, but who knows when and if they would even show up. This was just another minor non-event in the life of a day in the city.

By the way, CVS was out of the flu serum, again. It took three trips to finally get the shot.

I want to take a moment and explain my stand on dangerous situations. Either stand tall or go low, if you know what I mean. As the years have gone by, I've tried many styles of holsters and weapons, even carried a Charter Arms revolver in my belt band with rubber bands on the handle for extra grip, but I've come to the conclusion that the five-round S&W is the perfect gun for me. I could actually hit what I was aiming at, and my hope is that I never have to use it in anger.

When I stand tall, I have my hands atop each other at belt-buckle height. The right hand is resting lightly on the left, and the left is holding the edge of my jacket or coat. In one easy movement, the left hand lifts up the jacket and the right acquires the pistol's Hogue grip handle and extracts the weapon smoothly. My trigger finger is on the right side of the frame—ready for action, but not on the trigger. When and if you ever have to pull, keep your finger off the trigger. Some loud noise, event, or action can cause an involuntary jerk, thus discharging the weapon. Often with tragic consequences for an innocent bystander and for you. Don't show your weapon unless it is necessary, and I'll say again, keep your finger off the trigger until it's time to shoot.

Aim and shoot well. Hit what you aim at, not some old lady in the row house across the street—my guiding life principle passed on to me from my father. I want to die able to say that I've never killed anyone, but more important than that, I want to be able to say that I was never killed by anybody.

With everyone wanting high-capacity magazines, why (you might ask) do I carry an old-style five-shot revolver? Good question. The answer is simple. Every semiautomatic pistol I've ever owned or shot has jammed at one time or another. My revolver has not jammed in all the thousands of rounds I've put through it. If I get a bad primer, I simply pull the trigger again, and it goes bang. I've lived in Detroit for forty-five years, and thus far, I've only had to fire one round to end a bad situation.

I trust my wheel gun with my life.

CHAPTER 50

The Only Way to Get Over
the Loss of a Dog

Woodbridge
Mid-October 2014

T he only way to get over the loss of a loved dog is, first, to mourn the loss and then get another one. By September of 2014, we were ready to adopt a young pup—another Rottweiler, of course. Once you learn the temperament of a breed, you stick with it. I wanted to train the dog and mold her into the perfect companion and protector for our old age, but other plans were being made.

At that same time, our son, Bob, and his girlfriend, Linda, had decided to build their own house in the outskirts of San Antonio, Texas. They knew that we were looking for a new dog, and they just happened to have two Rottweilers that needed temporary shelter. They proposed that we take them—a big male named Echo and a little girl of mixed ancestry, primarily Rottweiler, named Aero—for about six months during construction. With building a house and his out-of-town assignments, Bob couldn't properly care for them.

We talked it over and said we would take his dogs for up to a year. Bob could come up and take them back home any time during that year, but we warned him that we wanted to get our own pup in the near future. I had always liked his big male and had been with him many times on visits. The female I knew nothing about. We met halfway in Branson, Missouri (a fun place to visit); put the dogs in the back of our van; had lunch; and headed back to Detroit. The big guy, Echo, was prone to car sickness and liked to issue earsplitting barks at nearby cars. The little girl, Aero, curled up to sleep, saving her energy for that night when we finally found a pet-friendly motel near Indianapolis, Indiana. We were up and out early before the management came around to evict us for disturbing the peace.

Echo was used to a suburban fenced-in yard and spoiled, while Aero was an unknown without any social skills. Urban life requires a lot of interaction with other species, and it calls for judgment as to the danger of the situation. They have to learn commands and can't just go running off after the first stray cat or squirrel. I have to admit the first two weeks were pure hell. The big guy, Echo (at 120 pounds), snarled and barked at anyone, friend or foe, who came too near; and frankly, he would scare the hell out of everyone, including me.

During one feeding, all hell broke loose when the big guy knocked Aero aside and began to gobble her food. Luckily, I saw this through the storm door. He had never tried this trick before while I remained with them during their feeding. Storming out, I pushed him aside and grabbed his food bowl, which still contained his uneaten portion. As I whacked him on his head with the metal bowl, denting it in the process, the contents flew over the porch. He was stunned, not by the blow (because a Rottweiler has an unusually hard head) but because someone had checked his aggressive behavior. From then on, they were placed on sit command before meals, grace was said, and only after the sign of the cross, were they allowed to eat. They were becoming Catholic dogs, or at least dogs living in a Catholic home.

I tried to establish a daily routine of feedings, walks, work, training, and treats (when deserved). I was the boss and they were the followers—the members of our pack.

Aero seemed to be better tempered, but she was very busy and had no concept of a walk patrolling the neighborhood. She would go along for a while just fine but then catch the scent or sight of something interesting and go after it. She would sniff and pursue any scent of a squirrel, cat, or dog in the neighborhood. Our walks were a comedy of errors. I simply didn't know if I'd ever get them ready for city living with all the loud noises and confusion.

Erma suggested that we use full-body halters to attach their leashes rather than hooking them to the collars. This seemed to help Aero somewhat, but she was a bundle of nervous energy going every which way. After a few days, I was able to go back to the collar-leash hookup for Echo; but alas, Aero is doomed to wear the halter indefinitely into the future.

The other night, Erma removed Aero's halter to give her a good rubdown and, hopefully, a better night's sleep. But the little girl wouldn't settle down. Even after we all were in bed, she continued coming into our bedroom, pacing, moving around, and nudging our bed. After a half hour of this, I told Erma that she should put the halter back on her, but Erma said that it had to be something else. Finally, I got up and put it back on her, and immediately, she went to her bed and remained for the rest of the night. She likes her halter.

For the past month, our walks went something like this: "No, Aero." I would give a tug to counter her motion and try to get her back on course as Echo plodded on. "Stay alert!" Then I would give another corrective pull on her leash. Then, in a few moments, she would discover a new smell and begin to sniff at ground level in that direction.

"PAY ATTENTION, Aero, now," I ordered. Her constant pulling and generally mean disposition reminded me of back when I was a kid on my grandfather's farm. He had a couple of mules hitched up to a farm wagon. They were ornery and stubborn and knew I wasn't my grandfather. They thought they didn't have to obey, and so they didn't. Walking these dogs was like trying to drive that team of mules. The only difference is that I'm not my grandfather.

Because of their very serious anger issues with others, we began placing them in the backyard then asking very brave neighbors and friends over for coffee. At some point, I would open the door, and the dogs would come in to investigate the visitor. After introductions, some smelling of the guests, followed by some petting and affectionate touching, the dogs went to their respective mats happy and at peace with the world. We didn't lose one friend or neighbor during this period.

The only bad incident was during one such visit when I tried to move a bone out of the middle of the floor, but a lightning-fast snap of Echo's jaw got my left hand. I pulled a red bandanna from my hip pocket and staunched the blood while I finished the visit. Then I checked the injury. It was pretty bad, and I drove over to the nearby WSU emergency hospital.

Over the next few hours, I had dozens of doctors, nurses, interns, and others come by and check on my hand and discuss procedures among themselves. Finally, someone closed the wound, gave me a shot, and sent me on my way. When I got the statement and invoice from the hospital, it was $1,500. It seems as if everyone on the staff had made a visit and given an opinion and submitted an invoice. Now I know what they teach there: creative accounting.

We were walking early one morning in the north end, an area recently plagued with car thefts and stolen wheels. A middle-aged black man driving a pickup truck pulled up and inquired about puppies. I informed him that they were both fixed. He said he was looking for a female Rottweiler for protection.

"Really?" I said. "You want a female? Here, you can have this one."

"What, you'd give her away?"

"Yes, take her." Aero looked up at me with those big brown eyes; and I saw, for the first time, that she understood the trouble she was putting me through. If she wanted to be a part of the family, she would have to give a little. The man shook his head in suspicion and drove quickly away.

"Eureka," I shouted as the idea came to me while working out with a chest-pull exerciser. It contained several metal springs and had come with extra ones to increase the tension during exercise. I would take one of the strong metal springs and attach it between Aero's lease and her collar. When she lunged at something, the spring should pull her back in place. Wow, what an idea. I wondered if I could patent it and make millions of dollars. I couldn't wait to try it out.

It was simple enough to attach, and I went on a walk with Aero sans Echo. At first, things progressed beautifully. She made her move toward a bird and lunged, and the spring's tension pulled her head back. Wow. It worked. As we approached a big German shepherd in a fenced-in yard, I thought this would be the supreme test. I had never dared take her near this animal for fear that I couldn't control Aero. The shepherd came out, snarling and snapping; and Aero, true to form, leaped toward him. Luckily for me, there was a fence separating them because the spring was stretched beyond its strength and sprung out in a long coiled strand of metal. I hauled Aero back, detached the now-worthless spring, and tossed it in a nearby garbage can. But the idea might be sound. The next day I purchased a stronger spring at the hardware store but came away with the same results. Again, I tried; but the only one Aero couldn't spring was an industrial-grade spring, which was so strong I couldn't pull it. It just hung there like a metal bar, worthless. Thus ended my dreams of millions.

Luckily, Erma located a device that linked the two dogs together in tandem on which one leash was attached. I had forgotten about it. We had used it for a while on two unruly Rotts years ago. The big guy's bulk and his steady plodding would check the little girl's tugs and starts toward who knows what. The big guy had been taught to heel and would walk along at his master's pace. The little girl had been taught nothing.

We found out later that she had been found running wild in a parking lot in San Antonio. She had deep scratches on her head, and the fur had been rubbed off her rear leg where a wire had once held her in check. She has had a checkered history.

No training was evident for the little girl. Now the little girl would get pulled along by the big guy, without effort on his part. Her lunges and movements were often checked by the big guy, and she was forced to proceed along the path I intended. It was beginning to work. It's a beautiful sight to see two big Rotts in tandem, walking down the sidewalk with their master lightly holding the leash. People step aside. Even groups of gangbangers stand frozen in awe as we march by.

I was eager to get Echo into carting and tried him pulling the dog cart around the neighborhood a few times a week. I think he is going to be a natural carting dog. You do know that the breed was known for pulling the butcher's cart in Germany.

Soon, six months had passed, and I called Bob to see how his house was coming along and when he wanted to pick up his dogs.

"Dad, we've got a problem here. No, not with construction. But I just found out myself that Linda is afraid of the dogs. It seems that she can't control them. Dad, it's her or the dogs, and I really love her. I just finished our dream house. What should I do?"

In truth, I really hadn't come to know and love Linda at that time, so I said, "If it were me, I'd take the dogs."

"You'll take the dogs," Bob said excitedly.

"Well, no, that's not exactly what I meant to say."

"Oh thanks, Dad, you are the greatest. Sorry, but I've got to run. Talk to you later. Love you."

"Wait. But, but," I said into a disconnected phone.

"Erma, I've been bamboozled…again!" Later that afternoon, we drove to a restaurant in Dearborn named Bamboozles and took a selfie in front of it. By the way, they have excellent pizza.

CHAPTER 51

Mayberry R.F.D

Woodbridge
November 5, 2014

D awn broke with radiant sunshine and a light fanning breeze. It was a perfect fall day in Michigan as we walked home down Avery Street. I was taking our dogs out for an early morning stroll.

I had voted early the day before in the midterm election, and the results this morning showed a clear move to the Republican right nationally. That is, everywhere but in Detroit and the other urban areas held in a vice by the Democrat party. The GOP now controlled both the House and the Senate nationally; and in Michigan, the GOP retained the governor's office and the legislature. Things were looking up.

Granted, things were beginning to improve economically. More traffic was on the expressways, and it was getting harder to find street parking downtown (that's how I judge the vitality of the economy). New restaurants and legitimate businesses were moving in. Old bars that that had been vacant for decades were being bought up, renovated, and reopened. Midtown Detroit was beginning to happen. The old Hoots on Trumbull had recently opened under the strange name "UFO Factory." Would I ever live to see Detroit become a real world-class city?

Our morning walks were becoming delightfully uneventful. We walked from one end of the neighborhood to the other, checking all the alleys and side streets and meeting and greeting neighbors as they left for work or returned home from who knows where. As neighbors waved greetings, I thought that this was really becoming a little like the old Andy Griffin sitcom *Mayberry, R.F.D.*

I was taking Erma's advice this morning and had picked up a nice limber switch about a yard long. Each time the little female dog (she was only eighty-seven pounds) would tug or pull one way or the other, I would gently tap her on the hind quarter or on her collar to get her attention. This generally corrected her misbehavior and put her back on course. On several occasions, where another dog or a cat was involved, it took a little more than a gentle tap along with my verbal cues and admonitions. The big guy just plodded along, occasionally turning to me for recognition and a "Good Boy."

It is common knowledge that Rottweilers need space and exercise. You've got to take them on daily walks and let them play tug-of-war. They need regular opportunities to stretch out and to run. They also need to have a job. That's why I'm trying to teach the big guy to become a carting dog, but more about that later.

Rottweilers must be socialized and learn not to be so territorial, especially while walking down a public sidewalk. They have to learn to step aside and go on a sit command and allow folks to enter or exit their vehicles. You have to learn to control their instincts on command, especially if they are older dogs and unfamiliar with their new environment.

The smaller mixed Rotts, like Aero, can be aggressive with other dogs of the same sex, cats, squirrels, and birds. Bad behavior must be checked, and checked hard, before it gets out of hand. Both of our new Rotts wanted to be the boss and had to quickly learn their place in the pecking order. It doesn't mean you have to be mean, just firm and in control.

They will respect a strong master who knows how to lead and command them. Once the master is firmly in control, life becomes fun. The Rott is a cool companion to have at your side during an emergency, and they are just fun to have around. And two good dogs are even better. As I always say, if given a choice, I would always pick a Rottweiler over a .45.

It was turning out to be one of our better walks. Neighbors waved in greeting and wished us a pleasant day. All was well with the world. The question came to mind, Just how much strength does it take to control a brace of Rottweilers? How do you know if a Rott is too much of a dog?

Try this simple test. Almost every home has a simple floor scale for registering your weight. Pick it up firmly in both hands, take a deep breath, and squeeze it as hard as you can. What did you register? Try it a few more times, and take your highest score. I can register 145 pounds without too much effort. If you can't break one hundred pounds, I wouldn't recommend a big dog unless it is well trained and highly disciplined. There are times when you must check a negative attitude, and often, that takes raw strength.

Because you need a certain amount of strength and agility to survive on the streets of Detroit, it means that you have to develop a daily ritual of exercises. I like working out at home, listening to the news, or watching a television program. Erma likes to go to the gym where the swimming pool is the center of attraction. Either way, it works. Get into a daily habit of exercise while you are young, and stay with it. Just keep the routine going as long as possible. Besides, you've got to be able to run at least fifty years to avoid danger and find cover. It's easier done when you are still young.

Detroit is a mean city, no doubt; and its thugs have no sympathy for the old or the weak. The punks and thugs will beat down and run over a handicapped person as easily as an elderly. They'll shoot a child as quickly as a senior citizen. The street creds among the young punks is time served in the juvie. Middle-class black families move to the suburbs as quickly as whites. Most of the private Catholic and Lutheran schools have closed or moved out of the city. The choices for the middle-class families are fewer and fewer. There are so many negative influences in the city, and the young people are pushed to try drugs and get involved in criminal activities.

CHAPTER 52

Communication in the Twenty-First Century

Woodbridge Community
December 13, 2014

A neighbor recently asked for the name, address, and phone number of a contractor I had used and was satisfied with. I had the information stored on my desk computer. I asked my neighbor for his e-mail address and told him that I'd send it to him. I was surprised to learn that he didn't have a computer.

"I don't believe in them," he said. I was a bit confused as to how someone would not believe in the existence of a computer. They were everywhere. I soon learned that was not exactly what he meant. After a pause, he said, "The internet is the Antichrist, or maybe Satan himself." He said this in all honesty.

I remembered a few years ago when they had that big power outage from Canada through the Midwest and along the East Coast. Erma and I were driving back from visiting Bob and his family. At that time, he was stationed at Fort Meade, Maryland, but spent most of his time in the Middle East.

We were on the Ohio Turnpike, running a little low on gas, when I pulled in to a service plaza and learned of the power outage. The pumps didn't operate, the cash registers failed to function, and all the lights and power were out. The coolers and freezers were out, and yet no one panicked. Eventually, backup generators came on, and the fuel flowed. The ice-cream shop did give out free samples. I wondered what would happen if the lights had not come back on.

I thought of this as my neighbor went on to explain that the computer was the gateway opening all sorts of evils and filth into the American home. It was, in his words, "the gateway to perdition." He believes that mankind will end not through a thermal nuclear war or an invasion from outer space but through our total and complete dependency on computers, which will eventually break down. And then we will all be engulfed in death and destruction of the end-time. It will be dog-eat-dog and every man for himself. I tried to point out the many benefits computers had bestowed on mankind but was only met with a scoff and a brisk "You'll see."

I must give this some thought. We remembered when we had been prepared for the Y2K chaos that failed to materialize because everyone was prepared. We had stockpiled emergency food, water, and fuel. It took us years to finally use up the stock, and I still have a case of MRE in the basement.

But as I thought of it, I had to admit that he had a point. Our whole economy was tied to the Net. How long would we survive as a people if the power really went out? It is said that society is only three meals from a revolution.

I always viewed computers as a necessary evil, but as I've gotten older, I've come to appreciate some of their functions. I certainly wouldn't be able to write this narrative without one. How can one use them without becoming dependent upon them?

One home computer has a program called Neighbor to Neighbor. I believe it's under Facebook for residents and business owners in a specific geographic area. You can report a suspicious person or vehicle in the neighborhoods or call attention to be on the lookout for a little lost puppy or kitty. Hundreds of alert and active citizens, mostly newer residents, who seem to have their smartphones permanently either embedded to an ear or held like a priest's prayer book, are then alerted. It informs the community of special events such as block club meetings and parties. This one application of technology has improved communications and made the neighborhood safer for its citizens.

In December of 2014, we joined the multitude of smartphone users; and now we get the alerts and messages from concerned citizens. What follows are the comments I sent to my neighbors in mid-December 2014.

> Hello neighbors,
>
> I'd like to talk about Woodbridge for a moment. We just got back from our daily walk around the Woodbridge neighborhood (I'm the guy with the two Rottweilers), and I have a few thoughts I'd like to share.
>
> Today I had a runner come up behind us on Avery and sprint past us on the sidewalk. No problem, but it would have been better if he would have given us a heads-up, such as "Hello" or "Passing on right." Or better yet, it would have been better if the runner would move to the street, if clear, or to the other side of the street. My dogs are pretty secure and don't get easily rattled, but dogs can get nervous when someone unexpectedly runs up on them. This is not a complaint, just a thought.
>
> You notice that my dogs are on leashes. And when we see a runner coming toward us, we'll move aside and I put them on a sit command, or if there's time, we go to the other side of the street. It's just a matter of courtesy and safety for all.
>
> I firmly believe one of the reasons why our little neighborhood is becoming one of the safest in Detroit is because of the many folks who walk their dogs. The bad guys stay away from this neighborhood when our dogs are out walking the community.

By the way, we love our new neighbors. I can't tell you how glad we are to see the mothers pushing baby carriages, runners running, joggers jogging, and cyclists biking on the streets. We've lived here for over forty-five years, and this is the best we've seen the area. I added a post to the Facebook page: welcome, welcome, welcome to our new neighbors!

Sincerely,
Dave, Erma, Echo, and Aero

CHAPTER 53

Concealed Carry

Detroit, Michigan
December 30, 2014

"How was your morning?" Erma inquired as she placed her little backpack on her desk. She had just returned from swimming at the Y and shopping. She was busy laying in supplies in preparation for the New Year. Her family has long and deep roots in the foothills of the Missouri Ozarks; and so traditionally, we have black-eyed peas, ham, and cabbage for our New Year's dinner. Why?

"It's for good luck for the coming year, and so we won't have money problems."

I asked her to please explain why these specific items are on the menu.

"We always have, always will," she answered.

We also don't travel, write checks, use a credit card, or spend any money on New Year's Day. If you spend absolutely no money on the first day of the year, according to her family tradition, you'll have no money problems and a prosperous new year. I have no problem with either of her family traditions and understand why the early church Fathers incorporated many pagan practices into the life of Holy Mother Church.

Family superstitions are interesting. In our Suttner family, as an example, we don't have rolling pins in our homes. This one I could not, for the life of me, understand. We love pies, schnitzel, dumplings, and other items needing a rolling pin; but none are found in our home or, as far as I know, in my parents' or grandparents' kitchens. My mother used a glass bottle as a roller for her pie dough.

"Why?" I once asked my mother. I was only told that my father forbade them in the house and that was enough for her.

Once, early in our marriage, we were visiting my folks before driving home. Erma later told me that she had retrieved a rolling pin from a box of kitchen utensils she had picked up from her family to take back to our apartment. She decided to surprise my family and prepare dinner while my parents were out on some church business. She was busy in my mother's kitchen rolling the dough out in preparation of chicken and dumplings, a favorite in both of our families. My little brother and I were in the backyard playing pitch and catch and were unaware of the unfolding incident.

Dad walked in first and stopped in surprise. I can just picture Erma smiling and see her with a bit of flour smudged on her cheek, smiling and rolling out the dough, unaware that she had broken one of the family taboos.

Years later she told me that my father, in no uncertain terms, told her that rolling pins were not allowed in his house; and then he left the kitchen. He neither explained nor did she inquire. Surprised and a little afraid, she immediately took the offending object back to the car and later returned it back to her parents' home. Throughout our life's travels, we've never had a rolling pin in our kitchen. Erma uses a large wooden dowel!

I'm sure something bad was witnessed in bygone days involving a rolling pin, but no one has been able to tell me what. Now that generation is gone, and it will remain a mystery.

So you see, our family has its share of superstitions. For example, if we talk about a plan or hope for the future, we knock on wood so as not to offend some little spirit. Otherwise, we'd have bad luck. Tapping on wood is to keep from jinxing something. If there is no wood around, we simply rap our own skull a few times with our knuckles, thus implying that we have a wooden head to even suggest such a thought.

This device is used when you make some optimistic statement and fear that it might not come true. The person hearing this optimistic statement can help reduce the danger by quickly saying, "From your lips to God's ear." By saying this and the rapping on wood at the same time, one can avoid the danger.

I understand that this practice goes back to the forests of Northern Europe when the Germanic tribes believed in the gods of nature and had to ask permission before entering the forest by rapping on the bark.

The practice in our little family has been for women never to carry their personal weapons in the purses. I preach against this common practice, calling to mind the number of times I've witnessed women leaving their purses unguarded at a restaurant table or in a church pew.

My belief has always been that a woman needs to keep her weapon on her person, in a holster, in a belly bag, or in her pocket. If you separate it from her person, she might as well not have it. Erma bought into this philosophy and keeps her little .32 in a small leather holster in a jacket pocket.

"Yes, we had a good morning," I answered. "We just got back from a walk in the field. It's too cold out to enjoy a long walk." I helped put away the groceries and asked, "Did you read about the tragedy in Idaho yesterday?"

"No, don't tell me they killed another police officer?" She stopped and looked with concern.

"No, but a young mother, while shopping at a Walmart, left her two-year-old son in the cart with her purse to examine some product or other. The little boy reached in her purse and grabbed her small-caliber pistol that she kept for protection. It discharged once, killing the mother."

"Oh my," Erma said, "how tragic. You say the child was only two?"

"Yes, just two years of age. The liberal press and commentators are going to have a field day with this one. You know what makes me angry?" I paused then continued, "This young mother, by all accounts a loving, caring mother, felt compelled to carry a pistol. And now her family is without a mother, and the little boy will learn about this and be scarred for life. It's very sad."

"Oh my, but it was an accident. It wasn't the child's fault, and really, it wasn't the mother's fault either." Erma sighed.

"Well, who's fault was it then? Was it the manufacturer that produced a pistol that probably didn't have a safety? Or if it had one, did the owner forget to have the safety on? Was it in a specially designed purse with a gun pocket built in? There are a lot of unanswered questions here. Should some hotshot litigator sue the gun manufacturer?"

"It wouldn't surprise me if someone did file suit. But no, of course, I don't agree. It was a tragic accident, no one is to blame. Why, my .32 doesn't have an external safety. Bad things just happen. Besides, what an awful society we live in when a young mother feels she must carry a gun to protect her family."

"True, very true, but you don't keep your weapon in your purse." Erma nodded in agreement.

For years, I've preached gun safety to my young wife, our son, nieces, granddaughters, and goddaughters. And I've always emphasized two points: first, keep your weapon on your person at all times while carrying, and second, keep your finger off the trigger until you acquire a target and are ready to engage.

Where was this young mother's older brother, father, or husband? Men have an obligation to protect their families, and part of that involves proper instruction for wives and children as to the proper carrying, handling, loading, cleaning, and storage of a weapon. Why is it that professional gun-safety classes accept the purse-carry method for women? Purses are now designed with specific pockets for pistols.

Erma's first pistol, and still a favorite, is a little .38 special S&W with a shrouded hammer. It's a perfect pocket pistol. True, it is a bit heavy, but it has no external hammer to snag in a pocket. Unfortunately, its recoil was a bit rough for Erma's hand, so I modified it with a Christmas gift several years ago of new Hogue grips for her .38 special. I had placed a set on my S&W .357 and was pleased with the results. There is nothing better than a warm pistol tucked up against your belly on a cold morning.

CHAPTER 54

Celebrating Detroit Style

Woodbridge
Midnight, New Year's Eve 2015

E rma and I decided to celebrate the New Year by staying home with our new dogs. A little after midnight, someone on Grand River Avenue let loose with a long barrage from what sounded like a 9 mm semiautomatic. *Bam, bam, bam.* The shots continued. He must have had a large-capacity clip, for it kept going on for at least fifteen rounds. Then others opened up. It sounded like a firefight from the jungles of Vietnam.

We have an interesting custom in Detroit relating to New Year's celebration. At midnight, folks go out into their yards and fire their guns up in the air in celebration. Unfortunately, what goes up will come down, and I'm told by cop friends that they park their squad cars under overpasses for thirty minutes before and after midnight. For years, the politicians have tried to get the people to give up this practice and instead use handbells to ring in the New Year. Fat chance of success. Old customs die hard.

Gunfire and firecrackers erupted all around the city. True, it wasn't as bad as when we first moved in. Over the years I've found scores of spent rounds in the garden and around the house.

I have to admit that when we first moved in, I would go out and fire a gun in the air with my neighbors. Then Erma said, "No more." For the next few years, she allowed me to fire black-powder blanks from a .36-caliber cap-and-ball 1851 Navy Colt. (For a while I thought I would get into Civil War reenacting. Have you ever seen an old black-powder revolver go off at night when the cylinder has been well lubricated with lard or butter? It's a beautiful sight.) But that didn't last too long either.

Next, I had to go with traditional fireworks that I would purchase down in Missouri during summer vacation and bring back for the New Year's celebration. Now, I'm not even allowed to shoot off fireworks. We just sit home and watch the ball drop in Times Square.

This was the first time the new dogs, Echo and Aero, had spent a New Year's celebration in Detroit. They both jumped up from their beds and began to howl and bark anew with each burst of gunfire and fireworks.

Erma immediately quieted them down by saying, "Good dogs. Thank you, thank you very much," and such. She stood up and patted each on their head and thanked each dog individually for alerting us to the danger. They circled their beds a few times and then settled down until the next gunfire erupted, but they didn't seem to be as anxious.

We had learned that trick from a UPS driver many years ago. The driver had come to the door with a package. Our dog was up and at the door with a vengeance. The dog threw himself with such force against the door that the house shook. He snarled, barked, and snapped at the person coming up the steps. I had to pull the dog away by force in order to open the door. I would then step out on the porch to sign for the package. The dog's barking was incessant. My telling the dog to shut up and quiet down did no good. It only made him more aggressive. We had come to accept the fact that he always went nuts when anyone came up on our porch.

We were visiting family in Missouri in the midseventies when someone threw a brick through the front-door glass to gain entry and looted the place of what little we had. Upon returning, I considered installing bulletproof Lexan in place of glass in the front door.

At the shop, I had watched a man fire a .38 special point blank into a sample. It left a deep puncture mark in the plastic but failed to penetrate. I then ordered and installed it with one-way lag bolts and a custom wrought-iron grill on the inside of the heavy oak doorframe. It could now withstand the dog's assault, but I still had the wooden screen and storm door. Not much of a deterrent there, so I ordered a wrought-iron storm door with a mail slot built in.

Erma placed dark car window tinted plastic on the inside lower half of the storm door window. In this way, the mail would be placed in the chute and drop between the two locked doors. No one from the outside would be any wiser if we were home or gone.

The new iron storm door swung out, and the main reinforced oak door swung inward. I was proud of the security measures I'd taken on the front entry and didn't worry too much about the dog. By the way, that was the last time a robber's entry was obtained via that door.

After signing, the UPS driver gave me the package. He started to leave, paused, and then he said, "Mister, are you open to a little advice?"

I said that indeed, I was open.

He said, "I deal with dogs every day, and yelling at them to quiet down just won't work. It only makes them more excited. They are doing just what comes naturally. Some punk comes up on their porch, and they are there to protect. As long as he's there, they bark and go crazy. Then he goes away, and they feel that their barking chased him off. Your yelling 'Bad dog' or 'Be quiet' only adds to his confusion."

"So what should I do?" I inquired. "I can't have him going nuts each time someone comes onto the porch, even though it does serve one good purpose. People know that you have a vicious dog on the premises."

"And that's a good thing, but there is a better way. And the bad guys will still know that a dog is on the premises." He paused to gauge my reaction.

"Sure, tell me."

He continued, "I see you have a 'beware of dog' sign on your front window."

Actually, it says "Beware of Rottweiler. The remains of trespassers will be prosecuted."

"That's a good thing," he continued, "but it's not helpful if your dog scares away your visitors. I suggest that you have a neighbor or friend come over, have some treats handy, and have your neighbor stomp as he comes up onto the porch. When the dog begins barking and going crazy at the door, in a firm voice simply say, 'Good boy.' Use his name and say thank you. Give him a nice rub and some pats and a little treat. It may take a few times, but he'll settle down."

"I'll try it. It does make sense," I conceded.

"Sure," he continued. "The dog's job is to alert the master and protect the home, especially the Rottweiler. It's built into him. He hears some punk coming on his property, and your yelling at him only increases his fear and anxiety. By petting him and giving him a little treat, he knows that you are aware of the threat and he has done his job. You watch. It works."

We learned that little trick many years ago, and it really does work. Both dogs received their rubs and pats then stretched and resumed their slumbers and began to ignore the disturbances.

CHAPTER 55

"No Go"

Detroit, Michigan
January 12, 2015

E rma planned on having her second knee replacement in early
February, so we decided to stay in Detroit the entire winter.
Besides, the two new dogs needed constant attention.

By 11:30 a.m., I had finished my morning exercises, read four
chapters from the pile of books I kept on the kitchen table, and finished shoveling the snow. This was a good morning in which to catch
up on the news.

The commentators on the right were lambasting France for
allowing the radical Muslims to gain control of enclaves around Paris
known as "no go" zones where only the law of Sharia was apparently
enforced. This permissive approach was blamed for the recent assault
on the satirical magazine, which claimed the lives of twelve employees, and the attack on the Jewish grocery store, which claimed even
more lives. I heard more than once how this would never have been
permitted in the good old US of A. These folks had obviously never
lived in Detroit.

Near our neighborhood, squatting on the edge of the John C.
Lodge Freeway, the Jeffries high-rises towered above the streets. It
had been designed for low-income folks coming to the city needing
public housing, but by the 1970s, the punks and thugs had taken

over. The drug gangs were beginning to organize and operate out of the high-rise towers. The senior citizens were frightened and intimidated. They would call the police, and no one would come. It was truly a "no go" zone.

Once I heard on the radio an urgent broadcast that someone was on the roof of the Jeffries and taking potshots at the traffic flowing on the John C. Lodge Freeway. By the time a squad of police arrived, the sniper had vanished. No one was killed, but a few cars were hit. More whites and well-to-do blacks moved out of the city. Another time, some hoodlum dropped a bowling ball off the overpass into the oncoming traffic. A huge pileup resulted. Again, no one was apprehended. The next summer, the road crews began installing metal mesh around all the overpasses to protect the suburbanites going to and from work.

Back then, before I gave up on organized religion and went my own way, we went to Saint Dominic on Trumbull Avenue for mass on Sundays. The church had once been Protestant, then when the neighborhood changed in the early 1900s, it was sold to the Catholics. It had a strong congregation of mixed race and income.

I got very involved in the church's mission and its congregation. Several older black ladies lived in the Jeffries Projects and walked the mile or so to the early mass that we attended. They told me that things were quiet on early Sunday mornings and that they felt fairly safe. But they were frightened to return after the service and asked if I would drive them home.

This I had no problem doing. Not only did I drive them home but I also parked the car, and with an air of bravado, I escorted the ladies into the building, past overflowing trash bins, and into the elevators smelling strongly of urine and disinfectant.

We were spotted entering the building, and word spread that a white man in a suit and tie was "in the house." I walked the ladies to the door of their apartment, and after wishing them a good day, turned and was confronted by a baker's dozen of black teens and others loitering in the corridors, just wanting to watch a show.

"Mister, got a smoke?" I was asked by one jive-acting black youth. He looked high, or was he just acting?

"No. Don't smoke," which was a lie. I smoked at that time and had a pack in my coat pocket and carried a classic Zippo lighter. I had just come from church and had lied. I would have to think about that. I pushed on.

"How about a light?" the punk asked as he pulled a cigarette from behind an ear.

"Sorry, I don't have a light or any money," I added as I continued hugging the wall as I made my way to the elevator and pressed the Down button. I turned to face the gathering crowd. My right hand slipped into my jacket pocket where it rested comfortably on my cigarette lighter, on what I hoped would sound like a weapon as I clicked open its cover. The faint metallic click carried to the members nearest me, and they began to move back to a more discreet location. I didn't carry a weapon to church in those days.

For some reason, I didn't seem to be able to intimidate the fool with the cigarette now dangling from his lips. The crowd had backed off a few feet to give us some room in front of the elevator.

"Are we going to have a problem?" I inquired in my best teacher voice. He gave no response. He just eyed me. I punched the Down button again on the elevator again and heard it shudder and take its time in arriving.

Suddenly, I heard the commanding voice of the black lady I had just driven home. The sweet little lady had changed into a commanding presence. "What's the problem here, Jerome? You leave that nice white man alone." The little lady parted the crowd and walked up to the elevator.

"Oh, Auntie Mary, we ain't bothering this...ah...nice white man, is we?" He glared at me, waiting for my response.

The little lady got right up to the teen and spoke. "If 'en I'm your auntie, just which one of my sisters' children are you, for I don't have no brothers? I'm going to have a conversation with my sister about the manners of her child toward me. You sure don't act like any nephew of mine. Now, Jerome, you and your friends run on. The man just drove me home from church, that's all."

"Yes, Auntie Mary, I'm...ah...I didn't know but that he was a cop, ah...we're leaving." The young man, eyes downcast, walked away; and the crowd dispersed. The show was over, and there was nothing left to see. The elevator arrived, and the door creaked open. I stepped back in and pressed the Down button and called out, "Goodbye, and thank you." She stood guard until the door creaked closed.

Each week, for several months, I drove the ladies home and once had tea with them before returning to my car. I would nod and greet the locals on my way out, but I no longer seemed to attract much attention. They accepted the fact that I wasn't a cop. I was like a mailman or a repairman; I simply didn't matter to them. Amazing, but for some reason, my car was not vandalized once while parked at the Jeffries Projects. I admit that I was elated and relieved each time I saw it where I had parked it in the lot. In those days, the youth of the black community respected and cared for their elders. Most of the older women knew the young men and had babysat and taken care of them in their infancy. It had been a closed community, but there were rules. Those days are long gone. I don't know if anyone is respected in Detroit today.

CHAPTER 56

Value of Literature (by the Pound)

Woodbridge
Early April 2015

I 've had a long-running battle with the workers at the recycling center just north of Woodbridge community. Don't get me wrong, I support the concept and practice of recycling. Just the physical act of sorting and placing all the trash from our daily lives into their proper bins is therapeutic. You begin to appreciate the economy and abhor waste.

As you separate the clear glass from its colored neighbors and deposit the "dead soldiers" in their coffins, you remember the tastes and delight and, at times, the misery and grief each bottle gave. The plastics are sorted by numbers, and paper is divided into its many forms. The one troubling issue is what to do with old books. Not telephone directories and discarded catalogs (that's simple) but real literature.

Books of literary value were being dumped in the bin along with circulars and sales pamphlets. I took the time to explain to management that it was wrong to destroy good literature and society is judged on how it treats the historic literature of its past. I reminded them of the book burners of history and asked if they really wanted to keep their company after they passed from this mortal coil. It seemed to work.

They installed a bookshelf next to the book recycle bin where books of value could be placed, and a sign saying "Free Books" told the world that they were available for the taking, For the past few years I have retrieved wonderful volumes of Twain, the Brothers James, Pushkin, Dickens, and so many more.

I also returned with books I had read and enjoyed and shelved for others to read and, hopefully, appreciate. We sang the praises of recycling even when the city began to issue blue recycling bins for home pickup. Novels, histories, philosophy, and nineteenth and twentieth century literature were exchanged for armloads of books each week. I looked forward to visiting the recycling center weekly as much as the Detroit Public Library on Martin Street where they sold their unread books at $0.10 each and fifteen for a dollar. I enjoyed it until today.

At the center today I first noticed that the bookshelves were moved away from the book bin to a location behind the employees' station. This would mean that a person bringing books would no longer have the shelves next to the bin. He would have to search out and transport the literature to the shelves. The result would be that the books would simply get dumped in the bin and be recycled along with other paper waste.

It was wrong, and I found an employee on which to express my opinion. He shrugged his shoulders and said it wasn't his responsibility and that I would have to speak with the manager. A few minutes later, a second employee approached me and said that people could still place books on the shelves and they would remain free.

"Don't you see?" I replied that most people who bring boxes of old books now simply dumped them into the recycle bin. "They don't shelve them. I usually reach down deep into the bin and retrieve books for the shelves. Most people's arms aren't long enough to dig deep for books of possible value." I then asked who made the decision. A young man driving a hi-lo was pointed out.

"Can we speak?" I asked. He turned off the machine and climbed down as I pointed out the problem, and he listened as I gave all my classic arguments without the slightest effect.

"Look, mister, I made the decision to move the shelves. People can still place books on it. But if they don't, then the bin books will be disposed of. Besides, they're old and most are trash. They have no value. Other than you and a few others, no one cares."

"Oh, people do care," I said with a little too much emphasis. "And one day you'll learn the value of books..."

"Besides"—he thought of another argument—"all those books are online, and you can download them on your tablet for practically nothing." By this time, a small crowd gathered to hear our exchange.

"Do you think that's all it's about?" I was getting hot, and the volume of my voice went up several clicks. "No, the books disposed of often have their key sentences underlined and margins filled with notes. Prior readers speak to you along with the authors. You are destroying another link with our past, our history. I believe there is a special place in Dante's *Inferno* for the destroyers of our literature and history."

"Oh, you do, do you! You think I'm going to hell because other people throw books away, do you? Those books are trash. Blame the ones who throw them away, not me." With that, he turned his back and called me an "asshole" as he climbed back on his machine in order to move a filled bin out and bring in an empty one.

I was livid and my blood was up. I was ready to haul him off his machine and have a knockdown, drag-out fight to see who was right. I stood there fuming, and Erma came up and said it was time to go, NOW!

I arrived home filled with sadness and concern for our society. "We are losing the links with our forefathers," I said. "One by one, the strands that bind us are being cut." I began to fill with anger, and I told Erma, "It'll be a cold day in hell when I ever go back there again."

At home, I worked on repairing the broken wing of a garden angel that the dogs had toppled in their play. "I've repaired the fallen angel," I said. "I'm going to read before lunch."

I had been reading *The Sayings of the Desert Fathers*. They were early Christians who removed themselves away from worldly temptation to live in small communities of monks in the desert. I had stopped with saying number 17 of Abba Macarius of Egypt.

In number 18, he said, "If you reprove someone, you yourself get carried away by anger and are satisfying your own passion; do not lose yourself, therefore, in order to save another."

Was Abba Macarius speaking directly to me? I reread it a second and then a third time. I had found myself losing my temper more often. I'd have to work on that. I remembered my dad saying that "a man is like steel, worthless when he lost his temper."

CHAPTER 57

Gays with Guns

Woodbridge
Mid-April 2015

"Mr. Suttner, hold up, wait for a minute."

Tom and I were on an early morning walk with Echo and Aero through the northern parts of Woodbridge when we heard a woman's voice. Pausing, we turned to see a neighbor hurrying along to catch us. Judy was deeply involved in dog rescue and prevention of animal cruelty. With our mutual love of dogs, we had formed a friendship lasting over the years. She is far-left liberal, while I've been accused of being to the right of Attila the Hun. She is openly gay while I live a straight life. Yet we like and respect each other.

After greetings and introducing her to my friend Tom, she took a moment to rough up the fur on Echo's head and give him some loving. He adores her and would follow her home.

"Mr. Suttner"—I interrupted her, asking her to please call me Dave. She continued—"Dave, I've decided, after a lot of prayers and thought, that you are right."

"Okay, about what?" I inquired.

"I'm going to get a concealed-carry permit, but I don't know anything about guns."

"What made you change your mind?" This was one of the hard-core liberal beliefs that she had held for the past generation, so now why the change?

"You heard about the shoot-out on Rosa Parks Boulevard the other night. Well, that happened just behind our house. Bullets were flying around everywhere. It was like something out of the Wild West. Then there was the girl who was kidnapped and sexually assaulted from the corner gas station last week. She was lucky to get away with her life. Things like this keep happening. I thought the neighborhood was getting better."

"Yes, we are having a spike in crime rates. Why? Because the thugs know that the neighborhood has a lot of young well-off residents—white and black, straight and gay—moving in. It's only going to get worse with the good weather."

"I know. Will you help me?"

"Sure. Get some of your friends together, and I'll take you to the range. I'll see if Erma wants to go. She has several smaller-caliber pistols."

"Oh no, not for me," she said. "I don't want any little ladylike pistol. I want big hulking cannon."

"All right, Judy. I'll give you a call."

She left, and Tom and I continued our patrol, ah…walk. The first few weeks of spring brought out a new crop of punks and hoods, along with the crocus and early buds.

A kidnapping and sexual assault of a young woman from the gas station at the end of the block had disturbed the community. The neighborhood Facebook was abuzz with rumors and feeling as to what should be done. Several vehicles had been sideswiped during early morning street races, and sporadic automatic gunfire was heard more frequently from the commercial streets bordering the neighborhood. The police were constantly being called to the apartment complex across Grand River.

After thinking about it, I decided to renew my efforts at neighborhood walks with Echo and Aero. I would do more front yard work and porch-sitting with eyes and ears wide open. I decided to engage my neighbors in an attempt to get to know them. I would hire another one of the local men who lived in a halfway house up the street, who aimlessly roamed the streets, and train him as my yardman. I also installed an inexpensive wireless alarm on the front porch to alert us to anyone coming up onto the porch.

We had lost a wrought-iron rocking chair from the front porch last winter. It was one of my favorite chairs for reading and had a nice cushion. After bringing back an older chair from the backyard and placing new cushions on it, we hoped we and our friends would be the ones to enjoy the chairs this summer.

CHAPTER 58

A Glass of Beer, or Two

Corktown
June 20, 2016

"So how long have you been around here?" I had struck up a conversation with the fellow seated on the barstool to my right. Wednesday evenings, we usually biked over to Nancy Whiskey's, where I had PBR beers for a dollar each and Erma had her Diet Coke. We watched a game on their big-screen TV and chatted with the bartender. Erma, seated on my left, had just received her drink and was checking out something on her cell phone.

"Only about a month," he answered. "I moved down from the UP." He sipped his beer and continued, "Got a job, and well, here I am. Do you live around here? I noticed that you two had ridden your bicycles over. I saw you locking them up outside the door."

Interesting, I thought, *he is observant of his surroundings.* "Yes, we've lived down here for almost fifty years." Then, by way of explanation, I told how we had moved into the area in the late sixties to attend WSU; liked the area, the people, the old neighborhoods; and decided to stay on.

"Wow." He let out a deep breath. "You've seen it all. How did you survive during those really bad days? I've been hearing stories about how rough this area was back in the day. With the shootings, carjackings, gangs, and street muggings…what kept you here?"

"Oh, part of it, I'm sure, is just plain stubbornness. I don't like to be pushed around. We were born in Missouri, and I guess, it's just part of who we are. Another part is, I discovered how to blend in and keep a low profile."

"Really? Explain."

"Well"—I took a long drink from my bottle and allowed my thoughts to gather—"it's hiding in plain sight, as it were, because to the really dangerous inhabitants, the predators, you are ignored and not really noticed. They may think, 'Is he dangerous? Don't know, but leave him alone. He doesn't look like he has much value on him.'"

"We were new to the area, having first moved up to the little town of Milford, which we both hated. We spent time in both Ann Arbor and in Detroit. I wasn't sure which university I liked better. Ann Arbor was more upscale, and Detroit was more down-and-out but had opportunities. I learned to dress appropriately for the situation. I soon learned the higher your profile, the easier you make yourself a target. For years, when I was out and about in the neighborhoods, I wore an old green Army jacket from the Vietnam era. My brother, who served during that period, gave it to me. It was well-worn and frayed, but it did help in the job of making me unnoticed because there were hundreds of vets wandering around the streets. It was a form of social camouflage."

"Why aren't you wearing it now?"

"Times. They are changing. That was then, this is now. Younger folks are flooding into the area. They have their own style of sorts. Now, look around. What kind of a clientele frequents this place?"

He swung his body on the stool, first one way and then the other, to take a look around the main room.

"Observe, but don't be obvious," I quietly commented.

He stopped, took a breath, and then let his eyes dart around the room (actually, he was just as obvious to the observant person). But he saw people standing in clusters, laughing and drinking. He saw several knots of folks sitting at tables watching the game or engaging in laughter and conversation. Several individuals were hunched over, engrossed in social media. "I don't know. They look just like regular people."

"Exactly," I said. "That's the point. You have young and old, men and women, white and black. It's a good mix. A good feeling abounds. You notice that you don't have the really down-and-out nor do you have the upper crust in thousand-dollar tailored suits with a limo parked out front. You and I, we both fit in. Granted, I could come in here with a business suit, take my jacket off, loosen my tie, and fit right in. You could also ride up on your Harley, wearing black leather, walk in, and also fit right in. This place has a wide range of acceptability. It's a friendly neighborhood bar. Besides I can get PBR on Wednesdays for one dollar a bottle."

"Hmm." He nodded. "Then you are saying that you must first be observant of your surroundings and then fit in."

"True, but does everyone follow it? It takes patience and practice to become observant. Someday it may pay off and save your life or the lives of others. Take, for example, where you are seated and compare it to my seat."

"Well, you are at the corner of the bar. Oh, I see, you can observe both doors and the main room and the way to the patio."

"Yes, and everyone going or coming to the johns must pass by me."

"Sounds like too much work."

"Not really. It becomes second nature. for example, sitting with your back to the wall, or if at the bar, positioning yourself to be in the best position to see what's going on and, in the rare occasion, be able to react." He nodded in agreement.

"Besides," I continued, "things have improved so much around the old neighborhoods that I can now wear pretty much what I want to and go where I want. But you still can't overdress on the street, or you'll get stopped by the panhandlers on every corner. The way I'm dressed now, my wife and I slide right by them on our bicycles, and no one even notices us. Besides, now we have thousands of bicyclists in the area. Back in the midseventies, during the oil embargo, I began riding a bicycle. There weren't many riding in those days. Now we even have dedicated bike lanes on Rosa Parks Boulevard from our house all the way here."

"That raises an interesting question. How do you react to the bums and panhandlers?"

"Good question. First, I don't believe in giving money to folks on the streets. If asked, give them directions to the nearest church with a food pantry. But in reality, most don't want food. They want money for alcohol or drugs. It's best not to engage in conversation. Just keep moving and firmly say, 'Sorry, can't help.'"

"Does it work?"

"Usually," I answered, "unless it's a woman with a small kid. I'm a sucker for a woman in distress. I guess I'm a romantic at heart. It's the way I was brought up to respect women. Yeah, I know I shouldn't, but I often dig in my left pants pocket for the few dollars that I keep for such an occasion. That way, I don't have to pull out a wallet or search for cash. Never pull your wallet out in public. I can hand the few bills over, give a word of admonition, tell her where the church pantry is located, and move on. The difference is that I know I'm probably a sucker, but I am who I am. I'm not going to change at this stage of my life. Besides, what if, on the off chance, she is telling the truth and really did just run out of gas in a bad neighborhood?" We both smiled at that old song-and-dance routine.

"I asked my priest once what did he do when confronted by the panhandlers on the corner. He said that he goes to Costco and buys a case of water and a big box of power-energy bars. When he is asked for money, he says that he has no money to give but offers them food and drink instead. It works for him. Most accept the offering and thank him. But on occasion, he is cursed and the person demands money. When that happens, he just moves on."

"Have you noticed," the young man asked, "the number of young people, my age or younger, both men and women, begging? You see them at the freeway exits. You didn't use to see that, only old folks down-and-outs."

"True." I nodded. "It's really sad. With more young white people flooding into the area, you are going to have an increase in panhandling and, sadly, mugging and robbery. What saddens me is when you see a young woman begging on the street. Where are her father, brothers, uncles, and family? The family as I knew it is shot to hell.

It's gone. When I was young, I heard tales of family members taking some guy aside who had abused or insulted a female relative and giving him an old-fashioned whopping. You don't see much of that anymore. The family is pretty much shot to hell."

"Why do you think that is true?"

"I know it's true, and I can tell you the year it went to hell. It was 1973. Yes, two events happened that year. In Michigan, the courts ruled that marriage was then and forever 'at will.' Now a person could get rid of his or her spouse 'at will.' Just say, 'I divorce thee.'"

"It can't be that simple?"

"No, but you get the point. It's still an adversarial proceeding, but one party can't stop the other from the divorce. Now it's all about asset division and visitation and child support." He nodded in agreement.

"The other event was Roe versus Wade, which allowed for the killing of the fetus for any reason or no reason. Put those two together, and the American family is on the ropes."

"How long have you been married?"

"Let's see. We've been married fifty years and together for fifty-five, yes, fifty-five years. Let me tell you two bits of advice. First, the first fifty years together are the hardest, the rest is all downhill. And second, 'happy spouse, happy house.'"

Erma finished with her search on the smartphone, and I introduce her to the young fellow on my right, finished my second beer, and settled my tab (two dollars for the beers, one dollar for the pops, and two dollars tip.). That's another reason we love Detroit. We got on our bikes and rode home before it got too dark.

CHAPTER 59

Another Glass of Beer

Detroit, Michigan
September 2016

Erma and I slid onto barstools at the small brewpub on Abbott Street. There was not much in the way of ambiance, just a bar and stools sitting in the center of a hard angular space carved out of a warehouse; but it created some of the best brews in Michigan, and I had been thinking about a tall glass of draft Stroh. They were bringing back a traditional formula into the Detroit market years after the company had been bought up, the executives had moved out, and the facility was torn down.

Unfortunately, the barkeep informed me that he was out of Stroh's beer on tap, so I settled for a bottle and checked out the monitors for a game. Several college football games were on, but I didn't have a dog in any of the fights. The beer was good, clean, and crisp; and I was with Erma. All was well in the world.

A young white fellow entered and took a stool on Erma's side. He began to question the barkeep as to the beers and carefully chose an IPA, a bit hoppy, if my memory serves. As time passed, those of us at the bar talked beer and discussed the quality of different beers, pubs, hops, and techniques.

Erma asked the young clean-cut white fellow if this was his first time visiting this establishment. He confessed that he was new to

Detroit and was attending a weeklong conference on history and museums and something else I didn't catch because the group around the shuffleboard had roared with approval at a good point being scored. He reported to us that he brewed his own beer at home and enjoyed traveling to different breweries to compare with his.

Turning to face Erma, he asked if she was interested in history. She replied in the negative with a shake of her head but said that her husband (nodding in my direction) was interested. I had always fancied myself a bit of a history buff. Erma then asked if he taught history at a college or university.

"No," he confessed but said he was the director of a museum out west that chronicled the life and times of the Japanese Americans interned there during WWII. He asked Erma if she was familiar with this dark episode of America's past. She said she was familiar and nodded toward me with an invite to explain our family's connection with a story I was fond of telling.

"Actually, yes, we are familiar. You see, my stepfather was with Chennault during WWII, in the South Pacific, Burma, and the whole thing. He was a mechanic on the Flying Tigers and lost a lot of good friends during the war. He often told us stories about the friends he lost to the cruelty of the Japanese soldiers. To put it mildly, he hated them." The stranger visibly became agitated.

I then explained that my younger brother had fallen in love with a Japanese American girl and had planned on bringing her home, a little town in southeast Missouri, to meet the family. My brother was concerned about the reception and called me to discuss the situation. I told him that Erma and I would come down from Detroit and looked forward to meeting his future wife. I then chatted with my future sister-in-law and asked her about her family history. She told how her family had been interned in a camp during the war and provided some family history.

I started doing a little research and discovered that her uncle had joined the 442nd Regimental Combat Team, made up primarily of Japanese Americans from the camps, and had fought against the Germans during the war. He had received a medal for valor, and his unit had been highly decorated. Armed with this information, I met with my stepfather at the VFW hall for beer and talk (prior to my brother and new sister-in-law's arrival) and showed him the evidence. My stepfather was a great guy, and we had a close relationship.

He was interested in the information I had brought and, thinking about it, said he had heard about that unit. He said it was one of the most decorated units of WWII. I think all went well during their visit.

I had just read an article in *Military History Matters* magazine dealing with the Nisei unit (second generation with parents born in Japan) and how it also gained fame in Southern France by rescuing the Lost Battalion. The article told of how an American unit had pushed too far into German-held territory and had been surrounded and cut off. The Germans beat off repeated rescue attempts by American troops when the Nisei troops were called on to attack the entrenched Germans up the hill. They succeeded with high casualties; but unfortunately, due to the discriminatory wartime attitudes, they received lesser medals than due. This wasn't corrected until the 1990s. I was mentally composing my postscript when I was cut off by Museum Man.

"Yes, America was, in those days, was full of bigots and racists. You could say America was a nation of racists. Racism is based on greed and ignorance. They forced thousands of hardworking Japanese Americans from their homes, stole their property, and moved them inland to places like my museum. I work at the museum that was once an internment camp."

"Well, as I said, my stepfather changed his opinion. And the Japanese Americans, just like the German Americans in WWI, proved themselves loyal. It was hard, but those were different times. They proved themselves loyal Americans." I finished my little homily, and feeling pretty good, I took a long drink of my beer.

Museum Man's voice increased in volume with each word. Several patrons turned his way as he said, "America was built on racism and greed. That's the only reason we relocated them. There was no other reason." Several patrons stopped to listen.

"I don't know about that," I continued. "Hindsight is 20-20, but at the time, we had just been attacked at Pearl Harbor and our

Pacific fleet of battleships sunk. The Germans also declared war against us and were sinking our ships on the east coast. The Japanese were sinking our ships on the west coast, and a Japanese submarine even shelled an oil refinery on the California coast. Luckily, they didn't do much damage, but people were scared. The entire West Coast was in a panic, and this brings out the worst in folks."

"Bullshit. There was no legitimate reason to relocate thousands of loyal citizens except to steal their homes."

"Look, it was a bad decision on the part of FDR, one of his worst. But to say everyone was racist is just wrong."

"Bullshit," he said.

"No reason to use vulgarity. Just saying that you have to look at it from their times, from their point of view. And not all Americans were racists. We were in a shooting war against declared racism, and folks were scared, jittery about a possible invasion."

"Now that's f—g bullshit. There was no possible invasion. There was not one episode of a Japanese American engaging in espionage during the war. The hysteria, based on ignorance and prejudice, was just an excuse to grab their land." His voice was high and on edge.

"Look, let's keep it civil. There is no reason to use such language in front of my wife and the other ladies here, and I'm not sure if what you say is correct. Japanese were active on American soil—"

"Such as?"

"Such as, for example, keeping track of the comings and goings of our fleet in Pearl Harbor. There are other examples—"

That's a f—g lie. They weren't Japanese Americans. No Japanese American was ever arrested during the war for treason."

"Once again, watch your language, please. Let's not parse words. There were Japanese spies on American shores, and they were out to do us great harm, as in Pearl Harbor, by informing the Japanese Navy about the whereabouts of our fleet and our planes. Yes, many took advantage of the wartime hysterics. And a lot of loyal, abiding Japanese Americans were moved into camps during the war and suffered as a result, but—" I didn't get a chance to finish.

"Don't you f—g get it? The few engaged in espionage were Japanese military, not Japanese American citizens—"

I interrupted. "Right, but that's the whole point, we didn't know—"

He cut me off with "Bullshit! Why do you say 'we.' I don't want any part of that society."

"Citizens or not, *we* (I emphasized) were at war," I continued. "We were unsure who was loyal to their emperor and who was loyal to America. We were at war."

"Don't be stupid. Don't you know anything? I'm sick of the bullshit you are spouting, the excuses you are making for a generation of bigots and racists—"

"Look, buddy." Everyone in the bar had stopped their activity and were now listening to our conversation. Erma reached over and patted my right hand, which I had subconsciously balled into a fist.

She whispered, "Don't worry about it. He's obviously had too much to drink. Let it go and let's go home." Erma quietly tugged my arm as the other patrons silently watched in anticipation, waiting for the climax.

Museum Man started to respond. I never gave him a chance. I shot my right arm straight out in his direction in the universal gesture to stop, palm up, and said, "Enough already, this conversation is over."

Rising up from his barstool, he began to wag his finger toward me and began to loudly speak when several patrons, all unknown to me, objected with comments such as "Watch your mouth" and "The man said that's enough, leave it alone."

Someone from the shuffleboard group shouted out, "We don't need to listen to your loud mouth." Others chimed in with agreement.

He sat back on his stool in a daze. Turning toward Erma, he said, "Sorry if I offended you, but let me explain my position—"

"Enough," I said. "This conversation is over. May I have my bill, please?" The barman brought over two bills and laid the first down in front of Museum Man, who quickly paid and bolted from the establishment. Next, he placed my bill in front of me and nodded an affirmation.

"Where does he get off with his version of history? Good riddance," the lady at the other end of the bar commented loud enough for all to hear.

The Japanese Americans were given a raw deal during the war, and many Americans took advantage of the scare to take their land and property. They were forcibly relocated to degrading internment camps, and yet in spite of all that, they remained loyal and their young men fought and died for us. I'm proud of them and what they went through. My dad was first-generation American and was too old to fight in WWII, but he worked in a defense plant building bombers to smash the fatherland. I'm very proud of his generation, the greatest generation.

Really, Museum Man and I were not that far apart. It might have been fun to discuss the facts with him but for the fact that his position was frozen. Like so many young people today, they have a point of view, and if you don't agree, then they begin calling you a blanking idiot. *In Detroit,* I thought, *that might get you hurt or even killed.*

"I'm proud of you," Erma said. "You let it go. He's young and had too much to drink. Take your time, finish your beer, and then let's go home."

CHAPTER 60

Driving in Detroit

November 2016

T he new license tabs arrived in the mail for our two vehicles. Pulling a couple of tissues from a box, I headed for the garage, tabs in hand. Kneeling behind each vehicle, I used a tissue and a little spittle to clean the area of the license plate where the tab is placed on top of the old one. I carefully peeled the tab from its backing and affixed it on top. After smoothing it down a bit with my tissue, I pulled out my pocketknife and made a hard, quick X across the new tab. The blade cut deep through the tabs into the metal plate. Then another quick rub with the tissue, and I was done. I repeated the process on the other vehicle.

You might ask, "Why go through this ritual?" For years in Detroit, it was common for folks to have their tabs stolen from their rear license plates (Michigan doesn't require front plates.). Sometimes the bad guys would use a putty knife and carefully pry off the tab; other times, especially in cold weather, they would use tin snips and cut off the section of the plate containing the tab. The bad guys would then use the tab or sell it to a local, who would affix it to their expired plates, thus giving the cops no probable cause for pulling them over.

They then cruised around the city unmolested, for the most part, often on a suspended license with an expired plate and with no insurance (a three-fer). How is that possible? Because most police cars were unable to connect to verify the authenticity of a plate and a cottage industry had sprung up providing illegal tabs, phony insurance binders, and temporary legal insurance binders that were just good enough to get a registration from the Secretary of State but soon to lapse (more of a civil matter than a criminal one).

That's why drivers in Detroit not only have to carry no-fault auto insurance plus collision (if your vehicle is worth enough) but also coverage for underinsured and uninsured drivers. Don't drive in Detroit unless you have these additional coverages. That's why we pay some of the highest insurance rates in the country. It's another social tax for the privilege of living in the city (many Detroit folks use a relative's address in the suburbs for their home address, thus receiving lower rates).

I once, several years back, fired a counselor at a black community center for a litany of abuses and was ready to escort him from the building. He demanded that he be able to retrieve his personal files. I told him that I would have his personal items boxed up and send them to him. This wasn't good enough. He wanted his "shit" and he wanted it "now." I finally had to threaten to call the police and have them physically throw him out before he would leave.

Later, upon going through his desk and file cabinet, I found out why he was so adamant about cleaning out his own desk. I discovered, hidden behind a drawer, piles of blank insurance forms and corporate stamps with legal-looking seals. I gathered the incriminating evidence and contacted the local police and was told to contact fraud division downtown.

After another explanation, they, in turn, told me to contact the Michigan Attorney General or the Insurance Commission and so on. Finally, after holding on to it for a few months and having no interest shown by any agency, I filed the evidence in my office and moved on. Another bad guy got away with it.

If you lived in Detroit during this period, you learn to let things go. So much of your energy goes to just creating a good life for you, your family, and friends that little is left to right wrongs and to protect the general community. You do what you can, and say, "Oh, well." Life has a way of righting old wrongs on its own. I've never seen much reason to get involved in revenge or become a vigilante.

I am reminded that the Greeks had a goddess of vengeance, retribution, and punishment—the goddess Nemesis. She was a she-dragon summoned by a god to punish another. Eventually, she was slain by a hero. Each of us must personally slay her before we can move on. The only thing that vengeance gets you is more anger, killings, and death.

Hear me out. Stand up for your family and property, but don't lie in wait or plan vengeance on others because they wronged you. If you can prove it, use the police and courts and try not to use self-help. But if you do, be prepared for repercussions. When justice fails, you may have no other choice but to confront the bad guys directly and openly or fall back and regroup. Hatred eats the soul and robs life of its joys. Even in the midst of conflicts, one can withdraw to his compound and regroup and recuperate before sallying forth again to do battle.

Life in the city is a trip. Returning to the Michigan license plate tabs, I can't tell you the number of times I had exited from sporting events or a bar downtown to see car after car with a vandalized rear plate, excluding mine, of course. Granted, that was years ago, before the advent of cops carrying working computers in their vehicles; but old habits die hard.

The X slash through the tab meant that it couldn't be pried off in one piece. It fell apart in their hands. But more importantly, it told the bad guys that I was a Detroiter. There was no profit in stealing from me. You'll get nothing but grief for your efforts. Better to steal from others.

By the way, I was recently told by a cop that often, most of the computers in the patrol cars are down. Often, after pulling over a car with a bad plate and no insurance, they just have to issue another ticket and let the bad guys go merrily on their way. That's how we roll in Detroit.

By the way, if you are rear-ended or T-boned in Detroit, it's probably by some dude drunk or high on drugs driving on a suspended license and without a valid plate or insurance. Often the car has been "borrowed." "No way, man, I didn't know it had been stolen" is the excuse.

I understand that in San Antonio, and other cities, their similar problem was dealt with by a simple law. The car is towed away to an impound lot awaiting judicial action or eventual sale at a police auction. The illegal car is taken off the street, and the driver is arrested. Unfortunately, our liberal friends in Michigan don't have the guts to do what is right, so they just nibble around the edges of the problem and leave it to the good citizens to deal with it.

CHAPTER 61

Kneel or Stand—Fight or Flight

Detroit, Michigan
December 8, 2016

"Did you hear the latest about that football jerk, Colin something or other?" I clicked off the television and turned to face Erma.

"Yes." She thought about it, then said, "Oh, yes, that football player who refuses to stand for the national anthem. I remember him. What's the latest?" Erma spread out some colorful Christmas paper on the kitchen table and began to measure a gift for wrapping.

"Yeah." I nodded assent. "Yesterday was the 75th anniversary of the attack on Pearl Harbor. Our commander of the Pacific fleet, Admiral Harris, made some remarks that clearly fit this situation. He said something about how you can bet that the men and women we honor today, and those who died that day seventy-five years ago, never took a knee or failed to stand whenever they heard our national anthem being played. Not an exact quote but you get the idea."

Erma stopped her wrapping and looked up. "So what did the audience do? How did they react?"

"I understand that he, the admiral, got a standing ovation with a lengthy rousing applause. There was even whistling and shouting of approval reported. I'd say there was wild approval. This could never have happened a month ago, before Trump's win. People are feeling freer to express their true opinions and blast the PC crowd."

"Was that football player there?"

"At Pearl Harbor? No, I don't believe so. But I read that he had been recently seen wearing a shirt with the image of Fidel Castro on it."

"Great." Erma finished wrapping the gift and raised it admiringly for me to see. I nodded approval, and she continued, "He won't stand for our national anthem, but he'll wear an image of a communist dictator on it." She sighed and began the process of wrapping another gift.

"My opinion is quite simple. Do you want to hear it?"

"Sure," she said.

"You kneel and pay homage to our God. Or in a country with a king or queen, you may have to kneel, genuflect, or bow, depending on the customs. But we are Americans. We don't have an earthly king. We only kneel before our God. Our government is not a supreme being over us, its citizens. We stand, look squarely at the flag, place our hand over our heart, and pledge faith and loyalty not to the flag itself but to the ideas it stands for. A lot of men and women have fought and died to give us that right. The flag represents the very best and highest ideas for our country."

Erma nodded in agreement and said, "You've changed a lot from your anti-war student days."

"True, but you see," I continued, "it's the same old problem of the message, or the messenger, that has been confusing folks since the beginning of time."

"Continue," she said.

"The message is clear. All men, and remember that the term men embraces all women"—Erma smiled at the old joke—"are born equal under the law and have the God-given right to life, liberty, and the pursuit of happiness. Now that's the message. Unfortunately, humans, being what they are, obfuscate, confuse, and double deal for their own advantage and trample other's rights underfoot. They are often the messengers. It's the same with the Holy Mother Church and the string of bad popes we had during the Renaissance and the priests who violate their vows by abuse. You have to separate the message from the messenger."

"Is that why they tell us not to kill the messenger?"

"I think that's a whole different topic, but back to the culture war, for that is really what we have here. Trump has advocated that anyone who burns or defiles the flag, even though it is currently legal under a Supreme Court ruling, should be punished and face the loss of citizenship. To me, burning our flag is the same as issuing a challenge, the same as fighting words. They disturb the peace and can lead to a riot. You know, in Missouri and much of the South, you could use the defense that someone insulted your mother to justify your assault. Unfortunately, most northern and eastern states have not adopted the "fighting words" defense. I think we had a much more civil society then. You knew where you stood. You either fought or you retreated."

"You know"—Erma smiled—"you have many more options than fight or flight. For example, you can negotiate, postpone until you gain allies, lay a trap, surrender, meld into the background, and wait for the right moment. You don't always have to fight like some people I know."

"You females are very devious, you know that. I think women have a different evolutionary experience than men. I guess it's because you had the extra burden of taking care of the young when we men were off hunting, fighting, and drinking grog. I'll have to give your ideas some thought."

CHAPTER 62

Organized at Last

Woodbridge
Early March 2017

Tom and I came in, unwrapping ourselves from our early morning walk. "The dogs were good today," I posited. Tom liked to walk with Echo, the big Rottweiler.

"He is such a good boy." Tom ruffled Echo's head. Smaller Aero, a female Rott mixed with who knows what and jealous as ever, pressed closer to me for attention.

"Okay, you two, outside," I commanded and opened the rear door. They bounded out.

I quickly set tumblers on the kitchen table and filled them with water from the refrigerator (Detroit usually has some of the best tap water in the world, but for the past few days, we had been under a "boil emergency" due to a backflow problem at a pumping station.).

"Well, at least it's not as bad as Flint," he said.

I clicked on the stove's gas burner under the teapot, set out two juice glasses, and retrieved a container of Clamato juice, a bottle of Worcestershire sauce (just a dash), and a bottle of Tabasco sauce (just a drop or two) from the refrigerator. In a few minutes, we were each enjoying fresh hobo coffee and a virgin Bloody Mary.

We settled in at the kitchen table, the heart of our home, sipping our drinks and discussing the latest speech by President Trump when Tom said, out of the blue, "Dave, send me the site on the film you said I might be interested in."

On our walk, I had told Tom about a Russian film with English subtitles I had recently discovered on YouTube entitled *White Tiger*. I had suggested that Tom and his son Robert (also my godson) would find it interesting. I told him that it had some of the best tank battle scenes filmed and asked him if he had ever read *Moby Dick* by Herman Melville. He said he hadn't and wanted to know why I asked. I told him that he would see the connection if he watched the film.

"Send it to me with the link," he stated.

"It's just *White Tiger* on YouTube. That's all."

It was during this discussion that Erma came in to join us.

"Look at this"—I tapped Erma's spiral notebook open in front of her. Today's date topped the page followed by a neat list of items— "Erma, tell Tom about it."

"It's my to-do list. I made a New Year's resolution this year to really get my act together. This one, for example, 'Return bottles' was on yesterday's list, and I didn't get it done. So it goes on to today's list. This way I don't have to remember anything. It's on the list. What I don't get done one day carries on to the next and will soon get done. This is Dave's system, modified for me. He's been trying for years to get me to adopt it."

"Does it work?" Tom inquired.

"We'll see. It's part of my New Year's resolutions, and I'm working on it. This way I don't have to remember everything. I just look at my notepad. I've tried this before, but in the past, I would usually lose my to-do list. But this is more than a list. It's my goals and ideas about things that are important to me. Yes, I think it will work."

"Tom, I told her that it was her subconscious mind forgetting where she had left her list. You see, no list, no problems." I chuckled.

Erma ignored me and continued, "I was having serious problems remembering things and falling farther and farther behind. It was getting very scary." Tom nodded in agreement.

"I've always told people that you'll never know when I become a senile senior," I added. "I write everything down, make lists, use calendars and hooks—it makes it hard to forget. I pair things. For example, if I need to take some papers with me, so as not to forget, I put them with my wallet or pistol, something I will not forget."

"You won't forget your pistol," Tom stated.

"No, I'd feel naked without it." I continued. "As a young man, I had the opportunity to meet an old-time bureaucrat in Washington, DC. He was totally nonpartisan. I was doing some work for the Department of Education, and we struck up a fast friendship. I was probably the only one who had ever shown any interest in what he did. One afternoon, while visiting him in his office, I was amazed to watch him answering phone calls, fielding quick questions from people stopping at his door, reviewing memos, replying to supervisors, and giving instructions to secretaries and subordinates. I loved watching this faceless, nameless bureaucrat. (It was so long ago I honestly can't remember his name, though I did write it down in my notes.) He made the machine of bureaucracy hum, and I wanted to be like him."

"How do you keep it all straight?" I had asked him as he slipped on his jacket with a telephone receiver tucked under his chin to make a final call before leaving the office. During lunch, he showed me his yellow legal pad, dated and filled with notes, symbols, things to do, urgent items, and highlights and with stars next to items, scraps of papers taped, and odds and ends found on his desk or in his pockets at the end of a long day.

He explained how he kept track of his time on an hour-to-hour and, at times, a minute-to-minute basis. He pointed out how he returned a department head's call followed by an LM (left message). Date and time would provide cover if and when the department denied having received his return call.

"It's all about organization and cover," he told me. He said something like, "Remember, your job is to move paper and stay out of trouble. Once you get a reputation for organization, people leave you alone. Every organization has to have a few grown-ups who aren't worried about their ego or getting credit. They just want to get the job done."

He told me about the number of times his compulsive organization had saved his career. He confirmed dates of meetings, attendance, and what was said at them. It provided him cover when it hit the fan, as it often does when a project goes south. He explained to me how easy it was to review his notes at the end of the day and set up his plan for the next. And with the use of his calendar, he gave prompts for assignments due in the future; and this was all before the handheld computer.

"When I fill up one legal pad," he told me, "I review it and make sure there are no unfinished items. And then I file it. Each year I dump files that are at least ten years old for proper disposal. We have a company that comes around to our department twice a year to destroy confidential memos and documents."

"Why ten years?" I asked.

"Why not? I don't have unlimited storage capacity. Besides the statutes of limitations on my contracts I deal with run within a ten-year period. Look," he explained, "I'm a bureaucrat. It's my life. It's what I do. I organize, collect, control, and follow up so my bosses have time to come up with the big plans and ideas."

CHAPTER 63

Amtrak Ride

California, USA
March 24, 2017

"This train has literally run out of a track." Tom smiled as we left the Santa Barbara station and boarded a bus for a nighttime run up the Pacific Coast through San Francisco to Emeryville, California.

Compared to our spacious and comfortable seats onboard Amtrak, the narrow, cramped seats of the crowded bus were not conducive to comfort, much less sleep. I'm a guy who brags that "I can sleep on a pile of rocks," and even for me, it was hard to catch a cat-nap; and for Tom—even at best, a light sleeper—it was impossible. So we talked.

Tom and I continued an earlier discussion as to the history and etymology of the term *red-eye*. Tom read from several online sources the idea that it came from an all-night flight that left one's eyes red and bloodshot.

"I bid to differ," I said. "As a kid, I remember my brother-in-law Richard telling me about cross-country flights. He was a pilot, and when flying west, it seemed forever for sunset to finally go down, the big red-eye in the sky. You notice it's not called 'red eyes' flight."

"Your theory is nowhere to be found," Tom enjoined.

"Okay, just think about this, and don't look it up," I requested. "What does the common phrase 'ball to the wall' mean?" We spent the next few minutes in serious discussion as to the origin and meaning of the term. (My brother-in-law Richard had also told me that its meaning came from early pilots pushing the ball at the end of the throttle all the way to the fire wall. Give it the gas, so to speak.)

As the bus rumbled north in a pitch-black night up the Pacific Coast Highway, it would occasionally brake hard, jolting the passengers. It would suddenly exit the smooth road to make a brief stop at a small unnamed hamlet where someone got off or on then accelerate, turning and twisting itself back on the highway. Then there was another brief run until the next stop. All night long, we followed the Pacific Coast in darkness and light rain. I noticed all the passengers entered and exited from the front of the bus, leaving all of us in the rear alone for the full ride.

Tom began to fall into a slumber as I began to pick up bits and pieces of conversations around me. Looking around, I noticed my fellow passengers appeared to be a hardened group of young men, twenty- to forty-year-olds, a bit on the rough side. Each had his overhead bin stuffed with bags, boxes, and bundles; and I thought we carried a lot.

The constant yammering from several men soon became an ever-present distraction from sleep. They spent hours discussing the various sleeping accommodations, flophouses, SROs (single room occupancies), food banks, church pantries, and other handouts in Los Angeles. I must admit they knew the lay of the land. At times they whispered sensitive information, for the other's ears only; then at other times, they spoke loudly and laughed openly about doings of "some old fool" who ran a charitable facility.

These men knew the best corners for handouts, every hobo camp for miles around (I had thought they had died out at the end of the Great Depression.), and convenience stores with poor security where a snack could be easily obtained. It was a graduate course on petty theft and survival for the homeless.

One said, "Yeah, I don't get drunk no more. You've got to have your wits about you to live on the streets."

"Very true," the other agreed. "I mainly get high smoking grass and dope, but you can't do that every place."

"Listen, man"—I realized the man now speaking sounded older, more experienced, than his seatmate—"don't get too high or too drunk. I myself just stay, you know, slightly buzzed." I could hear the cap of a bottle being unscrewed and a liquid swallowed, then the bottle was passed to another and drinks were taken. "Thanks, man. Good stuff."

"Yeah, only the best." The older companion continued, "I haven't been really good and drunk in almost six months. Los Angeles can be a mean Mother. Got to keep your wits."

Finally, after exhausting Los Angeles, the older man took up San Francisco, which I gathered to be their final destination. "It's still damp and a bit cold up there."

"Yeah, San Francisco is always a wet Motherf—er this time of year. I almost waited another week or two. But then I heard you were making the run, and I said, why not tag along, you know? It's good to have somebody watching your back."

"Sure enough."

The next hour they discussed the best places to sleep out-of-doors (the parks, behind public buildings) and, again, the best locations for panhandling and committing petty larceny. It sounded like a course right out of *The Threepenny Opera*.

Not familiar with *The Threepenny Opera*? Oh, you should be. It's a light musical opera by the great socialist German playwright Bertolt Brecht. I understand he adapted it from an older English ballad-opera called *The Beggars' Opera*.

Everyone knows at least one song from it; actually, it's better in English than German. The hero's name, Mackie Messer, in German just doesn't cut it, so to speak. It sounds better as Mack the Knife.

Our hero marries the beautiful daughter of the King of London's army of beggars, and he runs a school for interns into the field. The play has everything: a corrupt police chief named Tiger Brown, Queen Victoria, and civil protests and riots. I had recently found a 1933 German film of the play with English subtitles and couldn't help but replay scenes in my mind to entertain me during the trip.

When I find myself unable to sleep or need to stay awake, I replay films, plays, and books in my memory.

The interesting thing is that the majority of these young men appeared to be white; a few of the quieter ones had the hue of the desert, and a few remained quiet with heads down or facing the windows. The whole thing reminded me of a strange migration of wild birds coming back from a winter in the south.

In the wee hours of the morning, the bus toured through San Francisco and finally came to a halt near a bridge lit up with lights. The group in the rear got up, stretching, and gathered their belongings and exited. The final leg of our journey was peaceful; and I got a bit of sleep, waking as the bus pulled into its final destination, Emeryville.

Tom and I gathered our things and exited a now almost-empty bus. I noticed one woman—well, more of a white girl—exiting our bus as we entered the Amtrak station. She carried a backpack with a bedroll. Her blond hair was braided into long dreadlocks, and her face was smudged with dirt. She made her way to a far corner of an almost-empty lobby and spread her bedroll on the floor and laid down, disappearing from sight. We had made it to Emeryville and, in about four hours, would begin our cross-country return home. We both spread out in the padded lobby chairs, but for the life of us, neither of us felt like sleeping. It was still dark outside, but somewhere there must be an open diner.

CHAPTER 64

Not-So-Public Restrooms

Emeryville, California
March 25, 2017

Unloading our bags, we surveyed the station. There was an older bearded gentleman seated near the door in a wheelchair. He had several bags around him. I wondered how difficult it would be for him to use his power wheelchair and carry all those bags.

In addition to him, two others were in the lobby: a young white woman and a Hispanic man. He sat, legs splayed out, with his baseball cap pulled low over his eyes. The lights were on in the glass-enclosed Amtrak office, but it was unoccupied.

A young lady (probably a college student) hugging a pillow looked around cautiously as she paced the area near closed snack bar. We had several hours until our train departed, and we stood debating whether we should take a nap, go for a walk, or have breakfast.

"Well"—I looked at my watch—"what do you want to do?"

"I don't see any lockers around, do you?"

I replied that I also did not see any.

Tom accepted the situation and said "We can't leave the station unless we check the bags someplace, and no one is in the office. I guess we wait."

"Okay, Tom. Watch my stuff, will you? I'm going to hit the john." He nodded his assent.

Pulling my toiletry kit from the front zipper compartment of my suitcase, I headed for the restrooms. The restroom door contained a sign stating that the restrooms were for Amtrak passengers only and that a token could be obtained at the office. I glanced at the office area. It was still empty. I then examined the door and noticed that it was slightly ajar. The lock had not completely latched when the door had last been closed.

Carefully, I turned the handle and applied gentle pressure inward away from the lock (I had always suffered from being too heavy-handed and had learned to control my actions). With a *snap*, the lock clicked; but it had locked outside of the latch, so I swung the door inward and entered the restroom. I then closed the door and heard the distinctive *snap* as the lock closed behind me.

After a shave, use of the urinal, a GI bath, hair combing, and teeth brushing, I felt like a new man. As a kid, I had read a book—I still remember the title, *Escape into Action*—by some famous WWII soldier. He said that a shave and a bath were worth five hours sleep. I believe him. I was wide-awake and feeling good to go. Exiting, I held the door open and motioned for Tom to come over.

"You have to be careful, when you exit, not to let the door lock behind you so others can use the facility." Tom nodded and entered, and I approached our luggage; but before I could reach our seats, the pillow lady approached me.

"Sir," she said, "I noticed that you were able to open the men's bathroom. I wonder if you could open the women's. I have to go really bad, and there's no one in the office to give me a token."

"Sure, I'll take a look. But you have to come and stand near me. In case someone asks why I'm monkeying around with the lock of the woman's restroom, you can explain that you asked me." She agreed, but unfortunately, the door was completely closed and locked.

"Look, when my friend comes out of the men's room, I will keep the door from locking, and you can use it. I'll stand guard. It will be all right. I've done the same for my wife under similar circumstances."

"I'm sorry, but I can't wait." She had a pained expression on her face and now had her legs crossed.

"Look, you wait here. I'll be right back." I've always believed that once you put your hand to a task, you own it and you have to follow through. If you don't think you can do it, leave it alone, and someone else will try. Well, I had put my hand to the task, so I walked over to the office area and pounded on the glass partition. A woman in an Amtrak uniform, startled from her sleep in an inner area, came out of an inner office. She came out scowling and a bit put off and said, "We're closed until one hour prior to boarding."

"The lady over there"—I nodded toward the restrooms—"needs a token. She said it's an emergency."

"Oh, all right." She slid a small brass token through the opening in the glass and turned back toward her inner office.

"Wait. While you're at it, the others here need tokens. Five more please." Cranky and unhappy about the interruption of her nap, she passed them through the opening and turned to leave.

"Wait, please. Where can we check our bags? We are going out for breakfast." She wasn't happy at all but said we could bring our luggage to a side office door, and after a fee of $5.00 per item was paid in cash, we could leave them.

I distributed the tokens to the relief of some now-happy passengers, and a moment later, Tom opened the men's room door. I gladly paid the $25.00 in cash (Tom carried three bags and I had two) and asked for a receipt, which I asked to be stapled to my ticket (always keep like things together).

"Now for a nice walk and breakfast," I said and turned to put on a coat when the pillow lady exited the restroom and approached, saying, "Thank you."

"No problem, my pleasure," I replied.

"Sir, the vending machines here"—she nodded toward the closed snack area—"only take cash. I only carry a debit card. I was wondering if…" Her voice trailed off. "I could really use a cup of coffee."

I reached into my right pocket and removed my special travel wallet, which is attached to my belt, but I didn't unzip it. "You seem like a bright, nice young lady…student?"

She told me about her college, her major, and explained how she was on her way home to see her parents for a long weekend. She never carried cash because it was so dangerous.

"I understand that you are an independent young woman, able to take care of yourself. But you can't depend on the kindness of strangers for your morning coffee. Look, there are a lot of bad people in this world. It's better if you go out prepared, as best you can, to cope with every situation, rather than approaching strangers."

"Oh" was all she could say. She looked a bit confused.

"My wife, Erma, is a very self-assured lady. Independent, you know. She travels often by herself and always carries a hidden money belt. She carries an extra credit card, identification, and cash, you know, just in case. She has backpacked through Europe on her own and never had to depend on the kindness of strangers for her morning drink, which is Diet Coke, not coffee. But you see what I mean?"

She nodded and said, "Oh, you are saying that I need to be, you know, better prepared if I travel alone?"

"Yes, that's exactly what I'm saying. Now, I can give you some money for coffee and a snack, but you may have learned the wrong lesson. In life, you can't depend on the kindness of strangers, even old men who appear nice, which may not always be true. Do you want some money?" I began to unzip my travel wallet.

"Oh, thanks, I think I can do without it this morning. And thanks too, Mr...."

"You can call me sir," I replied. I liked the sound of it. "Now you are sure?" I asked.

"Yes, sir." She gave me a big smile, and I thought she hesitated and almost gave me a hug, I understand that it's common in California for folks to hug one another, but I'm not much into that.

Nodding, I returned my wallet deep into its pocket; and Tom and I exited the station.

She said, "Have a nice breakfast," but in a nice way—not with sarcasm but like she meant it. And then she gave me another smile. A smile from a beautiful young woman goes a long way to lighting up the life of an old man.

CHAPTER 65

Somewhere in the American Rockies

March 26, 2017

The next morning, after a wonderful breakfast of Bloody Slavs, our variation of a Bloody Mary recipe that we had been perfecting for days. We made our way to the observation car. By the way, a Bloody Slav is made with Clamato juice, not tomato juice, with a dash of McIlhenny's Tabasco sauce and a double dash of Worcestershire sauce, (Remember, it must contain anchovies, not just salt, to be the real McCoy. Yes, made from those salty little fish that people hate having on their pizzas.) and a nice sprinkle of celery salt, a replacement for the celery stalks usually found in the drink but, sadly, subject to wilting on long train rides. And of course, there must be Tito's Vodka, named after the former strongman and dictator of Yugoslavia? Maybe, not sure, but it seemed to be a great name for our drink.

Discretely sipping our "coffee" from covered mugs, we watched the mountains, rushing rivers, and valleys emerging from winter's grip roll by.

"This is better than any movie or television program," I affirmed. Tom nodded, busy taking pictures with his cell phone and posting them to family and friends.

Noise on my right caused me to turn in time to see Ms. Dreadlocks come up the aisle, balancing a cup of coffee with one hand while grabbing chairbacks and folk's arms and clothing with the other as she tried to keep her balance as the train took on a sharp jerking curve.

One has to gain their "train legs," so to speak. Think in terms of sea legs. It's the same concept. You see the experienced passengers and conductors walking up and down the aisle, kind of rocking as they walk in a sort of duck waddle with feet out a bit more, their weight balanced and shifting to compensate for the train's movement and jerks. Ms. Dreadlocks stepped into a seat on my right and sort of stretched out on her legs and gave a loud sigh of relief.

"I know you from last night, in the station." She turned and scooted her knees closer to me, now almost kneeling on her seat. "You were with that dude." She nodded toward Tom, who busily ignored her, concentrating on his pictures and texts.

"I saw you talking to that lady with the big pillow and helping her and others get into the bathrooms, then you two checked your bags and left. Where did you go? Breakfast I bet. Did you go out to breakfast? I thought about asking, you know…" Her thought and sentence ran out of space and died. She leaned closer and began to pick a real and imaginary bit of lint from my jacket, then she smoothed a strand of hair back across my temple and tucked it under my gray fedora.

"Don't do that," I smiled and whispered.

"I'm Brigid," and with that introduction, she tore into a detailed life history that began with an abusive early home life and then as a runaway to California and then to the Baja Peninsula with her dog named Rex and an assortment of boyfriends and hippie-esque companions.

I interrupted her narrative to introduce ourselves and told her that I had also noticed her early this morning in the station unrolling her sleeping bag in the corner and getting some sleep.

"Oh no, I wasn't sleeping," she purred. "You have to keep your eyes open, especially when you are, you know, a girl traveling alone. I left Jim—he's a bit of a loser and a small-time drug dealer—with

Rex. He's my best friend, and I really miss him." Her eyes began to tear up on cue.

"Jim or Rex?" I inquired. "Which one do you miss?"

"Oh, Rex, not Jim. He could be a real mean drunk. Better to keep him high of weed, never mind about him." She paused to take a long drink, so I took the opportunity to imbibe in a little more of my special "coffee."

"I'm headed back to Battle Creek to be with my main man, Mike. He's got a thirteen-year-old, and he has a dog and lives on a small farm outside of town. I could put out an organic garden and, you know, sell my produce at a farmer's market. Mike is a good guy. He's older, probably thirty something. But that's okay with me. I like older men. I want a home and a family, you know, and a dog." She went on, nonstop, telling me about her uncle Hunter who thought she was a bad influence on his girls and had kicked her out. "Someday I'm going back. Mike and I are going to drive up to his house in a big new car, honk the horn, say we are just stopping by to say hello, and wave goodbye. And then we are going to drive off."

"You remember the lady, the one with the big pillow at the station? She was also traveling alone." I then told her the story about the coffee and her decision to go without in order to gain some independence.

"You're not going to give me any money, are you?" She shook her head negatively and dangled her blond dreadlocks. "Not even breakfast?"

"No, I'm not."

As if on cue, she turned away from me and began to engage the older couple newly seated to her right in earnest conversation. I returned my attention to the observations of the view from my large picture window, turned off the neighboring conversation, and sipped my special "coffee."

Only a moment later I heard the older lady reply to Ms. Dreadlocks with a loud and indignant voice, "I voted for Mr. Trump. We're Christians and don't appreciate your language."

Turning more to my right, I addressed no one in particular with "What a view. Just look at those cliffs. The sedimentary rock has unusual curvature and colors. Beautiful!" The couple got up with a huff and exited, leaving Ms. Dreadlocks in mouth-open, stunned silence.

"You've got to cut older folks a little slack." I nodded toward the departing couple as the made their way out of the observation car.

She looked back at me for seconds in open-mouthed silence, a very rare sight, and then she said, "Do you think I came on too strong?"

"I can't say. I wasn't listening to your conversation. But it's like this. You come from a different world, I dare say, a world of open drugs, a free and easy lifestyle, fun, no jobs, and drinking with little or no responsibility. Now you are entering their world where older white folks are hardworking and opinionated. Many don't like where the country is headed and voted for Trump. You have to be a little more understanding or they'll just get up and leave."

"See, I don't work because I don't need to. Everyone, including those people, loves me. They give me what I ask for and need— drinks, food, weed, money, rides, whatever I ask for. Most people are very nice, not like some."

I deflected the comment aimed toward me with "Don't many of these folks want something in return?"

"Sure, at times, some do. But it's up to me. Most young guys are, you know, sniffing around and on the prowl for a little, you know, for some action. But old people—you know, like that couple—they just want to give me stuff." She held up her coffee cup. "Like, you know, buy me coffee and breakfast."

Old people, my eye, I thought. They were both at least twenty years my junior, but she did have a point. Older folks, especially Christians, want to help others. I call it the lost puppy syndrome. They don't want to take it home, but they will give it a bone and send it on its way.

"It makes them feel good, you know. They have extra money, and I don't ever seem to have enough. So it all works out."

"Yes, that may well be, but I think you scared that couple off."

"No, they love me. They'll come back."

"You are willing to put your life, your hopes, and your dreams in the hands of fellow travelers in life. Take from them, and maybe sometimes, give something private back to them. That's an interesting philosophy of life. Don't you want a life of your own where you don't have to depend on the goodwill of others? Where you make it on your own?"

"You mean a job?" Even the word mushed her mouth up with its sour taste.

"Sure, what's wrong with that? Being a wife, maybe a mother, and having a home and a loving family. What's wrong with that?"

"Oh man, that's not for me. I want to live, to travel, to see the world and have some fun. You know, meet some guys. Maybe one will take care of me."

Tom had heard enough, and getting up, he discarded his empty cup and began to make his way back to our coach seats. "I wish you the best of luck," I said. "Take care of yourself." I took the last sip of my "coffee" and also discarded my cup and followed Tom back through the observation car.

That evening after dinner, I again noticed Ms. Dreadlocks in the cafeteria car with a group of a rowdy college students, busy collecting empty beer bottles on their table. Bursts of laughter came from the group as I made my way by. She glanced up, caught my eye, and quickly returned to her drink. I smiled and nodded recognition as I passed by.

On the way back to our coach, I passed by the couple who had left Ms. Dreadlocks in a huff. Stopping at their seats, I smiled and nodded good evening. The lady pursed her mouth and said, "That young lady still infuriates me." Her man looked over and smiled his greeting.

"Yes, she is a piece of work," I answered.

"You can't do anything with people like that. She had the gall to say that President Trump closed down the federal parks a couple years ago. He's only just gotten into office, still in his first hundred days. The young people today." She paused and said, "They have no sense of history or manners."

"True. Sad but true. You folks have a nice evening."

As I moved back through the cars, I pondered the sad truth that we are losing thousands of young people to drugs, welfare, and poor parenting. So many young people just seem to float around the country, living by hook or by crook. They applaud the progressive left, and when they do vote, they tend to vote left of the Democrats. There is so much surplus wealth in this country that they have found a way to live off government programs, the charity of churches, and the generosity of strangers. I've seen them panhandling along the streets of our cities, taking handouts, and moving on. *Well, God bless them,* I thought, *and I hope they grow up someday and find what they are looking for. Dear God, please take care of Ms. Dreadlocks and all the fellow travelers as they make their way across this country tonight.* Everyone is looking for a little happiness and a place to call home. I hope they find it.

CHAPTER 66

We All Come Together

Detroit, Michigan
May 2017

E rma and I came through the Dakota Inn doors at our regular
time. Others of our group came earlier to hold the round
table, while still others would arrive later.

"Hello. Hello and welcome." Greetings came from the early
arrivals. A frothing glass of beer was poured and placed in my hand.
Ah, yes, the Dakota Inn on a Friday night. Cold beer, warm friends,
what could be better?

Well into the evening, I went up to the bar to my regular standing position and chatted with the bartender about his college classes
and job prospects. While standing at the bar, I leaned against the
pillar, so as to keep an eye on the door for the arrival of additional
regulars. In that way, I could be the first to give salutations and offer
a welcoming beer.

The door slowly opened, and a strange character walked into
the entryway. He was a young small-framed black man dressed in
drooping pants and wearing gym shoes. But what caught my attention was the way he had his black hoodie pulled down low, covering his head with the drawstring pulled tight. Only a small area of
his cheekbones and eyes showed. He reminded me of the cartoon
character seen in the raunchy television comic series *South Park*. Not

only could we not get a good look at him but he also had limited his field of vision to a small circle straight on. He had lost his peripheral vision and couldn't see me and the group at the round table.

Carl, the proprietor, also noticed his arrival and courteously approached. The area has some street folks who wander in from time to time, when they are off their meds (street or prescribed). And they can usually be dealt with patience and firm guidance. We've been going to the Inn since the late sixties and have never seen a fight or problem that got out of hand. I am proud to say that during the late seventies I was the doorman (a.k.a. bouncer) and never had a problem I couldn't deal with without the use of violence.

Glancing toward the round table, where Erma sat with her lady friends, I caught her eye and glanced toward the door. With a nod of her head, she was up with her purse and moved to the end of the L-shaped bar on the other side of the pillar to my rear. She now had a clear line of sight at the door where the stranger was engaging Carl in conversation. We couldn't hear a word they were saying because of the music and singing coming from the main room.

With one hand holding up his pants, the young man's other hand went into the pocket of his hoodie where it grasped some object. I stiffened and glanced back at Erma. She recognized the danger and assumed a shooter's position with her hands hidden in her open purse.

Damn these gun laws, I thought. Michigan gun laws forbid a holder of a concealed-carry permit to carry while drinking. If you have to use your weapon after having a few beers, you are going to be in a world of hurt. It's a good law, I suppose; but I felt totally naked with the realization that I had slipped Erma my pistol in the car. She had placed it, along with her gun, in her purse. She had been my "gun moll" for years. As a teetotaler, she could legally carry in such an establishment because she did not drink alcohol and it served more food than alcohol.

Carl stepped toward the stranger to hear and was told something that caused him to immediately step back one or two paces. Now Erma and I both had perfect views of the situation. Erma, with her new .380 Kimber with laser sight, had a clear shot while I had what? Nothing. I decided to watch and wait. If he pulled a gun or knife, I could maybe rush him. But that would put me directly in Erma's line of sight. Thinking of no better plan, I imagined that I had my trusty weapon in a shoulder holster and moved my hand under my jacket and tensed in anticipation.

A quick glance told me that most of the customers at the round table were unaware of the situation. Only Ronny, who had recently arrived and not had anything to drink and was seated next to Erma's vacant chair, was intently watching the door with his hands under the table. He would have a hard shot with customers between him and the target, but he was the best shot at our shooters club. Erma was the only one with a clear shot.

Carl, shaking his head in the negative, mentioned something to the intruder, causing him to look around with a startled expression. With one hand still holding up his pants and the other in his hoodie pocket, the young man looked in our direction and saw several patrons, including me, glaring directly back at him, waiting and watching. The piano music and singing still poured through the establishment. I held my breath.

After a long second, the intruder glanced around again and quickly backed out of the door and disappeared. I heaved a sigh of relief and looked back toward Erma and gave her a big smile and a nod, knowing that she had my back, literally.

Carl walked over to the bar and, placing both hands against it for support, leaned down and took a deep breath.

"So," I said to Carl, "what went on? What did he say?" Erma closed her purse, slung it over her shoulder, and moved around the bar to stand next to us. Ronny now also joined us at the bar. It seems as if we were the only ones in the bar aware of the incident.

If Carl was a bit shaken, he didn't show it. In a remarkably calm voice, he said he would tell all. At that moment, John came around the corner from the main room where he had led the singing of the "Schnitzelbank," the signature song at the Dakota Inn Rathskeller. The barman had been watching John and listening to the music and seemed oblivious to the entire event.

I ordered a pitcher of beer and poured as I said, "Carl is just about to tell us what happened, but first he needs to call the police."

Carl left for the privacy of his office to make the call. He soon returned and said, in a matter-of-fact way, "I saw that young dude walk in, and to say the least, he was dressed suspiciously, almost like a terrorist or something. I came up and asked him what he wanted. At that point, he put a hand into his jersey pocket and said 'The money!' I stepped forward to hear better, with the music and all, and he said, 'You don't want to mess with me. Give me the money from the till.' I began to wonder if he really had a gun and stepped forward. He told me to step back, which I did. He made a final demand and said 'You don't want me to pull this gun.' I told him to look around. 'We don't have money in the till. Everyone uses debit and credit cards. There is no money.' He began to look around and saw you all at the bar and Ron at the table and left."

The police arrived quickly and talked privately with Carl then went to the parking lot to talk with the attendant.

The regulars gathered at the bar to analyze the incident. Erma was roundly recognized for saving the situation by taking immediate action.

"Would you have shot him?" She was asked.

"Probably not"—Erma paused, thinking, and then continued—"unless he tried to hurt Carl. I was glad when Carl stepped back to give me a clear shot. Yes, had he pulled a gun, I would have fired, not to kill him but to end the threat." Everyone raised their glasses and toasted Erma's bravery. I basked in her reflected glory.

One of the wives seated at the round table with her back to the door said to Erma, "I didn't see anything. Why didn't you tell me?"

Erma calmly replied, "There wasn't time. I had to get into a safe shooting position. Dave doesn't have his weapon, and I had to back him up." Then fixing her gaze directly at her friend, she said, "If I ever say drop, do it. Don't question it or look around. Just hit the floor. Okay?"

"Okay." Her friend nodded.

Ronny's wife came up to him and asked, "Did you have a gun on you?"

"It doesn't matter. At that point, I was legal. I hadn't had a drop of beer."

"But did you have a gun?" she persisted.

"I'll never answer that. I'm taking the Fifth."

CHAPTER 67

Dogs Go to Heaven

Woodbridge
Mid-June 2017

"How do you know when it's time to…time to…put him down?"

"That's a good question," I replied to Erma. "What did the vet say?" We were discussing the medical status of Echo, our "Big Guy," the Rottweiler we had…ah…inherited from our son, Bob (or should I say we had been bamboozled into accepting?). We had fallen in love with the old boy. He had settled into our routine and become a great house dog as well as an active cart dog. He would take passengers for a ride through the neighborhood. It was great fun. But over the past few months, he had suffered a series of ailments. In addition to limping, knots bulging under his skin, and soreness, he was becoming ill-tempered.

"The vet diagnosed him with probable bone cancer. The next step is to get him on an expensive nerve blocker called Gabapentin. If that doesn't work, we'll bring him in for x-rays and blood work. And then he'll be put under for an operation. I asked the vet, 'What if he has cancer?' She said, 'Then we amputate immediately. 'I fear,' she continued, 'that it is advanced in his right forepaw and onset in his left rear leg.'"

Erma asked the obvious question, "How is the big guy going to survive if they lop off his right front and left rear leg?"

"Not sure if he would." I sat in thought and continued, "I told her we want him to be comfortable and free from pain, well-fed and loved during his endgame. I told her there will be no amputations." I looked at Erma's eyes that were welling up in tears. "Do you agree?"

She nodded and left the kitchen.

We received a second prescription for Echo that afternoon. It was for an opioid named Tramadol with a sticker on the plastic container warning that its use "may cause drowsiness and dizziness. Be careful using vehicles, vessels, machines."

"Well, there you go, Big Guy. No more driving your cart while on drugs," I quipped and gave his muzzle and head a good rubbing with affection. Echo's days of pulling Erma and the neighborhood kids in his dogcart were over. Erma began to also pet and love on him.

"Well, he's on his meds, so he won't be in pain. He still has a good appetite and likes to sleep, so we're not going to worry about his diet. As long as he is comfortable and can move around from one area to the next—he can still make it up and down the stairs and go outside to do his duty—he'll remain. He's too big to carry, and he gets testy if you touch an area where he's hurting. So for the time being, we'll wait and see."

Echo's condition continued to worsen during the following weeks. Finally, he began sleeping outside, away from us. He had been sleeping on the floor in our bedroom, and I had to be careful getting up in the middle of the night because a black-and-brown dog was invisible at night.

Even Aero, the pesky little stray who loved to tease and torment the big guy, knew something was wrong and left him alone. While in the house, all he would do was get up, stagger to his water bowl for a drink or out into the yard to relieve himself, then plop down and sleep. His time was running out, and he knew it.

We had alerted all interested parties as to his condition and were surprised to learn how many people cared for him and expressed real concern. So we had a family telephone conference call, arranged by Erma, to discuss his condition.

Our granddaughter Selena took it the hardest (he had been her dog before she moved out for college). She was finishing her bachelor's degree at Trinity College in Texas and always wore her heart on her sleeve. Christina, our other granddaughter, was more pragmatic—what was in Echo's best interest?

Questions were asked and answered as to the vet visits, treatment, medications, and options. Selena asked if she could talk with Echo via Skype. Of course, she could. Everyone finally agreed, and I called the vet and scheduled an appointment for the following day at 2:20 p.m.

The process was quite simple. We helped Echo into the van, and Erma first stopped at McDonald's for his favorite treat: a cheeseburger with fries. Then we drove to the vet's office where I first checked in, leaving Erma to wait in the van with Echo and have some private time.

When everyone was ready, I went out to help escort him in. I was asked to use a muzzle on him and had a bit of difficulty getting it on and tightened. Once inside, he collapsed on the floor. The doctor was wonderful. She brought in two aides to assist. She said it was fine to leave him on the floor. We didn't have to move him up onto the examination table. We had had a problem with this in the past. Echo did not like being placed on the examination table and let people know it.

The vet got down on the floor and shaved the fur from Echo's rear leg, the one not in pain. He was panting loudly. The injections were performed, and his labored breathing slowed. Erma, who had insisted on being with him to the end, was given permission to remove the muzzle. She stroked him as he relaxed and passed on. The doctor listened for life with her stethoscope. Finding none, she pronounced him dead at 2:35 p.m.

Why do I bring up this painful subject? Because dogs are an integral part of our family and provide a layer of defense in the inner city. They make life better. But we become so attached they truly become part of the family, and then we have trouble letting go. Trust me, you'll know when it's time. Can the animal control its bodily functions? Can it move around the house on its own? Is it dangerous? Does it have a good appetite and enjoy the comforts of home? The endgame is important, and we should embrace a dying animal with loving care during this transition.

We asked for his ashes, and they are now on the mantel in Erma's room with the other dogs we have loved during our lives. Our son has promised to bury the ashes with us in our family plot down in Poplar Bluff, Missouri, though I'm not sure about Echo's. Should I ask Bob and Selena if either wants to be buried with him? I can't think of a better companion for eternity.

CHAPTER 68

Lawn Care and Maintenance

*Woodbridge
Late July 2017*

I had just finished the yard work and stopped to admire my manicured lawns and gorgeous flower beds when the sudden roar of an accelerating engine caught my attention. Coming fast, a red pickup truck with a damaged front end blew through the stop sign and flew through the Avery Street intersection. The driver, a young black man, sat wide-eyed and frozen in panic. Was it drugs, alcohol, or a mechanical failure? I didn't know.

"You IDIOT," I screamed and shook my rake at him as he flew by, gaining speed. The pickup hit the curb near my garage driveway, and I thought he would fly out onto Grand River and collide with its heavy traffic. But instead, the driver turned hard right and tore across the empty field, making a wide loop. I stood in amazement. He was still accelerating. The engine was roaring, and I thought, *My God, he's coming back—at me.*

I stood watching, transfixed, unsure which way to jump. The pickup left the grassy field and hit the street, going back the way it had come. Then it slid, and its rear end caught traction and headed straight for me. I stepped aside at the last second as the truck came up onto the grassy strip between the street and the sidewalk. Its left front tire smacked into the high curb and came to an abrupt halt.

The driver sat frozen, hands gripping the steering wheel, eyes wide in terror.

"You idiot!" I screamed again. "I'm going to kick your ass. You idiot, you almost hit me." I grabbed for the passenger door, and my presence seemed to bring him out of his trance. Seeing me, as if for the first time, he turned the wheels hard left. The engine came to life, and the truck bounced off the grass and over the curb back onto the street and again shot through the stop sign, now going back the other direction. Just as before, his luck held and the intersection was clear. I walked into the street and watched as he ran another stop sign and disappeared, going north on Trumbull Avenue.

"What happened?" Erma had opened a second-floor window and leaned out to get a better view.

"An idiot just blew through the stop sign at Avery, did a circuit thought the field, and drove up on my grass, almost hitting me. The idiot!"

"Are you all right?"

"Yeah, but look what he did to my grass!"

Picking up some of the tufts of torn sod, I tried to place them back and pat them down. Over the years, I've had numerous vehicles hit curbs, cut across my lawn, and once, drive through my garage; I was upset and pissed off.

"Just calm down," Erma intoned.

Looking back east toward Trumbull Avenue, I was surprised to see a figure walking toward me. It was the same guy.

"I see you, son of a bitch," I thought, or maybe said. "You're coming back. Well, come on. I've got something for you." Sucking in a lungful of air, I exhaled and started walking toward him. We met in the middle of the intersection, which he had blown through a moment before. We stopped about ten feet apart. I turned my left shoulder toward him, right arm cocked and fist balled, and said, "You almost hit me. You blew through three stop signs that I counted and tore up my lawn. What the f—is wrong with you?" I spit out my words.

"Look, mister," he said, "I knew I had to come back and...to apologize. I'm really sorry."

"What? You mean you didn't do it on purpose?"

"No, I swear. I only just bought the truck, and somehow the brakes failed. And I, well, I just panicked. I hit the brake pedal, and it went to the floor. I kept stomping and must have hit the gas. I'm really sorry, mister. I saw that open field and managed to slow it down. I got the truck out of gear and into neutral, and man, I'm really sorry. I almost hit you. I'm really sorry about your grass. If you like, I'll come over and help you. I'm really sorry. You were there shaking and yelling at me, and I panicked and drove off."

"How did you stop it after turning on Trumbull?"

"I hit and killed a fire hydrant. Smacked right into it and broke it off. Lucky for me it wasn't working, so no water came out."

"My goodness, are you all right?" The young man began to tremble and shake and began making little sniffing sounds.

"Yes, I'm just so sorry."

"Look, I'm all right—no harm was done, no big deal with the lawn. Look, no one was killed or hurt. Do you have auto insurance?"

"Yes, I've got car insurance."

"Good. It's not for me. We're okay. But you'll need it for the truck."

He gave me his name and said that he had an apartment on Trumbull. He had just got out of the Marines and came back to go to college. We moved out of the intersection to allow a car to pass and stood chatting on the corner.

"Look," I said, "you see me all the time working around here. Stop and say hi. When you see a group on the porch, stop and have a beer with us. In the meantime, call your insurance company. All is okay here, no problem."

"I'm really sorry."

"I accept your apology." Reaching over, I grabbed his left shoulder and gave him a reassuring pat. "Look, you're okay, I'm okay. There is a lesson here for both of us." We shook hands, and I walked back to retrieve my rake and work on the lawn a little bit more.

Strange how I was ready to fight. I was angry because of all the times I had been subjected to violence and not been able to fight back. I felt really bad, thinking the worst about my fellow Detroiter.

I could only imagine the courage it took that young man to come back and face me. I also knew that my anger and bad attitude had contributed to the problem, not helped solve it. I would give that some thought and prayer and work on my anger.

"I saw you go down the street after him. What happened?" Erma showed concern in her voice. "I came out to check on you and saw you two talking in the street."

"Yes, everything turned out all right. It was a mechanical failure on his part, and I guess I have to call it a human failure on my part."

CHAPTER 69

A Winter Tale

Woodbridge
Mid-February 2018

The snow, already a foot deep, kept falling, covering the several inches of hardpacked snows earlier in the month. Funny, I thought, how both Ash Wednesday and Valentine's Day both would fall on February 14 this year. On the one hand, our Catholic traditions demand that we sacrifice by giving up some of the frills and luxuries (like chocolate and sweets) for Lent; then on the other, our commercial culture expects husbands to give their wives flowers and heart-shaped red boxes of chocolates. To play it safe, I gave Erma flowers and gave up chocolate and evening snacks for Lent.

It was the Sunday before Fat Tuesday. The day before Lent begins when the snows begin in earnest. I had just come in from shoveling the sidewalks and helping to push cars out of the intersection. A cup of coffee and a glass of tap water later, I was back at it, reshoveling the sidewalks and pushing another stranded car.

I actually like shoveling snow. I have my own unique method. I push the snow forward with a big bladed shovel until it piles up on its curve. Then I make a ninety-degree turn and push the pile to the side, then from that point, I push forward again and then do another turn to the other side of the walk. This creates a crazy checkerboard pattern along the sidewalks. But on the way back, I take the cleared path to stand in while shoveling. It's my own practice. As far as I know, I'm the only one who uses it.

In shoveling snow, as with most lawn work, you immediately see the results of your labor. You plan the work then work the plan, and in no time, you have the job completed.

I was engaged in the process when I heard a rumbling, grinding sound and, to my amazement, saw a snowplow going down the center of Alexandrine. It shoved a ridge of snow and ice up against the vehicles parked on the street. This was the first time since the 1970s that I had witnessed a snowplow on the residential streets of Detroit. Next, I dug out my granddaughter, Selena's car, which was buried, and continued helping stranded motorists. That night, the temperature rose a few degrees, and the snow changed to a freezing rain and snow mix. It turned cold again, and everything froze solid.

Selena and I ventured out to the Polish Club in Warren for a traditional Polish dinner. We were invited by the Dakota Inn's Just Right Club to join their members and lady friends for dinner. The Just Right Club is a male-only club, but once a year, it arranges an outing in which the ladies are invited to attend. Erma had decided to stay home, having just been advised by our doctor that she had tested positive for strand A of the flu, a virus that was then sweeping the country. Yes she had her flu vaccination. So Selena took her place.

We enjoyed the traditional Polish dinner and purchased a variety of paczkis (pronounced sort of like a *punch* then a *ski*) to be eaten before Lent. By the time we got to our neighborhood, everything was snowed in and locked tight with ice.

Our van hung up making the turn in our intersection. Selena immediately hopped out without asking and, lickety-split, grabbed a shovel and began digging out around the tires. And then she grabbed a handful of salt from the bag kept in the rear of the van and threw it under the front wheels. A gentle rocking forward in low gear and then backward, and we soon were around the corner and safely home with our van in the garage. That's our girl! Freezing rain continued to fall throughout the night.

By early morning, the weather system had moved east into Canada, leaving a four-inch layer of ice covering the neighborhood. I first tried to move it with my big snow shovels, but no luck. The layer was frozen solid on the walks, steps, and porches.

Abandoning the snow shovels, I went to the tool shed and examined my options. There in the far corner stood an old coal shovel that I had inherited from my father. It was rusty with a well-worn wooden handle. I hefted the shovel, and my hands slid along the same wood that Dad had touched generations ago. I would go old-school.

I positioned myself on the sidewalk and slammed it hard into the ice on the walk. The heavy steel bit through the layer and under the ice. I then used the shovel to leverage up, and a large section of ice rose and snapped off. It was easily flipped off to the side.

It was real work, honest, I was sweating with the same tool my father had used generations earlier. My gloved hand gripped the same slight depression caused by thousands of movements. I was happy and at peace, just taking my time and working up the sidewalk, when I heard tires spinning freely on the ice. *Ziz-zzzz, ziz-zzzzz,* and finally, *ZIZ-ZZZZ* as the driver gave it the gas. The tires spun helplessly, sinking deeper in the ice. Steam and smoke poured out from the buzzing tires.

"Hey, buddy," I called and cautiously approached. He took his foot off the gas and allowed the car to idle. The driver was a well-dressed middle-aged black man. The car was an expensive late-modeled sedan and pretty useless in this stuff, especially the way he was driving. His front wheels were turned to make the turn in the intersection.

I guess he didn't hear me with the noise and all, so I rapped on his window. He jumped and looked at me with big eyes frightened at the sound. I stepped back and motioned for him to roll the window down. After a moment of reflection, he complied. He was fully alert, his cautious eyes measuring me as he sized up the situation. Could I be trusted, or was I a threat? I had already decided that he posed no threat to me. His tan cashmere topcoat half covered a briefcase on the passenger's seat. I had priced them out last year, and they began at over $500. He was no threat.

"Okay, buddy," I said, "let's see if we can get you on your way."

Stepping back, I assessed the situation and began to pry and dislodge chunks of ice and snow from beneath his frame and away from his wheels. The snow shovel's long handle quickly freed the vehicle and cleared a path to escape on. After a quick circling around the car, I again stopped at his window and again had to motion for the window.

"Okay, first straighten your wheels…no, the other way. That's got it. Okay, now, nice and easy, put it in the lowest gear."

With a dumbfounded look, he said, "Drive?"

"Does your car have low gear? Often you have to put it in Drive, then move the gear lever just so." I showed him with a hand motion.

The "D" on the instrument panel changed to a "D1."

"Good," I nodded. "Now gently, don't gun it." I leaned into the doorframe and said, "Now." The car moved forward a few inches. "Now put it in into Reverse. Easy does it." The car rolled back a good twelve inches before spinning.

"Go forward, don't turn. Go straight onto Grand River. Stay in the ruts, and you'll make it." I tapped the top of the car and stepped back out of the way.

He nodded assent and smiled and said, "Thanks, mister. Do you live around here?"

"Yes," I nodded and turned my head toward the corner house. "I've been here forever."

"Can I pay for your trouble?"

"No, it was my pleasure. Just trying to help."

"You say once I get moving, I just keep going to Grand River?"

"Yes, you can get on easily there. Good luck."

"Well, I want to thank you again. Not many people would help someone, a stranger, you know."

"This is a great neighborhood," I said. "You know, neighbors helping neighbors."

I gave him a final push, and his car gained traction on the icy path I had cut. I smiled and waved as he rolled forward and got into the ruts and disappeared. I hope he remembers to get it out of low gear.

After a break, I resumed the clearing of the ice from the sidewalks. A corner house has both good and bad points. On the good side, you have more space for planting bushes and flowers. On the negative side, there is more lawn to mow and sidewalks to clear. Oh well.

A half hour later, I had worked my way to the front of the house when a passerby stopped and asked, "Mister, I'm a little short for bus fare. Could I get a buck from you?"

He was a young well-dressed black man. He was wearing an expensive Carhartt jacket and good work boots with the laces untied. Many of the young black men in Detroit have an interesting dress code. They wear traditional high-quality work clothes and boots but do no manual labor.

"No, I don't give out money. But if you need to make a few bucks, I can find something for you to do."

"Like what?"

"Oh, you can continue the progress of removing the ice from the sidewalks. Here, let me show you how it's done." I forcibly slammed the coal shovel under the ice sheet and lifted up, breaking off a large section. With a turn of the wrist, I flipped it off to the side. "See? You try."

He took the shovel in hand and struck the ice, sending a shower of icy shards off in all directions, but the ice sheet remained intact. He took a few more licks and handed the shovel back and, with a smile, said, "No thanks, mister, too much like work. I'll go to the gas station, and someone will give me some money." With a smile, he sauntered off down the sidewalk and out of the neighborhood.

CHAPTER 70

I've Seen It All

Woodbridge
January 2019

Detroit was basking in a beautiful respite from winter, with temperatures in balmy low fifties, with plenty of sunshine. It was a rare and blessed winter thaw that pushed Detroiters out of doors. I was raking up the leaves and trash revealed by the melted snow when a white cargo van pulled into the side drive in front of the garage, setting the dogs to barking and howling.

A stocky middle-aged man, looking to be of Middle Eastern descent, got out of the driver's side and pulled his stocking cap down low over his ears said, "Hey, mister." He walked toward me, "Mister, you don't remember me, do you?"

I took his measure and thought, *Work clothes, Carhartt quality but not worn. Ethnicity probably Middle Eastern. Language, born here or longtime resident.* And then I said, "Can't say I know you. What's your name?"

"My name's Frank, Frank Wilson (an alias?). I did some work for you a few years ago." He stuck out his hand, so I gave him a bone-breaking handshake and asked how he was doing. His hand was soft, and I doubted if he'd ever done an honest day's work in his life.

"I suppose I'm all right, and you?"

I stepped back and moved the rake between us, holding it casually in my left hand, and answered, "Fine," and followed it with a Missouri phrase, "What can I do you for?" I found that changing the order of the last two words also changed the meaning.

"I'm not doing so well. My dad passed, and my mom is taking it hard (sad face). I've got to spend a lot of time taking care of her and keeping up her house too. She's a basket case."

"Sorry to hear that. When did he pass?"

"Uh." He thought a bit. "About six months ago."

"Yes, it's really hard on a couple who've been together for a long time. How long were they married?"

"How long?" he repeated. Thinking hard, he said, "Fifty or fifty-five years—anyway, a long time."

"Yes, it's difficult. But she has you, and I'm sure you'll do the right thing by her."

"That's what I'm trying to do, make some extra money for my mother. I do most of my work in the city now, and I just finished up a job nearby. I've got seventy pounds of high-quality exterior acrylic solution left over. It normally sells for eighty dollars a pound, but I need to get home and check on Mom. I'm willing to do the exterior work around here on your basement window frames and interior basement walls for six dollars a pound. We can do it right now." He turned to walk toward his van. He signaled the passenger, a young black man who got out and came around to the side sliding door, and started to remove gallon buckets from the interior to the sidewalk.

"Hold on," I said. "Sorry, but I never have any exterior work done in the winter."

"But it's a beautiful day," he objected, "and this stuff dries immediately."

"Well, let's walk over and look at the product." I was curious to see the label on the bucket and maybe get his license plate number.

The dogs started going nuts again and were just behind the fence when he asked, "Will those dogs bite?"

"Yeah, sure, all dogs bite (my stock answer). The little female is only eighty pounds, but she's mean as sin. The big guy is my granddaughter's pit bull and as tough as they come. But if you worked here in the past, you will remember that I always introduce the contractors and tradesmen first to the dogs. You would stand there, and they would sniff around you, get your scent. Then you close your fingers and put your hands out, palms down, like this," I demonstrated. He was becoming more and more anxious by the moment. "They again sniff you, and if they lick your hands"—he cringed—"then you are all right. If they don't, then you don't get the job."

"All right," he said while opening the driver's door and instructing his assistant to place the bucket back in the van, close up, and get in. He quickly backed out and drove off in a hurry.

Normally, its spring when the con men and scam artists, along with the crocuses, come out. Property values are rising in the old neighborhood, and folks are making home improvements. Old folks are seen as easy marks. His was a classic ploy, and it should have worked.

First, the con man establishes a bond with the mark (e.g., "I worked here a few years ago" or "I just finished some work at a neighbor and have some leftover materials").

Second, he tries to get your sympathy: "My dad just died" or "I'm trying to make some extra money to help my dear old mother."

Third, "Such a deal I have for you. This is a onetime offer. Take it now or else… It normally costs $70 a pound, but just for you, I'll give it to you below my cost so I don't have to return it." You get the idea. Everyone wants to save money, and the con man plays on the mark's greed.

There are many variations to the script, but often, they make a deal for cash and are often invited into the home to be paid. Often, one will ask to use the restroom or a telephone or will ask for a drink of water and wander about, checking out possible items of value. Even if they don't do the actual B&E later on, they sell or trade information with others who specialize in that sort of work.

The city is full of scams to be aware of. Over the years, we've had trouble centered in and on the corner gas station. We've seen everything from shootings, robberies, beatings, drugs, drinking, carjackings, fights, and loud music late at night come from the station.

Recently, on a cold evening, I noticed the tank in the little Chevy HHR was low and asked Erma to ride with me to the station. The lot was filled with an unusually large number of vehicles jockeying for position at two pumps where two young black men were directing traffic, gassing up vehicles, and accepting cash (strange, to say the least).

Another white man was in line in front of me. He got out and walked toward the convenience store office, ignoring the young black man's offer to fill his tank "at a discount." With a firm "No," he gassed up and sped away. Erma slipped her .380 from her purse as I said, "Lock the doors and keep your eyes open." She nodded in the affirmative. I knew I didn't have to say anything, but it made me feel better.

On the way in, I saw the cashier ensconced behind bulletproof glass in the convenience store, watching the activities in the lot. I was then asked by the man at the pump, "Say, man, you want some gas? I can help you."

"No thanks," I said. "I pay my own way." As I walked by, the expression on his face changed to a dumbfounded look of disbelief.

"Whatever, man," he replied.

All the customers were young blacks driving upscale and customized vehicles with lots of chrome and expensive wheels. They probably learned of this scam via social media and were told to come to a certain location and bring cash. As I gassed the HHR up, an older black man pulled in on the opposite side and leaned out, saying, "What's going on here?"

"Look, mister," I said, "it looks like a credit card scam. Be careful."

He nodded thanks and ignored offers to pump his gas and went in to also pay. As we pulled away, Erma sent an e-mail to a police officer friend, explaining the situation, and asked if the fraud division could do anything.

A few weeks later, the place was raided and a variation of the theme of credit card fraud was discovered. In this scenario, scores of gift cards were obtained with stolen credit cards. The gift cards themselves were legal, for a short time. They, in turn, were used to purchase gas at the station. Such is life in the big city.

CHAPTER 71

Late for Her Own Funeral

Woodbridge
February 2019

I have German heritage. Have you ever heard of the term *punktlich*? Roughly, it translates as being punctual; but in our family, it was more so.

I remember once, in grade school, I was coming back from a Boy Scout meeting and a little late. Our Sunday suppers were promptly at 5:00 p.m. I ran home as fast as I could and entered the house as the clock began striking the hour. My mother stood at her place nearest the kitchen door. My two older sisters sat at their places, hands folded. My little brother sat in his chair at the other end of the table from my father. I made it to my chair as the last chime sounded the hour.

My father looked at me with disapproval and said, "Almost late."

In our family, one had to be five minutes early to be on time.

Later, I met Erma and her family. They came and went as freely as sparrows in a courtyard. No one seemed to have any notion of timeliness. Their Sunday dinners began earlier and lasted later with relatives, employees, friends, and customers dropping by, eating, drinking coffee, having dessert, and departing. The foods stayed on the stove and in the oven as people came in and made themselves feel at home. It was a different world, and I loved it.

Over the years, I can't tell you the number of times I called out to Erma that we were going to be late and sat in the car waiting for her. I told her that she was born late and would even be late for her own funeral.

When we moved to Detroit, I often found myself sitting alone in an office or a conference room, having arrived early for a meeting. I always said that if I was even in a position to control meeting schedules, we would start and end on time.

Later, in my career, as I began to accept the position of secretary for various boards and committees, I learned a valuable lesson: The Detroit culture runs about fifteen to thirty minutes late, so if I want a meeting to begin, say at 8:15 a.m., I would schedule the meeting to begin at 7:45 a.m. with breakfast, plenty of coffee and juices, and lots of pastries. Detroiters love free food and drink. The actual agenda would begin at 8:15 a.m. and end on time. I would arrive early to make sure everything was arranged—tables, seating, food, coffee, materials, signage, etc. No detail was too small or insignificant. As I began to take over the control of more and more meetings, I remained in the background, always seated at the right hand of the chair or president. I was ready to take notes and look up information. I also became a compulsive notetaker.

As I ran around Metro Detroit attending meetings and visiting sites, I couldn't help but be occasionally late. I learned to tap down the anxiety of being late with a call to the office, and my secretary would call to say that I was on the way but caught in traffic and so on.

In 1986, I leased a Mustang convertible and installed a wireless telephone (this was before cell phones were common). I also learned to keep reading materials, journals, texts, etc. in the car at all times, in the event I was caught when someone else was late. There is a pecking order in Detroit: the senior management can keep the subordinates cooling their heels but not the other way around.

It was only after retirement that I recognized that much of my anxiety about being late was due to childhood upbringing. Now if we were late, so what? With the exception of church and an occasional film or play, there was nothing to be late for. I still kept reading material around just in case I had some free time (*Military History* and the *Rifleman* were two favorite magazines.).

As Erma prepared lunch, I asked her if, as a girl, she had watched the *Twilight Zone* television series in the early sixties. It had not been a family favorite, but she had seen it.

"Well, I'm recording them and watch one a day while I do a set of exercises. They are really fun. I saw many of them in the early sixties…good entertainment."

"That's nice."

"Well, I was thinking about a *Twilight Zone* episode I'd like to write and direct. Do you want to hear about it?"

"Sure."

The setting is a hallway. A man is seated in a large ornate chair, his foot restlessly bobbed up and down. He looks at his wristwatch and called up the stairs to his wife. "We're going to be late again." He sighs to himself and thinks about being late again. "We're running late," he calls out.

"Go out and warm up the car. I'll be out in a few minutes" comes the response from the second floor. He examines his watch yet again, and the camera goes in for a close-up. His face is etched with the frustration of waiting. The camera (everything is in black-and-white) pulls back and pans the room to show, first, a loudly clicking clock, three minutes past eight o'clock when it comes to rest on Mr. Rod Sterling, the host. He's standing in a corner and casually smoking a cigarette (remember, this is 1960). He makes his usual utterances about a trip into the *Twilight Zone* and breaks for commercials."

In the next scene, the husband we met earlier is seated at a booth in a busy cocktail bar. The camera shifts from him to another man chatting with two ladies seated at the bar. He pays for his drinks and carries them over to the booth. He sits the fresh drinks down, moves two empty glasses over, and slides in next to his friend.

"Wow, the joint is jumping tonight." His friend nods in response. "Two lovely ladies at the bar expressed an interest. Are you up for calling the little missus and telling her that you will be working late? Say, what's the matter with you? It's Friday night, and we had a tough week with that Conner account. But we got it. It's time to celebrate."

They chit chatted about the snow, and the husband says he had better get going if he is going to be home on time for dinner. His friend says that women need to understand that men are in the trenches fighting to bring home the bacon. "We can't be tied to a short leash. If we need to stop off for a drink or two, then let the little lady put the roast back in the oven."

"That's not my problem. All I have to do is call and tell her I'll be late. But I'm always on time. Tell me, what do you do when your wife is always late?"

"That's easy. I give her a good dose of my being late but always with just cause—example, working late on the Conner contract.

"Drink up. Ready for another one?"

"No, I've got to get on the road."

"That's your problem. You're henpecked. Give her a taste of her own medicine. Don't call home. Just come in late and see how she likes it. Tell her there was an accident on the way home and you had to wait for an ambulance to arrive. It was awful."

Fade to commercials.

The next scene is at the same cocktail lounge but not as crowded.

The two men are seated in the same booth, and a waitress takes their drink order.

"Tell me," said the friend, "how did it work out last week with the little woman? You know, when you had to work late and then there was an accident on the highway?"

"Not so great. She said she was frightened that something happened to me on the way home. She sat by the telephone for hours, praying that I would be all right. She was so relieved when I came in she had forgotten to fix any dinner. I had to fix us an omelet and toast, she was so upset."

"I see. You've got quite a girl there. She plays it well. All right, two can play at this game. We'll move it up a notch. You need to really teach her a lesson. Are you still planning on taking her with you to the buyer's convention this Friday?"

"Yes, she is really looking forward to it. I checked, and there is no extra expense if I have a guest. They didn't even care if it was my wife."

"Is she still in the habit of being late?"

"Yes. I think she was born late. I tell her that she will be late for her own funeral."

"Right, here's what you do." Camera backs off, showing the man's friend in consultation, and fades to commercials.

The new scene shows the husband is on the telephone with his wife. "I know. I'm sorry, but I have to get the report out before I leave. It will be all right. Just take a cab to the airport. Remember Gate 19, Pan Am. I'll head to the airport as soon as I'm finished and will meet you there with your ticket. Just don't be late. Planes don't wait. All right, see you then. Love you. Bye." He hangs up, and the camera backs up, showing him at the airport terminal with his friend. They have already checked in their bags and each carries his briefcase.

"Nothing to do now," the husband said, "but to have a drink and wait and see if she arrives on time." Scene fades.

In a new scene, their glasses are empty when the loudspeaker announces, "Pan American flight boarding at Gate 19. Business passengers may board."

"She hasn't arrived." Both men look around the gate area. "No, I guess not."

"Okay, let's get onboard and find our seats," says the friend.

"Maybe I should wait. We can always catch a later flight." The husband is undecided.

"Sure, but then what have you taught her? She's beaten you. I know women. I've been married three times, and if there is one thing I know about women, it's that you have to be in control, take charge. You have to have the upper hand." The friend gets up to leave.

The camera fades back and captures both men getting into the line of boarding passengers. Each is carrying his briefcase.

The new scene is onboard the plane. The captain comes on the PA and tells passengers and crew to return to their seats and fasten seatbelts. The turbulence in the plane increases. Overhead bins pop open, and two briefcases tumble to the aisle. Passengers are screaming in terror.

The husband, seated at the window, looks out as a bolt of lightning strikes the plane and an engine flares out. The plane begins a rapid descent. He looks at the empty seat that should be occupied by his wife and chuckles. Smiling, he says, "Late for her own funeral."

"What?" screams his friend as he grabs the armrests in white-knuckled fear. The camera has close-up.

The camera moves to a close-up of the husband. He is calm, tranquil, especially under the circumstances. "Oh, I just said that she'd be late for her own funeral." Fade to darkness.

In the final scene, the camera focuses on a distant scene of smoldering debris scattered across a muddy field. Firemen are putting out the last flames.

The camera swings to Mr. Sterling, still smoking a cigarette. "A valuable lesson has just been learned in the *Twilight Zone*." Fade to darkness.

CHAPTER 72

The Endgame

Woodbridge
Spring 2019

I stood on the back porch this morning, drinking a cup of hobo coffee, and watched as heavy gray clouds rolled in from the west, snuffing out the sunlight. Soon snow began to fall; and in minutes, the grass, rooftops, and sidewalks were covered in a thin white frosting. Quickly, the clouds raced east across the Detroit River into Canada. Soon thereafter, the radiant sunshine appeared to melt the freshly fallen snow.

This is a metaphor for Detroit. It's coming out of a deep hard winter of discontent. We are living in the early spring like days of the rebirth of a great city. We have lived in the heart of a declining city for the past fifty years. We know that the frigid cold of racism drives people to abandon their homes and neighborhoods and leads to economic despair that wrecked and destroyed a once-proud city. I, like everyone else, was sold a bill of goods that said race was the most important element in American life. Because it was believed by all, it became so. In truth, I've learned over the years that it is probably the least important. Middle-class families—black, white, Hispanic, and Asian—have the same drives and desires for their children. During the past half-century plus that I've lived in Detroit, the overwhelming majority of my clients have been black and Hispanic. I've come to know and respect the overwhelming majority, while the most vicious criminal elements in our neighborhood were Southern whites, abandoned in the city by the retreating tide of white neighbors.

We live in an ideal location on an international waterway directly north of Windsor, Canada. In a few hours, we can be in the Northwoods, camping, bicycling, canoeing, and communing with nature. In four hours, we can drive to a score of major Midwestern cities or, within a few hours, fly to the majority of destinations in the USA. We have decided to remain and live out our retirement years here. We have survived the worst and now intend to enjoy living in (what we hope and pray will soon be) a world-class city. Soon the leaves will bud and the flowers reappear. Detroit is on a comeback.

Our son, Bob, and wife, Linda, a marathon runner and a real foodie (believe it or not, they are not mutually exclusive), came for a visit last month. In addition to a family visit, Linda wanted to visit Al Almeer's restaurant in Dearborn (the winner of the Beard Culinary Award for new restaurants). After an exquisite Mediterranean meal, we visited the new Japanese world-class restaurant, the Katsu, on Trumbull Avenue in Woodbridge for tea and sake. (Linda was so impressed that she returned for a traditional Japanese dinner.) The next day was followed by a full seven-course meal at the Prime and Proper Steak House in Downtown Detroit. (I was told it is very expensive, but I was not allowed to see the tab or give the tip.) It was one of the most memorable meals we have ever had, but in truth, I am blue-collar in taste and attitude. But it's nice to know that such a restaurant exists only a few minutes away. After a wonderful meal, we stopped by the new Shinola Lounge for drinks and conversation. (I still can't believe the price of a cocktail.)

For years Erma and I discussed our endgame. Where did we want to wind up during our declining years? We traveled around the country and asked, "Is this the place?" Thus far, we have never found a better place to live. Sure, in the past, other places had far less crime, better city services, less political corruption, lower taxes, and better job opportunities—but it wasn't Woodbridge!

Why stay in Detroit? Now that our community is hot, hot, hot, and the homes values rocket skyward, we stay to enjoy the remainder of our days. I have to figure out a way to make peace with the majority of my left-leaning neighbors and stop using so much self-help. I'll be glad when I can keep my weapons locked in a safe, but that day has not yet arrived.

We believe in the rebirth of Detroit so much that we purchased a Ford 150 pickup truck to pull our little seventeen-foot trailer on camping trips. Why is this important? Because it is too big to park it in the garage at night. For the first time, I have a vehicle that I must park on the street. Thankfully, Bob's Christmas gift was two ring cameras that I mounted, one to monitor the front porch and the other to keep an eye on the new truck. At night, bright lights come on to record all movement in the area. Someone parked his vehicle next to our new truck and started to break in by jimmying the plastic panel between the driver's window and rear window. The light came on, the camera was activated, and the miscreant drove off in a hurry. It's still not a perfect world, but it's getting better.

It's hard to believe, but the city had a team of tree trimmers on our block cutting down dead limbs. Last winter, a dead limb fell during a windstorm and smashed the cab of a neighbor's vehicle. We have asked the city for trimming services for years with no luck. With Erma holding the ladder, I extended my reach to cut limbs; but it was never a truly professional job. Will wonders never cease? We've lived here for over fifty years, and this is the first time I've seen the city take care of its trees.

We purchased electric-assist bicycles last fall, and yesterday, we completed our first ride of the year. E-assist means that you must still pedal, thus you get plenty of exercises; but in the event of a steep overpass or incline, you hit the throttle and zoom up. Today is Sunday. We will be biking over to Saint Anne's for mass, and then after a nice ride, we'll wind up at one of the many new restaurants for lunch.

We must remain vigilant, but with spring comes hope. When you come to Detroit on your next visit, after you've enjoyed the professional sports; casinos (We have three in Detroit and one in Windsor, Canada.); entertainment; and restaurants, come over to Woodbridge.

Afterword and Dedication

Woodbridge, Detroit, Michigan
June 2019

J oy and delight changed to sadness and anger as I first looked at the white tag inside the brim of my new NRA cap. I had received the headgear as a promotional gift for renewing my membership. Printed on the white tag were the following: "100% cotton. Made in China." What the hay? With all the grief the farmers are taking on behalf of this country on this tariff business with China, the least one could expect would be NRA support for goods made in the USA. The good news is that I have time and energy to be concerned about international politics and not just neighborhood and local problems. Wayne La Pierre, executive vice president of NRA, will soon be hearing from me.

My thanks goes out to Erma for sticking with me during the hard times and for her help in editing this manuscript. Thanks to our son, Bob, and his wife, Linda, for caring, visiting, and checking up on his old man and mom every now and then. Thank you Isabel for joining our family and becoming the mother of our two precious granddaughters, Christina and Selena, who are so tough that they "vacation in Detroit."

A special thanks goes out to my siblings and their spouses and families. My sisters, Jo Ann and husband, Dave and Barbara and Dick, (always remembered), and our brother, Danny Mac and J.K. (great addition to the family), were there for me in the past, are there for me in the present, and will be in the future. Thank you to

Erma's sister and brothers and their spouses, Marie B., Jack, remembered as a great guy, Chris his wife, Alita, Greg his wife, Michelle and Leonard Browning and for all the love, support and lively excitement. Best wishes to all the great friends and neighbors we've had over the years (especially Bill and Ella, and family, Bill (always remembered), Dennis, Ed, Melissa, Chuck, Robert, Hank, Andrea and Keith (always remembered), Ron, John, Michele and the Dakota Inn friends and their families. You are all the stand-up friends and great neighbors).

Thanks to our good friends, Tom and Sherry, for help in proofing this manuscript.

A special "thank you" to Marilyn Lundy and all the wonderful folks at Casgrain Hall and Orchestra Hall. Your dreams live on.

Postscript

January 2020

The news of early autumn 2019 was filled with dire predictions of presidential impeachment, tariff wars with China, Iranian aggressions, domestic mass shootings, conflicts in the middle-east, and an angry dominant progressive culture. We were happy to "get out of Dodge" and spend much of November touring Europe, with highlights being the Vatican City, Colosseum and Pompeii followed by a cruise around the Western Mediterranean.

We had also planned a trip to southern California for December with a visit to the Getty Villa, an antiquity museum built by oilman John Paul Getty, who is said to have believed that he was the reincarnation of Roman Caesar Augustus. Getty had his villa built on the plans found of an ancient Roman Villa destroyed by the eruption of Mount Vesuvius. A visit to Catalina Island and a day driving along the costal Pacific Highway 101, plus visits to the Nixon and Reagan Museums and Libraries rounded off our vacation.

I had always heard that the worst traffic in the world is found in Los Angeles during rush hours and I wanted to experience it myself. We started north of LA, got on the south bound I-5, and spent the next three and a half hours averaging a grueling five miles an hour. In the background we heard the constant wailing of police and emergency sirens. The drive was indeed horrific with cars frequently changing lanes while motorcycles roared between vehicles frequently creating mayhem. They call it lane splitting, and it's legal in LA, California, and Rome, Italy, two of the worst cities to drive in.

We would be cruising along at 65 mph in the express lane when a vehicle with only a driver would roar by (the express lane requires one or more passengers), and then it would suddenly dart back into the six lanes of traffic proceeding south at a snail's pace. The driver was trying to avoid an expensive ticket $435.00 for driving in the express lane without a passenger. They seemed to know where the check points were located.

The traffic radio station reported that the I-5 experienced four major accidents that afternoon, which caused much of the stalled traffic. Never again will I complain about our traffic in Detroit or our drivers. No wonder the folks in L.A. are a little off center.

Our flight back to Detroit arrived late (almost midnight) on Saturday, December 21st. Our granddaughter, Selena picked us up at the airport and in turn, we had arranged to drive her to the airport the next morning for her flight to visit family in Arizona and Texas during the holidays.

With no time to spare Sunday morning, Erma and I had a hurried breakfast at a local diner and made it on time to the 10:00 A.M. mass at Most Holy Trinity. Things were running like a well-oiled machine. Returning home, I reviewed the pile of mail and paid bills, and soon it was time to leave for the airport.

All was going well. We were zipping along westbound I-94 toward the airport. We had just passed the huge tire that came from the Ferris wheel at the 1964 New Your World's fair, when my world came apart.

I had just popped a cube of gum into my mouth and began to chew. Traffic was light and we were cruising at about 75 mph when suddenly, without warning, my mouth began to burn and tingle—it was as if I had received a massive dose of Novocain. My lips, mouth, both inside and out, felt like pin-pricks and began to go numb. I spit the gum into a tissue and checking the mirrors slowed down and moved to the right. I was losing all sensations in and around my mouth, and it was spreading to my tongue. What the heck was going on? Had I ingested some toxin? My lips and tongue were numb and I wasn't sure I could articulate the problem when suddenly…blinding lights with flashes of color and double vision shattered my eyesight.

I tried blinking first one eye then the other, but it did no good. I was rapidly losing my sight.

"Erma, I have a problem. I'm having trouble seeing. Help me to pull over…please." I tried to be as cool and calm as possible. I put the blinkers on and began to edge over. "Is it clear? Is the shoulder clear? I'm losing my vision." Both Erma and Selena gasped in unison and Erma, always the dutiful partner, followed my request.

"Yes," she said, "it's clear. Slow down and pull over a little more. Now slow down, not too far. Keep it straight. You're on the shoulder. Good. Good. Now stop."

I stepped hard on the brakes bringing the big Ford 150 to a jerking halt.

Opening the driver's door I heard and felt the rush of air as a big semi passed within inches of my partially open door. I squeezed out and closed the door as another semi-truck blasted past with a gust of air and a long warning scream from its air-horn. I had parked too close to the traffic lane and didn't want to open the rear door of the crew-cab on the driver's side for fear it would be taken off by the fast moving traffic and me along with it. I managed to hold on to the truck body and felt my way around to the open rear door on the passenger's side. By now I was exhausted and barely able to support myself. I was totally drained, but with Erma's help I managed to haul myself up and in. She made sure I was in and closed the door.

I tried to explain my condition, but it made no sense. The words were hard to form. Erma asked Selena to slide over and take the wheel.

"Should I take him to a hospital?" Selena inquired.

"No." I grunted. Drive on to the airport. We are almost there." I didn't want her to miss the holidays with family and friends. I sat back and closed my eyes and witnessed a pyrotechnic display of blinding lights and starbursts. If it hadn't been happening to me it would have been interesting. Erma handed me a bottle of water with instructions to flush my eyes and rinse my mouth. I did as I was told.

Suddenly I began to perspire. Rivulets of sweat ran down my head and neck soaking my clothing as Selena pulled out toward the airport.

I don't remember much after that. Selena was dropped off at the airport and Erma quickly pulled out and sped back to into the city to Henry Ford Hospital's emergency entrance.

Well, at least things can't get any worse, I thought when suddenly my breakfast began to heave in my stomach and I was concerned about making a mess in the truck cab. "Honey, pull over. I'm going to be sick."

In no uncertain terms I was told "No." In a voice firm and commanding voice she said, "It will take too long. Here, take this." She handed back a large half-empty box of Kleenex tissues.

"Do the best you can to contain it, and don't worry," were the last words I heard before everything came up into the box I had carefully positioned under my chin concentrating to carefully capture my stomach's contents in the tissue box. I thought of our family rule that "sickies have no rights." The sick individual must obey the commands of the well person until such time as recovery is complete.

Next, waves of head-splitting pain were followed by gut wrenching nausea and more vomiting. When we pulled up to emergency, I was barely conscious and was helped down and onto a gurney by the medical team. Erma held my hand and told me, again in no uncertain terms, that I would be alright.

Thus, following the hospital stay, I began four weeks of tests, probes, bloodwork, MRI, EKG, CT Scans, and Lord knows what else. It was determined that I had suffered two mini-strokes (called TIA or Transient Ischemic Attack) by clinical assessment. I was suffering from a small flap of protein in my heart chamber that had to be removed (seems as if two small particles, "as small as grains of sand", had broken off from the flap and travelled up into my brain and short circuited some functions). Oh, and in addition, two of the four by-passes that had been installed in 2004 in open heart surgery had collapsed.

I'm currently at home, still undergoing more tests to determine if I'm a good candidate for surgery and I'm faced with a dilemma. I'm told that I have to remain reasonably physically fit, but I couldn't work-out, take my usual long brisk walks, or do-lawn work, including shoveling snow. I had to get exercise, but just the right amount so that more bits of protein don't break off and finish the job.

One good result from the enforced solitude is that we redrafted and updated our legal documents (deeds, wills and Durable Powers of Attorney). The Michigan Probate Code has changed many of the documents since I retired. Finally all is in order. Basically, I leave all major decisions up to Erma and she has done the same for me, with one exception. The other night we were watching a television murder mystery entitled "Vienna Blood," in which a gruesome scene depicts a young woman receiving electro-shock treatment. I want no part of that and the one power Erma does not possess is to authorize such treatment for me. Who says we are not influenced by the popular media?

As the weeks went by, I regained my vision and feeling in my mouth, the headaches and nausea have receded to a bad memory. I'm just biding my time. In a few days I go in for a pulmonary function test, bloodwork and more x-rays, to see if I am a suitable candidate, and then I hope to have the surgery.

Erma was able to reschedule our January flights and reservations for May to Arizona to visit our granddaughter, Christina. I had planned to be at home during February to take care of the anticipated heavy snows predicted by the Farmer's Almanac. Luckily, I was able to postpone our March trip to fly out of Boston to the Azores until later in the year.

I can't tell you how difficult it is to hear a vehicle stuck in the intersection and remain seated at my desk, or to hear Erma clearing snow from the sidewalks and do nothing to help, but she has ordered me to stay inside. Strange, I heard what sounded like multiple shoveling with folks talking. Looking out of the window I saw several neighbors had gathered to help out. What a great neighborhood. It's all about neighbors helping neighbors.

The other day I spoke with Holly, the editor on this book, and she said I could add this Postscript bringing folks up to date. Not sure how things will turn out, but I remember my grade school teacher, Sister Anatolia, telling the class that one should live every day as if it were the last, and the last like every other day.

Detroit is a tough town, especially during winter. It is certainly not for the weak of mind, body or spirit. Erma and I have agreed that we want to live out our days here as long as we are able to maintain and secure our compound. If, and only if, we are unable to do so we want to sell the property to a family willing and able to take over, but we hope this doesn't happen during our lifetimes. Whatever happens, it's a great life here in Woodbridge, and, thus far, I've never killed anyone, and more importantly, I've never been killed by anyone.

March 29, 2020

I came though the operation with success and was discharged in five days rather than the average of eight to twelve days. I had a wonderful team of surgeons and now I'm working my way out of rehab and back to good health.

Unfortunately, the Coronavirus Pandemic is now raging in Detroit, as elsewhere. We are under, what Erma calls "house arrest." Not so bad for me. I love being around the house and on good days spend time on the yard and take short walks around the neighborhood. We will also survive this and spring will come.